Unwelcome and Unlawful

BOOKS BY RAYMOND F. GREGORY

Age Discrimination in the American Workplace:
  Old at a Young Age

Women and Workplace Discrimination:
  Overcoming Barriers to Gender Equality

Unwelcome and Unlawful

Sexual Harassment in the
American Workplace

RAYMOND F. GREGORY

An ILR Press Book

Cornell University Press

Ithaca and London

First published 2004 by Cornell University Press
First printing, Cornell Paperbacks, 2004

Printed in the United States of America

Library of Congress Cataloging-in-Publication Data

Gregory, Raymond F.
    Unwelcome and unlawful : sexual harassment in the American workplace / Raymond F. Gregory.— 1st ed.
        p. cm.
        ISBN 0-8014-4250-8 (cloth : alk. paper); ISBN 0-8014-8927-X (paperback : alk. paper)
    1. Sexual harassment of women—Law and legislation—United States. 2. Sex discrimination in employment—Law and legislation—United States.
I. Title.
KF3467.G74 2004
344.7201'4133—dc22   2003023063

Cornell University Press strives to use environmentally responsible suppliers and materials to the fullest extent possible in the publishing of its books. Such materials include vegetable-based, low-VOC inks, and acid-free papers that are recycled, totally chlorine-free, or partly composed of nonwood fibers. For further information, visit our website at www.cornellpress.cornell.edu.

Cloth printing   10 9 8 7 6 5 4 3 2 1
Paperback printing   10 9 8 7 6 5 4 3 2 1

To

RAYMOND, PAMELA, AND GEORGE

with love

Contents

Unwelcome and Unlawful

Introduction

What is sexual harassment? University of Michigan law professor Catharine A. MacKinnon defined sexual harassment in her seminal work written in 1979, "Sexual Harassment of Working Women,"[1] as "the unwanted imposition of sexual requirements in the context of a relationship of unequal power." MacKinnon observed that women, in exercising control over their lives, want to choose whether, when, where, and with whom to have sex. Sexual harassment undermines that control and denies women the opportunity to work without being subjected to sexual demands. "Women who protest sexual harassment at work are resisting economically enforced sexual exploitation."[2]

Stanford University law professor Deborah L. Rhode's conception of sexual harassment, similar to that of MacKinnon's, describes it as a form of sexual abuse and a "strategy of dominance, exclusion, control, and retaliation—as a way to keep women in their place and out of men's."[3] Cornell Law School professor Kathryn Abrams agrees, stating that sexual harassment "functions as a means of establishing male control and expressing or perpetuating masculine norms in the workplace."[4]

Other legal scholars follow suit. Sexual harassment is a "type of incivility or disrespect," "a sexually discriminatory wrong because of the gender norms it reflects and perpetuates," "the institutionalization of women's subordination through the preservation of male control of the workplace," and a "tool used . . . by men as a method of undermining women's competence in the workplace and thereby blocking women from certain jobs."[5]

These views are grounded on the supposition that sexual harassment is primarily about "power, not sex." Although this characterization may be accurate with regard to certain types of workplace conduct, it is inappropriately applied to others. From the legal practitioner's perspective, sexually harassing conduct is more often seen as the product of sexual or erotic desire, conduct that is generally perceived as an expression of male sexuality, a sexuality run amok. Thus, although "the power, not sex" approach may provide an appropriate lens through which to view certain forms of workplace harassment, it should not divert our attention from what the law—developed over the past twenty-five years—defines as sexual harassment.[6] In determining whether an alleged harasser's conduct is unlawful, the focus of attention should be on the nature of his conduct and the circumstances in which it is translated into action affecting the working life of a female employee.

While accepting the premise that sexually harassing conduct more commonly reflects a sexual desire rather than a wish to dominate, we must be careful not to ignore the generally accepted principle that, irrespective of the harasser's motivation, workplace sexual harassment always culminates in the diminution of a woman's humanity and her status as a worker. Sexually harassing conduct reduces the workplace roles of women to objects of male sexual desire. We must also accept as accurate the legal scholars' view that conduct, based on traditional masculine conceptions of legitimate sexual behavior, tends to fortify and bolster male control of the workplace. Thus we accept the formula enunciated by University of Arizona College of Law professor Katherine M. Franke that "sexual harassment is sex discrimination precisely because it replicates and perpetuates a sexual hierarchy in which men possess and maintain their power by virtue of their ability to define women in terms of their sexuality."[7]

The chapters that follow center on sexual harassment as it is perceived in the courtroom. Sexual harassment is defined by law as unwelcome sexual conduct, sufficiently severe or pervasive to alter the terms and conditions of a woman's employment. It is also defined as unwelcome sexual advances or requests for sexual favors and other conduct of a sexual nature, culminating in a hostile or offensive work environment. These legal definitions, however, present more questions than they provide answers.

What types of workplace conduct are correctly classified as sexually harassing and what types are not? When is sexual conduct considered "unwelcome?" If a woman submits to requests for sexual favors, may she still establish that the conduct of the alleged harasser was unwelcome to her? When is harassing conduct perceived as severe or pervasive and when is it not? Under what circumstances will a worker's terms and conditions of employment be considered as having been "altered?" When is an employer liable for acts of sexual harassment committed by co-workers of a female employee? When is an employer liable for the sexually harassing behavior of its supervisory or managerial personnel? May an employer be held liable for the sexually harassing conduct of its customers, clients, or other persons not directly under its control? What are the obligations of a woman to report acts of sexual harassment? Should the implementation of the laws barring sexual harassment be based on a "reasonable person" or a "reasonable woman" standard? If a woman proves she has been sexually harassed what monetary damages may she recover? Are there remedies other than monetary damages to which she may be entitled?

An adequate understanding of the law barring workplace sexual harassment cannot be attained unless these questions are first addressed. Thus one of my objectives in writing this book is to provide answers to these questions.

In the process of providing these answers, we also must consider borderline conduct that may or may not be considered sexually harassing. Although "a slap on the buttocks in the office setting has yet to replace the hand shake,"[8] sexual mores exist in a state of continuous change. Conduct formerly held acceptable may no longer be so. Conversely, what was previously considered as sexually harassing may now be perceived as acceptable behavior.

Since sexual harassment encompasses only "unwelcome" conduct, the laws barring sexual harassment in the workplace should not be interpreted in a manner that would allow them to become factors negatively affecting ordinary male-female workplace social discourse. These laws were not enacted to provide a means of redressing the petty slights of the hypersensitive individual, or "to bring about a magical transformation of the social mores of American workers,"[9] and as the Supreme Court has noted, they were not intended to produce a "general civility code for the American workplace."[10]

On the other hand, we must be careful not to pass to the other extreme, viewing sexual harassment merely as a workplace nuisance, a view commonly advanced by some employers:

[Sexual harassment is] all "noise" cranked up to a loud pitch by a chorus of greedy, disgruntled employees looking for a way to stick it to their companies. . . . [Statistics] provided by the Equal Employment Opportunity Commission (EEOC) and by various studies and surveys are exaggerated, most of the claims are false, and the majority of the plaintiffs are . . . crazy. Some claims may be valid, but they are few and far between. . . . Because the financial awards being won by these cases are greater than ever, so are the number of frivolous complaints. . . . A tremendous amount of companies' profits are spent to defend employers against such charges.[11]

Rather, we should focus on a frame of reference adopted by more enlightened employers, those employers who view the existence of sexual harassment in their workplaces as aberrant and unprofessional conduct.

The reader's viewpoint of sexual harassment issues will undoubtedly be colored by her or his gender, as women and men exhibit vast differences in their views of the propriety of sex in the workplace. In an early study, a group of men and women were asked how they would feel if asked by a member of the opposite sex to engage in sex. Their responses are given in table I.1.[12]

Table I.1

	Males (%)	Females (%)
Flattered	67.2	16.8
"It depends"	8.9	14.4
Insulted	15.0	62.8
Neither (it would not happen)	8.9	6.0

Traditional differences in male and female attitudes are reflected in the varying standards used by the courts in their rulings on sexual harassment issues.

From the legal perspective, sexual harassment is a form of sex discrimination. An issue of critical importance in a sex discrimination case is whether members of one sex are exposed to adverse terms and conditions of employment to which members of the other sex are not. A woman cannot establish that she was subjected to sexually harassing conduct without demonstrating that such conduct was discriminatory, that is, she was treated differently than her male co-workers. If a woman is subjected to acts of sexual harassment but so are her male co-workers, then it cannot be said she was discriminated against, and her sexual harassment claim will be dismissed. Thus a review of the issues typically arising in a sexual harassment claim must be conducted within the context of the laws barring sex discrimination in the workplace. On the federal law level, that law is Title VII of the Civil Rights Act of 1964.

It has been argued, with some merit, that the courtroom is not the most appropriate forum to resolve sexual harassment issues. Highly charged emotional issues, such as those that nearly always arise in the litigation of a sexual harassment case, are difficult to resolve in an adversarial environment. Such issues generally are more effectively addressed in the work forum, where efforts to eliminate sexual harassment from the workplace are far more likely to be effective, especially in those instances where employers adopt and implement policies designed to prevent sexual harassment from occurring in their workplaces, and where they act aggressively to curtail harassing conduct when it does occur.

Employers, however, often are insufficiently motivated to expend the funds to accomplish those goals. But women are empowered to create that motivation. Sexual harassment charges levied against a supervisor and his employer, followed by a jury verdict and a huge damage award, together with subsequent widely promulgated adverse publicity, often prove sufficiently calamitous for an employer to force it to adopt a more enlightened view regarding the measures it is willing to initiate to assure a harassment-free work environment. In fact, an employer's fear of litigation may provide the requisite incentive for it to address sexual harassment issues, thus rendering it unnecessary for women to resort to litigation.

Women, far more often than men, are the objects of sexually harassing behavior. This is not to deny that on occasion women sexually harass men, that men harass other men, or that women harass other women. The sexual harassment of men by women and same-sex sexual harassment are discussed in chapters 15 and 16, respectively. Throughout other parts of the book, when analyzing legal issues I generally refer to the victim of harassment as "she" and to the harasser as "he." The use of these pronouns reflects the fact that more than 90 percent of sexual harassment cases involve the harassment of women by men. The reader should understand, however, that the use of these pronouns is a matter of convenience rather than of substance. In most cases, the gender identification could be reversed without affecting the underlying legal issues, since the legal principles barring the sexual harassment of men are the same as those barring the sexual harassment of women. Accordingly, prospective male sexual harassment complainants should find the book as useful as female complainants.

Although I am a lawyer, I have written the book primarily for ordinary citizens—secondarily for other lawyers. It has been written for workers who have been sexually harassed, those workers who are contemplating litigation and considering whether to engage an attorney, and those already involved in litigation and who wish to assist their attorneys in the litigation process.

A complainant cannot gain an adequate understanding of the legal issues that commonly occur in sexual harassment cases unless she is able also to view those legal issues as they are perceived by her employer. A one-sided view of sexual harassment issues will lead only to misunderstanding, and thus all issues should be viewed from the perspective of the employer as well as that of the employee. A balanced view is a prerequisite for a complete understanding. Because both views are presented in the chapters that follow, human resources, managerial, and supervisory personnel should find the book useful in evaluating commonly occurring harassment issues. Although not written primarily for attorneys, those attorneys not fully aware of the scope and range of the legal issues normally arising in the courtroom in sexual harassment cases may find the work to be of value.

Every attempt has been made to eliminate technical language and legal jargon and to preclude the reader's immersion in legal intricacies and technical data having less than general application. In the discussion of those areas of the law where some technical knowledge is required, emphasis has been placed on the general applicability of the law, without regard to its exceptions. The broad picture takes precedence over special circumstances that may be relevant only in a limited number of instances.

Since Title VII of the Civil Rights Act of 1964 has largely preempted state-enacted antidiscrimination legislation, the focus of the book is on federal rather than state law. Most of the court cases reviewed in the book were decided pursuant to Title VII and were litigated in the federal courts. The emphasis on federal law should not be interpreted as an effort to undermine the significance of various state laws barring workplace sexual harassment. Although many of those laws are similar to federal law, an analysis of their differences falls outside the scope of this work. Victims of sexually harassing conduct and their attorneys should remain alert to the possible advantages of proceeding in state court and in reliance on state laws. They should also be mindful of harassment claims that may be alleged as tort claims, such as assault and battery and the intentional infliction of emotional distress, and they should also consider the possibility—if not desirability—of alleging in a single lawsuit violations of state, tort, and federal law.

The laws barring sexual harassment were intended to eradicate unwelcome sexual conduct from the workplace. These laws have achieved a great deal since the enactment of the Civil Rights Act of 1964, but sexual harassment has yet to be totally eliminated. It will be eliminated only if American working women regularly challenge such conduct. This book has been written to encourage working women to commit themselves to accepting that challenge.

CHAPTER ONE

Sexual Harassment in the Workplace

An Overview

Women have always been sexually harassed at work. A study conducted in the early 1980s reported that up to one-half of all women experienced some form of sexual harassment during the course of their working lives.[1] A later survey, focusing solely on female attorneys, reported that 51 percent of the women participating in the study affirmed they had been sexually harassed.[2] Women employed in governmental positions have been treated no differently. A 1981 study undertaken by the United States Merit Systems Protection Board disclosed that 42 percent of the female federal employees responding to its survey asserted they had been subjected to acts of sexual harassment at one time or another.[3] Other studies have reported even greater numbers of working women who claim to have been sexually harassed, with one report concluding that incidents of workplace harassment occur in the lives of 90 percent of working women.[4] But studies and surveys are not needed to prove the point. I venture to say nearly all of the women reading this book have on at least one occasion been subjected to the sexually harassing behavior of a co-worker or supervisor. Unquestionably, sexual harassment is a condition of employment daily encountered by millions of women. It is a problem that "is not only epidemic, it is pandemic, an everyday, everywhere occurrence."[5]

University of Michigan law professor Catharine A. MacKinnon described the scope of sexually harassing conduct as it existed in 1979:

Victimization by the practice of sexual harassment, so far as is currently known, occurs across the lines of age, marital status, physical appearance, race, class, occupation, pay range, and any other factor that distinguishes women from each other. Frequency and type of incident may vary with specific vulnerabilities of the woman, or qualities of the job, employer, situation, or workplace.[6]

MacKinnon might very well have been describing current working conditions; the range of harassing conduct remains today as expansive as MacKinnon observed it nearly twenty-five years ago.

The number of women who formally report incidents of sexually harassing conduct has steadily increased. Between 1992 and 2001, the number of sexual harassment complaints filed by women with the Equal Employment Opportunity Commission skyrocketed, increasing by nearly 50 percent during that time.[7] Moreover, a far greater proportion of sexually harassed women—for reasons later discussed—refrain from filing formal complaints. A survey of female workers who held managerial positions at fifteen hundred major companies revealed that 60 percent of them reported having experienced some sort of sexual harassment at work, but only 14 percent had informed their employers of these occurrences, and less than 1 percent had filed formal complaints or lawsuits.[8]

The injuries suffered by a woman subjected to acts of sexual harassment may be economic or psychological or, in many cases, both. If the harassment leads to her resignation, the victim loses her salary, insurance, pension, medical and other benefits. If, on the other hand, she reports the harassment but remains in her position, she may be branded a troublemaker, subjected to co-worker hostility, blocked from further advancement, or suffer a retaliatory discharge. In general, sexual harassment impedes a woman's prospects for economic equality, reduces her productivity, lowers her job performance, diminishes her work aspirations, and limits her economic independence.[9]

The psychological effects of sexual harassment may be devastating and extend beyond the workplace. Victims of harassment frequently suffer mental turmoil, depression, guilt, anxiety, and loss of self-esteem, both inside and outside the workplace, and thus experience a diminished satisfaction with life in general.[10] In her book, MacKinnon, observing that victims of harassment often feel humiliated, degraded, ashamed, embarrassed, and cheapened, referred to comments reportedly made by harassed women in a survey conducted by the Working Women United

Institute. One woman's remarks were typical of those reported in the survey:

> As I remember all the sexual abuse and negative work experiences I am left feeling sick and helpless and upset instead of angry. . . . Reinforced feelings of no control—sense of doom . . . I have difficulty dropping the emotion barrier I work behind when I come home from work. My husband turns into just another man. . . . Kept me in a constant state of emotional agitation and frustration; I drank a lot. . . . Soured the essential delight in the work. . . . Stomach ache, migraines, cried every night, no appetite.[11]

But the most fundamental harm a victim of harassment suffers is a loss of personal dignity, a loss of self-esteem. Rosa Ehrenreich, a senior adviser to the U.S. Department of State, summed it up well when she described sexual harassment as "an insult to the dignity, autonomy, and personhood of each victim, [violating her] right to be treated with the respect and concern that is due her as a full and equally valuable human being."[12]

Occurrences of sexual harassment in the workplace may reflect a condition of inequality existing between male and female workers. The harassment of female employees often conveys the message that women are primarily perceived, not as workplace colleagues and valuable assets, but merely as sexual objects. While creating barriers to job advancement, the persistent presence of sexually harassing conduct also signals to women that they are welcome to remain in the workplace only if they subvert their identities as women and adopt—or adapt to—male sexual stereotypes.[13] A male worker's sexually harassing behavior expresses the age-old belief that women should be sexually available to men, and it simultaneously reminds them they are neither viewed nor respected as workplace equals.[14]

Since acts of sexual harassment generally culminate in a hostile and offensive work environment, the harassed woman is compelled to labor under abusive and antagonistic conditions each day of her work life. Every aspect of her employment status is thus undermined. Women, therefore, perceive acts of sexual harassment as material threats to their economic livelihood.[15]

Women generally react to sexually harassing conduct in one of four ways: "avoidance, defusion, negotiation, or confrontation."[16] In avoidance—the least assertive but the most common response—the victim of the harassment departs from the workplace, either by quitting, transferring to another position, or taking sick leave. In defusion, a somewhat more assertive response, the victim endeavors to minimize the intensity of the harassment by pretending to go along with the harasser so as to defuse the situation. She hopes the harassment eventually will cease, but often, the harasser interprets this type of response as encouragement to further harassment or even considers it provocative.[17] In negotiation, the victim asks the harasser to cease his offensive behavior, sometimes threatening to expose him to his supervisors. In confrontation, the most assertive and the least-utilized response, the victim of the harassment files a formal complaint with her employer and later may resort to seeking a legal remedy.[18]

All workplace conduct of a sexual nature is not necessarily of a harassing nature, since dating is common among co-workers, and many people find their marriage partners at work. Obviously, sexual attraction thrives in the workplace. But men and women in general differ concerning the appropriateness of sexual conduct in the workplace. Behavior considered offensive by women may be viewed as harmless by men. What is regarded by male workers as acceptable conduct may be considered unacceptable by female workers. In the 1980s study previously noted, 67 percent of the male participants in the study reported they would be flattered by a sexual advance made by a female co-worker, but only 17 percent of the women stated they would feel that way if made the object of a male's sexual advance.[19] In certain respects, a determination that a co-worker's conduct is harassing is dependent on a gender perspective. Which perspective should prevail—male or female? This is one of the issues later to be addressed, but first we must undertake a review of the existing legal provisions enacted by Congress to eliminate sexual harassment from the workplace.

In 1963, President John F. Kennedy proposed broad-based civil rights legislation, barring discrimination in places of public accommodation and in connection with voting rights, school enrollment, and employment. Although the proposed legislation included prohibitions against discrimination in employment based on race, national origin, and religion, it lacked any provision barring discrimination based on sex.

Even with growing public support for the adoption of a Civil Rights Act, the proposed legislation was not without its opponents and detractors. Congressman Howard Smith of Virginia, a leading opponent of the president's proposals, offered an amendment adding sex to the prohibitions against employment discrimination. His intent was not to advance the interests of women, but rather to defeat the entire bill by complicating the debate and confusing some in Congress who, although fully supportive of provisions insuring equality for African Americans, were less certain of the need to include protections for working women.

Smith showed contempt for his own amendment when he related having received a letter from one of his female constituents complaining about the "grave injustice" incurred as a consequence of the existence of more females than males in the country, which prevented every woman from having a husband of her own. This story was greeted with laughter on the floor of the House but also resulted in anger from the few women serving in the Congress at the time. Smith's ploy backfired. Once the question of discrimination against women was placed on the House floor it was difficult for many representatives to ignore it, and ultimately Congress adopted Smith's proposed amendment.[20] The inclusion of sex in the statute has had profound social implications.[21] What was first considered a ruse and a joke ultimately culminated in legislation providing the broadest set of workplace protections ever granted American women.

After enactment of Title VII—that section of the Civil Rights Act of 1964 barring discrimination in the workplace based on a worker's race, national origin, religion, or sex—the courts were pressed to decide whether sexual harassment was a form of sex discrimination barred by the statute.[22] Nothing in the wording of the statute even suggested that sexual harassment was a form of sex discrimination, and due to the course pursued by Representative Smith in introducing his sex discrimination amendment, the issue had not been discussed in congressional hearings prior to the statute's enactment. Without either a legislative history or a clearly expressed statutory provision to guide them, the courts were slow to respond to female worker complaints of workplace sexual harassment.

When some courts rejected the concept that sexual harassment constituted a form of sex discrimination barred by the statute, Catharine MacKinnon argued in her 1979 book that sexual harassment indeed was a form of sex discrimination. "Sexual harassment is seen to be one dynamic which reinforces and expresses women's traditional and inferior role in the labor force."[23]

> As a practice, sexual harassment singles out a gender-defined group, women, for special treatment in a way which adversely affects and burdens their status as employees. Sexual harassment limits women in a way men are not limited. It deprives them of opportunities that are available to male employees without sexual conditions. In so doing, it creates two employment standards: one for women that includes sexual requirements, one for men that does not.[24]

Concluding that acts of sexual harassment are discriminatory, MacKinnon was among the first to contend publicly that sexual harassment in the workplace is a form of sex discrimination made unlawful by Title VII.[25]

Courts continued to differ on the issue. In 1976, a New Jersey federal court judge ruled Title VII was not intended to prevent "a physical attack motivated by sexual desire on the part of a supervisor" merely because it "happened to occur in a corporate corridor rather than a back alley."[26] In another early case, involving a complainant's allegation that her supervisor had retaliated against her after she rejected his proposed "after hours affair," a District of Columbia federal court held that the substance of the complainant's allegations centered on her claim that she had been discriminated against, not because she was a woman, but because she had declined to engage in a sexual affair with her supervisor. According to the court, this was not sex discrimination: "This is a controversy underpinned by the subtleties of an inharmonious personal relationship. Regardless of how inexcusable the conduct of plaintiff's supervisor might have been, it does not evidence an arbitrary barrier to continued employment based on plaintiff's sex."[27]

Less than a year later, an Arizona federal court ordered the dismissal of the claims of two women who alleged they had been verbally and physically harassed by their supervisor, and that his conduct had continued unabated until each was forced to resign. The court ruled that although Title VII clearly bars discrimination of women by their employers, nothing in the statute renders unlawful the sexual advances of their supervisors:

> In the present case, [the supervisor's] conduct appears to be nothing more than a personal proclivity, peculiarity, or mannerism. By his alleged sexual advances, [he] was satisfying a personal urge. Certainly no employer policy is here involved. . . . Nothing in the complaint alleges nor can it be construed that the conduct complained of was company directed policy which deprived women of employment opportunities.

From the perspective of this court, an act of sexual harassment merely reflected a need to satisfy a "personal urge," and thus it did not violate the legal rights of the victim.

The court also expressed its concern that if it were to declare sexual harassment actionable under Title VII "every time any employee made amorous or sexually oriented advances toward another," it could culminate in a federal lawsuit. In such circumstances, the court opined, the only sure way an employer could avoid such charges would be to hire only workers who were "asexual."[28] Another judge remarked that if sexual harassment was covered by Title VII, the federal court system "would need 4000 federal trial judges instead of 400."[29] If the rationale underlying these decisions had prevailed, no working woman would have ever successfully advanced a sexual harassment claim against her employer under Title VII. Fortunately, not all courts were as myopic.

One year later, a District of Columbia federal appellate court reversed course, ruling that a woman subjected to acts of sexual harassment is indeed discriminated against, not merely as a consequence of her refusal to engage in a sexual act demanded by a supervisor, but simply because she is a woman:

> But for her womanhood . . . her participation in sexual activity would never have been solicited. To say, then, that she was victimized in her employment simply because she declined the invitation is to ignore the asserted fact that she was invited only because she was a woman. . . . Put another way, she became the target of her supervisor's sexual desires because she was a woman and was asked to bow to his demands as the price for holding her job.[30]

The court concluded, therefore, that an act of sexual harassment, because it is discriminatory, violates Title VII precepts.

Soon after, another federal appellate court ruled that if a supervisor, with the knowledge of his employer, makes sexual demands of a subordinate female employee and conditions her employment status on a favorable response to those demands, then he as well as his employer may be held liable for violations of Title VII.[31]

Following these cases, the Equal Employment Opportunity Commission issued guidelines formulated on the assumption that sexually harassing conduct indeed constituted a violation of Title VII. There the matter stood until 1986 when Mechelle Vinson's sexual harassment case alleged against Meritor Savings Bank reached the Supreme Court, presenting the court with its first opportunity to consider issues involving allegations of sexual harassment in the workplace.

Vinson had worked for the bank for four years, first as a teller and later as a head teller and assistant branch manager. Throughout the term of her employment, she had worked under the supervision of Sidney Taylor. When Vinson was fired, purportedly for taking excessive sick leave, she sued Taylor and the bank, claiming that during her four years of employment, Taylor had continuously harassed her sexually.

Vinson alleged that shortly after beginning to work at the bank, Taylor suggested they engage in sexual relations. At first she declined, but when he persisted, she eventually agreed, but only because she feared she would lose her position if she did not accede to his request. Thereafter, Taylor made repeated demands on her for sex, both during and after business hours, and as a result they had intercourse on numerous occasions. Vinson also claimed Taylor fondled her in the presence of other employees, followed her into the women's restroom, exposed himself to her, and raped her. Because she feared Taylor and was concerned for her job, Vinson neither reported Taylor's harassment to any of his supervisors nor took advantage of the bank's grievance procedures.

Vinson's case required the Supreme Court to decide three basic issues:

- Is sexual harassment a form of sex discrimination barred by Title VII?
- Is an employer liable to a female worker for an offensive or hostile working environment, an environment created by acts of sexual misconduct committed by her supervisor?
- Is Title VII violated in circumstances where a sexual relationship between an employee and her supervisor is "voluntary"?

The court's responses to these questions proved to be of paramount importance in the development of Title VII's role in resolving issues relating to the presence of sexual harassing conduct in the workplace.

In affirming a lower court ruling that a woman may establish a Title VII violation by proving that her supervisor sexually harassed her, the court quoted from an earlier appellate court opinion:

> Sexual harassment which creates a hostile or offensive environment for members of one sex is every bit the arbitrary barrier to sexual equality at the workplace that racial harassment is to racial equality. Surely, a requirement that a man or woman run a gauntlet of sexual abuse in return for the privilege of being allowed to work and make a living can be as demeaning and disconcerting as the harshest of racial epithets.[32]

In these circumstances, women and men are not treated on equal terms. Thus sexual harassment generates inequality. Accordingly, acts of sexual harassment violate Title VII's ban of workplace discriminatory conduct.

The Supreme Court then proceeded to set the standard the courts were to use in determining whether sexual conduct reaches the level of sexual harassment. Sexual conduct violates the precepts of Title VII only if it is sufficiently "severe or pervasive" to alter the terms and conditions of the harassed woman's employment, thus creating for her a hostile and abusive work environment. Without question, Taylor's conduct, as alleged, was sufficiently severe *and* pervasive to alter the terms and conditions of Vinson's employment, thus creating an abusive and hostile work environment in which Vinson was compelled to work. Vinson's allegations of Taylor's harassing conduct, if proved, would be sufficient to establish a claim of sexual harassment under Title VII.

With respect to the issue of the bank's responsibility and liability for Taylor's conduct, the bank had advanced the position that it could not be held legally liable for Taylor's behavior because its executive personnel were unaware he had engaged in harassing conduct, since Vinson had not reported his conduct to his supervisors nor had it otherwise come to their attention. Vinson's attorneys, on the other hand, maintained that since the bank had placed Taylor in a supervisory role over Vinson, it was liable for Taylor's misconduct, even if his superiors had not been apprised of the harassment. They argued that when Vinson received direction from Taylor, she in effect received direction from the bank. Thus, when Taylor exercised his supervisory functions, he acted as the representative or agent of the bank, and since the bank is legally liable for the actions of its representatives and agents, it was liable for Taylor's acts of sexual harassment.

The Supreme Court basically agreed with the position asserted by Vinson's attorneys. Since an employer delegates to its supervisors the power and authority to direct and control its employees, supervisors generally act as their employer's agents whenever they exercise that power and authority. Employers are thus generally held liable for their supervisors' misuse of the power and authority delegated to them. In some circumstances, however, such as in instances when a supervisor exceeds the scope of his authority or acts without authority, his acts may not be considered as those of his employer. Each case, therefore, must be judged on its own facts. The court must determine whether—in light of the facts existent in that particular case—the harassing supervisor actually acted as the employer's agent, thus rendering it liable for his harassment.

With regard to the issue of Vinson's "voluntariness" in consenting to a sexual relationship with Taylor, the court pointed out that the correct inquiry was not whether Vinson's participation in sexual intercourse with Taylor was voluntary, but rather whether the sexual relationship was "unwelcome" to her. The fact Vinson was not forced to participate against her will in a sexual relationship with Taylor did not undermine her sexual harassment claim. However, Vinson had to prove her participation was "unwelcome" to her. This is an element of proof that must be borne by any complainant in a sexual harassment suit—an element of proof that may be sustained only with persuasive evidence that even though she acceded to her supervisor's advances, his harassing conduct was nevertheless unwelcome. Since that issue had not been considered by the lower court, the Supreme Court remanded Vinson's case for further proceedings. Before those proceedings were conducted, however, Vinson and the bank agreed to a settlement of the case.[33]

Subsequent to the *Vinson* ruling, sexual harassment cases have appeared on court dockets with increasing frequency. These cases generally involve one of two categories of conduct, each held to be sexually harassing. The first is based on the abusive treatment of a female employee, treatment that would not have occurred but for the fact that she is a woman, and it usually entails demands for sexual favors either in return for employment benefits or under threat of some adverse employment action. This type of sexual harassment is referred to as "quid pro quo" harassment. Under guidelines adopted by the EEOC, quid pro quo sexual harassment exists when "submission to [sexual] conduct is made either explicitly or implicitly a term or condition of an individual's employment [or when] submission or rejection of such conduct by an individual is used as the basis for employment decisions affecting such individual."[34]

The second category of sexual harassment evolves from the nature or quality of a woman's working environment. When an employer encourages or tolerates a work environment replete with sexual commentary, sexual touching, or other forms of harassing conduct—conduct that is sufficiently severe or pervasive to alter the terms and conditions of a woman's employment—the employer may be held liable for "hostile work environment" harassment.

A sexually hostile environment is one that is both objectively and subjectively hostile. It is objectively hostile if any reasonable person would find it hostile, and it is subjectively hostile if the victim of the harassment also perceives it to be so. Whether a work environment is sufficiently hostile or abusive to support a sexual harassment claim is determined by viewing all the circumstances, including:

- the frequency of the acts of sexual harassment;
- the severity of the offensive conduct;
- whether the offensive conduct was physically threatening or merely verbal;

- whether the victim was humiliated by reason of the conduct;
- whether the harasser was a co-worker or a supervisor;
- whether other workers joined in the harassment;
- whether the harassment was directed at more than one individual;
- whether the harassment unreasonably interfered with the victim's work performance, thus altering the terms and conditions of her employment.

A survey of sexual harassment cases filed in the federal courts during the ten-year period following the *Vinson* case revealed that 70 percent of those cases were hostile environment claims and another 23 percent presented a combination of hostile environment and quid pro quo claims.[35] Hostile environment claims, therefore, predominate.

As previously noted, Title VII does not prohibit all sex-related conduct; the mere presence of some sexuality in the workplace does not render a work environment "hostile." Some forms of sexual behavior are harmless or wholly innocent. Moreover, the differences in the ways men and women routinely interact with members of the opposite sex rarely rise to the level of sexual harassment. Flirtation, teasing, off-hand comments, isolated incidents, and vulgar language that is trivial, even if annoying, are generally insufficiently serious to support a hostile environment charge.[36]

We now turn to a review of the various forms of sexual harassment as they commonly appear in the workplace.

CHAPTER TWO

Various Forms of
Sexual Harassment

Sexually harassing conduct generally appears in the workplace in one of two forms or in a combination of both. In "quid pro quo" sexual harassment, the promise of employment benefits or the removal of threatened adverse employment actions are conditioned upon a woman's affirmative response to the sexual demands of one higher in company hierarchy. Submission to sexual demands is made a condition of her employment. In "hostile work environment" sexual harassment, a woman is subjected to sexually harassing conduct sufficiently severe or pervasive to alter the conditions of her employment, requiring her to perform her job functions in hostile and offensive conditions. When quid pro quo conditions of employment culminate in hostile and offensive working conditions, a woman suffers both forms of harassment.

Sexual harassment may be physical or verbal in nature, and at times both physical and verbal. In most instances, a supervisor or co-worker targets one individual, but on occasion, a group of women, or even an employer's entire female staff, may be subjected to the harassing behavior of a number of male employees or even of an entire staff of male workers.

Sexually harassing conduct adversely affects the working lives of women employed in blue-collar and white-collar positions as well as women working in management and professional positions. Women in all industries, businesses, and professions experience its corruptive cast. The cases that follow illustrate the depravity and degradation of this common workplace scourge.

Quid Pro Quo Sexual Harassment

At the time that Paulette Barnes obtained an administrative assistant position with the Environmental Protection Agency, working under the supervision of the director of the agency's equal employment opportunity division, the division director promised to elevate her to a higher position within ninety days. Barnes later claimed that immediately after starting her new job, the director initiated a series of requests for sexual favors, repeatedly soliciting her to join him for social activities after office hours, repeatedly making remarks of a sexual nature, while suggesting that if she cooperated with him in a sexual affair her employment status would be enhanced. Barnes resisted all these overtures, informing the director their relationship would have to remain on a "professional" level. When the director ultimately concluded that Barnes truly meant what she said, he began to denigrate her employment status by stripping her of her job duties, and eventually he ordered the elimination of her position. Instead of receiving the promised promotion, Barnes was fired. This is a classic example of quid pro quo sexual harassment. Barnes's job was conditioned on her submission to the sexual demands of one having the power and authority to establish the terms of her employment.[1]

Carmelita Wilkes also was subjected to quid pro quo sexual harassment. After she submitted an application for an executive secretary position with Unichema North America, its personnel manager, Lance Chambers, offered her a lower-paying secretary/receptionist position. Wilkes agreed to accept that position. A few days before she was scheduled to begin work, Chambers telephoned Wilkes to advise her he was about to visit her at home to provide her with copies of the company's benefits package and various forms necessary to be completed prior to her first day of work. On his arrival at Wilkes's home, Chambers told her the benefits package and employment forms were located in his apartment and suggested she accompany him there so he could give her copies. On their arrival at Chambers's apartment, Wilkes discovered that the benefits package and forms were located in the briefcase Chambers had been carrying when he arrived at her home. When Wilkes asked why he had asked her to his apartment under a false pretense, Chambers responded that he wanted to be her mentor "and that if [she] opened up to him he was sure [she] would advance at [Unichema]."

During her brief career at Unichema, Wilkes split her day, working as a receptionist in the morning and as Chambers's secretary in the afternoon. Wilkes was not long on the job before Chambers made some sexual remarks she found offensive. He later made other suggestive comments, bragging of his ability, if given the opportunity, to sexually satisfy any woman in bed. On one occasion Chambers asked her why she would "settle for second best when [she] could have the best with [him]." When Wilkes failed to respond to Chambers's sexual remarks, he reduced her secretarial duties and later terminated her. Wilkes had a job as long as she played along with Chambers, and when she ignored or rejected his advances, she lost her job.

In order to succeed in proving a quid pro quo claim, the claimant must establish that the harasser's sexual conduct was linked to an employment decision affecting her employment status. Wilkes easily demonstrated a direct connection between her rejection of Chambers's sexual proposals and his decision to fire her. If each of Chambers's remarks had been considered separately, they might not have been deemed sufficiently offensive to support a quid pro quo sexual harassment claim. However, when Chambers's conduct was considered in combination—that is, when the totality of the circumstances surrounding his conduct, both before and after Wilkes began working for him, were taken into account—then it became clear Chambers terminated Wilkes once he realized she had no plans to accommodate his interest in a sexual relationship. Wilkes was subjected to quid pro quo sexual harassment.[2]

A quid pro quo sexual harassment claim is not dependent on proving that the harassment culminated in a termination of employment as in the *Barnes* and *Wilkes* cases. Consequences of lesser significance, such as a failure to promote, a denial of a choice job assignment, a refusal to provide training opportunities, or any other job action that substantially decreases a worker's potential or causes a material deterioration in her working conditions, may be sufficient to support a quid pro quo claim.[3]

Hostile Work Environment Sexual Harassment

Cynthia Stoll, a single mother of three boys, worked for six years at the Sacramento post office as a letter-sorting machine operator before literally fleeing the workplace to escape multiple acts of sexual harassment committed by a network of supervisors and co-workers. They repeatedly asked her to perform oral sex, commented on her body, shot rubber bands at her backside, bumped up against her from behind, pressed their erect penises into her buttocks while she was sorting mail, followed her into the women's bathroom, asked her to go on vacation with them, fondled her body, subjected her to continuous sexual commentary, and generally stalked her throughout the facility.

Stoll was described as "fairly shy" and was easily intimidated by her supervisor, who seemed to take sadistic pleasure in screaming at and tormenting her. Another supervisor intervened on her behalf and then demanded sexual services from her. Stoll rejected these advances and tried to avoid him, but he then raped her. Stoll had to resign to escape her tormentors.

After resigning, Stoll suffered severe depression and on four occasions attempted suicide. A psychiatrist testified Stoll was scarred for life, would never again be able to work, and probably would continue to try to kill herself. At that point in Stoll's treatment, the psychiatrist was solely focused on keeping her alive.[4]

The harassment Stoll confronted was severe, pervasive, and totally corrupting, culminating in a highly offensive and hostile working environment. A judge who heard her case characterized her working conditions as those no woman should ever have to endure. Although most women survive a hostile work environment suffering less severely than Stoll, hostile working conditions are frequently the cause of acute psychological pain and suffering. Hostile work environment sexual harassment may be as devastating for a woman as acts of quid pro quo sexual harassment.

On occasion, an entire staff of female workers may be subjected to hostile and offensive working conditions. Women working at the Eveleth Taconite Company in Minnesota filed a class action lawsuit against the company, alleging it allowed, and in some instances promoted, a work environment that was sexually hostile and abusive to all women. They submitted evidence demonstrating a pattern of sexual hostility that had long existed throughout the company. Company officials permitted sexually explicit graffiti, pictures, and posters to be placed on office walls, lunchroom areas, and tool rooms. Similar materials were exhibited in elevators and women's restrooms, posted in company-locked bulletin boards, and distributed in interoffice mail. In addition, women often suffered incidents of unwanted kissing, touching, pinching, and grabbing. Everyday workplace language reflected a male-oriented and an anti-female work environment. Offensive sexist comments, such as "women should remain home with their children" and "women deprive men of their jobs," were commonly heard in the conversations of male workers.

Sexually oriented offensives grew so pervasive at Eveleth Taconite that they became "standard operating procedure." First-line supervisors were well aware of the harassing behavior of nonsupervisory personnel, and some of the supervisors even participated in the harassment. The company was male-dominated in terms of power, position, and atmosphere. Male-focused attention on sex and references to women as sexual objects created a sexualized work environment, and the presence of graffiti and other sexual materials, together with the general sex-oriented conduct of male workers, reinforced stereotypical attitudes toward the women working for the company. The court ruled the company had maintained a sexually hostile work environment.

> It should be obvious that the callous pattern and practice of sexual harassment engaged in by Eveleth Mines inevitably destroyed the self-esteem of the working women exposed to it. The emotional harm, brought about by this record of human indecency, sought to destroy the human psyche as well as the human spirit of each plaintiff. The humiliation and degradation suffered by these women is irreparable. Although money damage cannot make these women whole or even begin to repair the injury done, it can serve to set a precedent that in the environment of the working place such hostility will not be tolerated.[5]

Quid Pro Quo and Hostile Work Environment Sexual Harassment in Combination

Quid pro quo sexual harassment underlay Mechelle Vinson's claims against Meritor Savings Bank (described in chapter 1). Vinson alleged she first consented to a sexual relationship with her supervisor out of fear of losing her position, and later complied with his repeated demands for sex only to save her job. She understood that if she rejected his advances, her continued employment with the bank would be placed in jeopardy. When the receipt of employment benefits or the elimination of threatened adverse employment actions are conditioned on a victim's submission to the sexual demands of her supervisor, victims such as Vinson may assert a powerful quid pro quo claim against her employer.

The circumstances Vinson confronted also afforded her the opportunity to allege a hostile environment sexual harassment claim against the bank. In fact, in its ruling, the Supreme Court emphasized that aspect of the case, noting that although her supervisor's harassment had not resulted in any economic loss for her, it unreasonably interfered with her work performance and created an offensive working environment. The court gave its approval to previously adopted EEOC guidelines that Title

VII "affords employees the right to work in an environment free from discriminatory intimidation, ridicule, and insult," and that the victim of such misconduct may sue her employer for having failed to provide her with a work environment free of hostility and offensiveness. Vinson's allegations that her supervisor made repeated demands for sex, fondled her in the presence of other employees, followed her into the restroom, exposed himself to her, and even raped her were fundamental to her quid pro quo claim, but they also served as a basis for a claim that her working environment was overtly hostile and highly offensive. Claims of both forms of sexual harassment were thus available to Vinson.[6]

Terri Nichols worked in an equally offensive and hostile working environment. Nichols, deaf, mute, and incapable of communicating with coworkers except through writing and sign language, worked as a night-shift mail sorter at the Salem, Oregon, postal facility. The night-shift supervisor, Ron Francisco, was the highest-ranking manager at the facility during that shift and was the only supervisor able to communicate with Nichols in sign language. Shortly after Nichols commenced work, Francisco asked her to photocopy some documents for him. He followed her into the photocopy room, started kissing her, and indicated he wanted her to perform oral sex for him. Initially she refused, but when he persisted, she complied because she was afraid she would lose her position if she continued to resist him. Her testimony later given during the trial of her sexual harassment case vividly describes how a harassed worked typically perceives a sexually hostile work environment:

> I remember that when this first happened I was just in shock. I was nervous. I was upset. I wasn't happy doing it, and I was hoping it would never happen again. And I just kept that all to myself. But then there was repeats and repeats and repeats, and I was more upset and I didn't want it. I didn't want to do it again and again for him, and I didn't know how to say, "Stop, just stop."

Although this routine occurred repeatedly over a period of six months, Nichols did not report Francisco for fear post office officials would not believe her and Francisco would then retaliate against her. Nor did she tell her husband:

> I tried to kill myself because I just didn't know how to tell my husband. . . .
> I was afraid he would take the children and divorce me. And so I was just
> stuck. I was stuck between the two and there was no one I could talk to. I
> was afraid other people wouldn't believe me. . . . [If I reported] the super-

visor I would lose my job. My husband and I had just recently bought a house and that house depended on my earnings, and I didn't want to lose everything. And that job was so important to the support of my family, so I was just stuck with the two.

Ultimately, Nichols grew depressed, anxious, and irritable and had difficulty eating and sleeping:

I was losing weight. I wasn't able to eat regularly. I didn't have enough sleep. I got real emotional at home. I was angry. I remember as time progressed, I was getting crazier. I hated that sex. I didn't want sex even with my husband.

Her fears about the reaction of her husband were realized when he sued for divorce. At the time, Nichols asked Francisco for a leave of absence to deal with her family problems. He granted her request but only after she again agreed to perform oral sex for him.

In the end, Nichols reported Francisco to the postal authorities and filed suit. Subsequently, she was diagnosed as suffering from a post-traumatic stress disorder and was granted federal disability benefits. By the time her sexual harassment case reached trial, the Postal Service had transferred her to another facility. She was then living with her two young children, her marriage having ended in divorce.

Francisco, as a supervisor and the highest-ranking managerial employee working on the night-shift, possessed the power to dictate the conditions of Nichols's employment, and he made submission to his sexual demands the predominant condition of that employment. The quid pro quo nature of his harassment of Nichols was epitomized in his demand for oral sex as the price for granting her request for a leave of absence. But Francisco's conduct also created a wholly offensive and hostile work environment, an environment sufficiently severe and pervasive to alter the conditions of Nichols's employment. The acts of harassment to which Nichols was subjected clearly supported a quid pro quo as well as a hostile environment claim.[7]

Physical Harassment

Lynn Fall worked in the South Bend branch of the Indiana University serving as a liaison between the university and the local community.

Shortly after Fall was hired, David Cohen, the university's chancellor, sent her an e-mail message requesting her to come to his office. According to Fall's testimony, when she entered Cohen's office, he closed the door behind her. After they had spent some time discussing university matters, Cohen told her he had used the e-mail message merely as a ruse to get her into his office. Fall immediately rose from her chair to leave, but before she could make her exit, Cohen put his arms around her, kissed her, and forced his hands down her blouse, groping her breasts. Fall broke from his grasp, fled the office, and ran to a restroom where she vomited.

Fall filed suit claiming sexual harassment. The court focused its attention on the fact that Cohen had committed a single act of harassment. Did Cohen's one and only act of harassment rise to the level of severity or pervasiveness required to support a hostile environment claim? First, the court noted Cohen's deception in luring Fall into his office, that his attack on her was calculated in advance. Cohen's preplanned sexual advance added significantly to the degree of severity of his conduct. Second, the court observed that the social context in which the offensive behavior was committed was an important factor to consider. He had not approached Fall in a social setting or out in the open where she could have more readily deterred or escaped his advances. Instead, Cohen's attack occurred behind closed doors within the confines of his office, and thus concealed from public view. But, even if these factors were not present, the determining factor in this incident was the physical nature of Cohen's harassment. He grabbed Fall and kissed her while groping her breasts. Although Fall alleged only a single act of sexual harassment, the court ruled that an incident involving physical assault, such as that experienced by Fall, may sufficiently alter the conditions of the victim's employment as to create an abusive work environment.[8]

Evidence of physical assault or the touching of a woman's breasts or genital area will nearly always be sufficient to establish a hostile and offensive workplace, even if the victim experiences only one such incident. The courts attribute a significantly higher degree of violation and transgression to acts of physical harassment than to acts of verbal harassment. EEOC policy is similar:

> The [EEOC] will presume that the unwelcome, intentional touching of a [woman's] intimate body parts is sufficiently offensive to alter the conditions of her employment and constitute a violation of Title VII. More so

than in the case of verbal advances or remarks, a single unwelcome physical advance can seriously poison the victim's working environment.[9]

Verbal Harassment

In contrast to the physical harassment suffered by Mechelle Vinson, Terri Nichols, and Lynn Fall, some women are subjected only to verbal harassment. A valid sexual harassment claim may be asserted even in the absence of any inappropriate physical contact, since an extended period of verbal harassment may prove nearly as demeaning and as humiliating as an incident of intimate touching.

Connie Blackmon, a security guard for Pinkerton Security, was the only woman on a five-member team working the night-shift at a manufacturing plant. From the beginning of her employment until the day of her termination, her four co-workers engaged in constant, graphic sexual conversations in her presence. They used lurid language to comment on the bodies of female employees, fantasized as to the sex acts they would like to perform with them, graphically portrayed their sexual conquests and fantasies to each other, and used vulgar language in referring to sex acts and the female anatomy.

When Blackmon complained about her co-workers' conduct and asked that it be halted, her shift superintendent, rather than addressing her grievances, accused her of complaining because she was not getting enough sex. The sexually explicit conversations continued unabated, and Blackmon continued to complain, advancing up the company's chain of command, and ultimately her complaints reached the office of Pinkerton's district manager. He agreed to conduct an investigation, but instead of considering the particulars of Blackmon's complaints, he focused on Blackmon herself. He obtained a written statement from one of her fellow workers averring that Blackmon used foul language. He then asked Blackmon's four male team members to maintain a written record of all conversations they had with Blackmon, and he encouraged them to make certain this written record failed to provide any support for her complaints. Obviously, the district manager intended to try to show that Blackmon actively participated in the conduct she complained of, or even to show she was the cause of it. Attacking the victim of sexual harassment is a typical employer strategy, and the best way of attacking the victim is to create a basis for her dismissal.

After Blackmon sued Pinkerton, a jury awarded her $75,000 in damages for emotional distress suffered as a consequence of the harassment and $100,000 in punitive damages. In light of the egregiously offensive language and verbal harassment to which she was subjected, these awards for damages were fully justified.[10]

A supervisor or a co-worker does not violate Title VII merely by initiating a conversation having sexual content or connotation. A line must be drawn between workplace conversation that is harassing and that which is merely vulgar or borderline inappropriate. In establishing that line, gestures, voice inflection, the presence or absence of other persons, and the place where the words are uttered all must be taken into account. As an example, a mildly offensive remark might be considered harmless if delivered in a public setting, but acquire a sinister cast if made in private.[11] In chapter 4 we will study at some length the types of workplace verbal conduct the courts have considered harassing and those types of behavior they have labeled as merely obnoxious, unpleasant, or inappropriate.

Sexual Harassment of Blue-Collar Workers

A blue-collar worker is more likely to be subjected to acts of physical harassment than a management employee or a woman employed as a lawyer, physician, teacher, or as a member of one of the other professions. One study disclosed that nearly 50 percent of reported blue-collar sexual harassment cases contain a complaint of physical harassment, compared with 32 percent of management employee cases and 38 percent of complaints asserted by women employed in one of the professions.[12] But in addition, as was the case in the Eveleth Taconite lawsuit, women working in a blue-collar setting often experience blatant, openly committed acts of sexual harassment.

Lois Robinson worked at the Jacksonville Shipyards as a welder. The shipyard, in the words of one of its employees, was a "boys club, a man's world." Few women were employed in most positions. In this man's world, pictures of nude and partially nude women appeared throughout the workplace. Two varnished, wooden plaques portraying nude women hung in the office of the foreman charged with the responsibility of dealing with personnel matters. Although magazines and newspapers were forbidden in work areas, cartoons and pictures cut from pornographic magazines were seen everywhere. Management condoned pictorial displays of nude women in common areas, and executives had their own pictures in their offices. One of the pictures displayed in Robinson's work area was that of a nude woman with long blond hair, wearing high heels and holding a whip. Robinson felt targeted by this photograph as she had long blond hair and worked with a welding tool referred to as a "whip."

In addition to subjecting Robinson to displays of nude and partially nude pictures, male co-workers inundated her with sexual comments and abusive language. Other female workers were similarly treated. The openly exhibited pornographic materials, the abusive comments, and the sexually oriented treatment that was forced on the shipyard's female workers openly sexualized their work environment, while subverting their work roles.[13]

Although this type of work environment is now less prevalent than in earlier eras, it nevertheless persists, as Julia O'Rourke, a Providence, Rhode Island, firefighter, can attest. Until 1992, the Providence fire department had never employed a female firefighter, but in that year, acting pursuant to a newly implemented affirmative action plan, it admitted O'Rourke and five other women to its six-month training program. Once she completed her training, O'Rourke was temporarily assigned to the office of the fire chief. During the course of this assignment, a male firefighter working near O'Rourke blew in her ear, rubbed his cheek against hers, and as she worked at the copying machine, stood over her with their bodies squarely touching. His conduct continued even though O'Rourke declined his many invitations to go out on dates with him.

Following her assignment in the fire chief's office, the department transferred O'Rourke to an engine company, the first woman ever thus assigned. Subsequently, her daily life as a firefighter was replete with incidents of male co-worker sexual misconduct. Stacks of pornographic magazines were located in the common sitting rooms, rest rooms, and other areas of the firehouse. She was told that a closed-circuit television camera had been placed in the bedroom that had been allotted to her. Posters of seminude women hung on the engine house walls. Pornographic movies were shown in the common sitting area. One firefighter kept pictures of nude women in his locker. Another co-worker attempted to initiate discussions with O'Rourke about oral sex. A poster, hung in the sleeping area portraying a seminude woman in a provocative pose, contained a handwritten reference to O'Rourke. Her working environment was overtly sexual, openly hostile, and wholly offensive.

The fire department's legal defense offered in response to O'Rourke's sexual harassment claim centered on the contention that its workplace should be evaluated in the context of a blue-collar work environment where crude language and sexual-oriented conduct is common. The court rejected this argument. A woman who chooses to work in a male-dominated environment does not relinquish her right to work free from sexual harassment. If the contrary were true, then the more hostile the environment the more difficult it would be for a female worker to prove the conduct she was subjected to was severe or pervasive. Women working in blue-collar jobs do not deserve less protection than women working in white-collar positions.[14]

We will return to the sexually harassed blue-collar worker in chapter 6.

Sexual Harassment of White-Collar Employees

Female white-collar employees are far less likely to find themselves toiling in the type of environment found at the Jacksonville Shipyards and the Providence Fire Department. Physical and verbal harassment may abound among white-collar and management employees but generally in a much less obvious and overt manner. Such a work environment, however, is no less offensive or hostile for the women forced to work in it.

Catherine Broderick worked as a staff attorney for the Securities and Exchange Commission's Division of Corporate Finance in Arlington, Virginia. During the entire period of her employment with the SEC, an atmosphere dominated by sex pervaded her department. Two of the department's supervisors were involved in ongoing sexual relationships with secretaries and another supervisor with a staff attorney. The secretaries and staff attorney were favored with salary increases, promotions, commendations, and bonus awards. Fully aware that her supervisors bestowed preferential treatment on those who submitted to their sexual advances, Broderick was grossly offended by the nature of the conditions in which she was required to work, and eventually this environment undermined her motivation and adversely affected her work performance. The conduct of the supervisors, apparent to all, created a hostile and highly offensive work environment, thus entitling Broderick and other women working in the department to relief under Title VII.[15]

Rhonda Mallinson-Montague, a white-collar worker, experienced harassing conduct of a more typical nature. She was offered employment by James Pocrnick, a senior vice president of consumer lending for the Professional Bank. Pocrnick first met Mallinson-Montague when he closed a consumer loan for her at the bank. Despite Mallinson-Montague's lack of banking experience, Pocrnick offered her a loan officer position, paying a base salary plus commissions computed on the basis of the number of loans closed. Although Mallinson-Montague had reservations about taking the job, she accepted the offer after Pocrnick assured her she would be properly trained and would be provided with sufficient leads to enable her to earn substantial commission income.

Immediately after Mallinson-Montague began work at the bank, Pocrnick began to harass her. On one occasion, he instructed her to meet him at a nearby park to review some business matters. When she arrived at the designated meeting place, he pressed himself against her, kissed her, and asked her if she could feel his erection. After Mallinson-Montague rebuffed these advances, Pocrnick denied her the business leads he had previously promised and began to reject loans she had originated. Apparently, Pocrnick had induced Mallinson-Montague to accept employment at the bank primarily for the purpose of facilitating his plans of sexual conquest. In fact, another female employee reported experiences with Pocrnick remarkably similar in nature to those described by Mallinson-Montague. Pocrnick's acts of retaliation following Mallinson-Montague's rejection of his advances only added to the severity and pervasiveness of his harassing conduct.

Soon after the incident in the park, Mallinson-Montague retained an attorney who wrote to the bank's president disclosing Pocrnick's behavior. The harassment then ceased, but Mallinson-Montague, believing her career at the bank had been compromised, resigned. When she later sued Pocrnick and the bank for sexual harassment, the jury rendered its verdict in her favor.[16]

Sexual Harassment of Management and Professional Employees

A sexually harassed waitress may resolve her problem by quitting and taking a job down the street with another restaurant, but a woman in a high executive position or one with an advanced degree is less likely to be able to satisfactorily resolve a sexual harassment situation in that fashion. Since her position is important to her, she wants to hold on to it, and thus she may be more vulnerable to the sexually harassing conduct of a superior. Her perception of sexual harassment is also likely to differ from that of the waitress, in that she more than likely has higher expectations for being treated in a professional manner, and thus may be more inclined to label sexual advances as harassment.[17]

Emily Bryson first worked at Chicago State University as a bibliographic instruction librarian but later advanced to full professorship with tenure. After several years as a professor, Bryson claimed she had been made the subject of quid pro quo harassment inflicted by the university's provost, Chernoh Sesay. Bryson alleged that Sesay, shortly after his appointment to the provost post, began to make sexually suggestive comments in her presence and attempted to engage in improper physical contact with her. For example, at a Christmas party, he approached Bryson, caressed her shoulders, pushed his body against hers and whispered, "When are you going to come over and start cooking for me?" Bryson responded that she did not cook for anyone. Two months later, while Sesay and Bryson were visiting another campus, Sesay asked Bryson to accompany him back to the hotel so they could "relax." On several occasions when she was in his office, he tried to kiss her. He repeatedly asked her to visit him in his room, and when she continued to resist him he told her, "You had better do what I say or you're going to be sorry." Subsequently, Sesay ordered her duties reduced and later directed her to return to her former position as bibliographic instruction librarian.[18]

Bryson's allegations of sexual harassment are typical of those asserted by women in the professional ranks. Even though sexual harassment in the professions is less likely to be openly displayed, on occasion it can be flat-out nasty.

After Jean Jew obtained her medical degree, the University of Iowa's College of Medicine appointed her an associate professor in its Department of Anatomy. At the time of her appointment, Terrence Williams was the head of the Department of Anatomy.

Throughout her employment at the University of Iowa, Dr. Jew worked closely with Dr. Williams as a research collaborator. They coauthored several articles for scientific publications and they had a close professional relationship. Although Jew and Williams's wife, also a professor at the College of Medicine, were friends, rumors circulated throughout the Department of Anatomy that a sexual relationship existed between Dr. Jew and Dr. Williams. The ongoing rumors accused her of using her sex as a tool for advancement in the department. Sexually suggestive cartoons and sex-based graffiti referring to Dr. Jew appeared on the wall of the men's room and at other places in the department. One of the male faculty members repeatedly speculated about a sexual relationship between Dr. Jew and Dr. Williams, and he told faculty, graduate students, and staff that Dr. Jew had been observed having sexual intercourse with Dr. Williams in his office. He called her a "slut," and accused her of having received preferential treatment based on her sexual relationship with Dr. Williams. Another male doctor also characterized Dr. Jew as a "slut" and also referred to her as a "bitch" and a "whore."

Dr. Jew complained to the Dean of the College of Medicine, advising him of the conduct of the male doctors in her department, and charged the college with ignoring the existence of a pattern of sexual harassment intended to discredit her professional and personal reputation. College officials advised her nothing could be done, that a single woman commonly encountered these kinds of difficulties in a small town, goldfishbowl type of environment.

Dr. Jew continued to author and coauthor with Dr. Williams a number of articles published in prominent medical journals. She received two grants from the National Institute of Health and another from the National Science Foundation. In due course, the medical school considered her for promotion from associate professor to full professor. In accordance with established procedures, school administrators placed the proposed promotion before the entire faculty of the Department of Anatomy for approval or rejection.

The same faculty members who had verbally harassed Dr. Jew were among those called on to evaluate her work and vote on her promotion. Two of the doctors who opposed her promotion were those who had labeled her a "slut" and a "whore." Another doctor voting "no" commented that Dr. Jew had received many more advantages than he had been granted. All of the voting faculty had heard the pervasive rumors and, not surprisingly, they voted against her promotion. Those who voted "no" expressed the opinion that Dr. Jew had not established her "independence" in the areas of research and publication.

When Dr. Jew later sued the university for sex discrimination and sexual harassment, the court, citing the conduct she had endured, ruled in her favor:

> The ongoing rumors, which were false, accused her of physically using her sex as a tool for gaining favor, influence and power with the Head of the Department, a man, and suggested that her professional accomplishments rested on sexual achievements rather than achievements of merit. Similarly situated males were not so harassed. . . . The sexual relationship rumors, of course, also implicated Dr. Williams. . . . Unlike the import of the rumors with respect to Dr. Jew, however, there was no suggestion that Dr. Williams was *using* a sexual relationship to gain favor, influence and power. . . . While some of the harassment of Dr. Jew may have been motivated in part by animosity towards Dr. Williams, it nonetheless remained sex-based harassment of Dr. Jew.

The court held that the rejection of Dr. Jew for promotion flowed directly from the harassing and discriminatory conduct of the male doctors in her department. The court directed the university to promote Dr. Jew, retroactively, to full professorship.[19]

In the chapters that follow, we will study in greater detail the types of sexual harassing conduct women experience during their work lives. We begin that study with an analysis of the welcomeness issue, followed by an evaluation of the levels of severity or pervasiveness of harassing conduct necessary to support a sexual harassment claim.

CHAPTER THREE

The Welcomeness Issue

During the course of her sexual harassment lawsuit against Meritor Savings Bank, Mechelle Vinson admitted she had consented to a sexual relationship with her supervisor, Sidney Taylor (see chapter 1). She testified that Taylor at first treated her in a fatherly fashion, making no sexual advances, but then invited her out to dinner and later suggested they have sexual relations. At first she refused, but when he persisted, out of fear of losing her job, she consented. According to Vinson, Taylor subsequently made repeated demands on her for sex, and over the next several years they had intercourse some forty or fifty times.

In defending against Vinson's harassment claim, the bank advanced the position that since Vinson's participation in sexual intercourse with Taylor was voluntary, her claim was without merit. The Supreme Court rejected this argument, ruling that even if Vinson's participation was voluntary—voluntary in the sense she was not forced against her will to participate in the sexual act—the question remained whether the sexual relationship with Taylor was *welcome* to her. It is not a question of consent or voluntariness, but rather a question of welcomeness. A woman may consent to sexual conduct, but not welcome it.[1]

Since sexual attraction is an element of social exchange between workers of the opposite sex, it is often difficult to discern the distinction between sexual advances that are invited and welcome, those that are uninvited but nevertheless welcome, and those that are neither invited nor welcome. And because of this difficulty, the issue of welcomeness often appears at the center of sexual harassment disputes.

At times, a harasser's actions are of such a degrading nature that a court will assume they were unwelcome, as any reasonable person would be grossly offended by them. In one such case, two female employees accused their supervisor of repeated episodes of sexual misconduct characterized by extremely vulgar comments and gestures. As an expression of his anger or dissatisfaction with their job performance, he would stand behind them and pretend to masturbate and ejaculate on them, and made other offensive gestures when their backs were turned. He repeatedly commented on their breasts, and on one occasion grabbed one of the women, leaving bruises on her arms. The court held no ordinary person would welcome this type of conduct. It constituted precisely the sort of demeaning behavior Title VII was intended to address.[2] Welcomeness in circumstances such as these is not an issue.

When the question of welcomeness is disputed, the complainant's position will have been materially strengthened if she protested the harasser's conduct when she first experienced it and reported it to company officials as well. If a woman immediately informs the harasser that his sexual advances or other sexual-oriented conduct are unwelcome and that he should cease from engaging in any further behavior of that sort, it is unlikely her employer will later argue she welcomed the harasser's conduct. For a variety of reasons, however, women tend to delay a confrontation with their harassers and such a delay provides an employer with an opportunity to assert the welcomeness issue.

In 1991, Anita Hill testified before the Senate Judiciary Committee, then considering the nomination of Clarence Thomas to the U.S. Supreme Court. She related to the committee instances of sexual harassing conduct allegedly committed by Thomas when they both worked for the EEOC in the early 1980s. A member of the committee asked Hill why she had not reported Thomas's conduct a decade earlier. This was her response:

> It is only after a great deal of agonizing consideration that I am able to talk of these unpleasant matters to anyone, except my closest friends. . . . Telling the world is the most difficult experience of my life. . . . I may have used poor judgment early on in my relationship with this issue. I was aware, however, that telling at any point in my career could adversely affect my future career. . . . Perhaps I should have taken angry or even militant steps . . . but I must confess . . . that the course that I took seemed better, as well as the easier approach.[3]

When a woman fails immediately to confront her harasser or delays in reporting his conduct, the question of welcomeness nearly always is asserted by the employer. If she really found the conduct offensive and unwelcome, why did she not tell the harasser to stop it? Why did she not immediately report it to his supervisors?

Although a woman's silence may give rise to questions of her welcomeness, that silence does not necessarily signify she welcomed the conduct. The circumstances confronting her at the time of the harassment may have motivated her to delay a direct response to the harasser's behavior. She may have feared the loss of her job—as did Anita Hill—or other act of retaliation, not an unrealistic fear, as employers often act negatively toward workers who complain of supervisory harassment. She also may have remained silent out of a feeling of shame, guilt, humiliation, or embarrassment, making it difficult for her to discuss her situation with anyone, even family members, much less her company's officials. And, of course, at the time of the harassment, she most likely was not considering litigation, and thus furthest from her mind were the steps advisable for her to take to preserve her legal position. Consequently, a woman's failure to immediately confront her harasser may inadvertently elevate the significance of the welcomeness issue in subsequent sexual harassment litigation.

When a victim of harassment decides she cannot any longer remain silent, she should notify her harasser that his conduct is unacceptable and unwelcome. Her message should be clear and unambiguous—*Stop it now!* In one case, the court noted that when the complainant asked her supervisor not to touch her, she failed to act with any sense of force or urgency. She sent out mixed signals, relying on various schemes to curtail her supervisor's behavior, but each involved a "hopelessly indirect action that delivered an attenuated message." Since she never sat down with the harasser and made a serious plea for him to stop, the court dismissed her case.[4] Other courts, viewing the issue less restrictively, have permitted women to establish unwelcomeness even though they failed to directly confront their harassers. A case in point involved Katherine Chamberlin's harassment charges against her employer.

Newly married and a recent college graduate with a bachelor's degree in architecture, Chamberlin applied for a position with 101 Realty in New Hampshire and was hired by Matthew Zsofka, president and owner of the company. Zsofka later made a number of sexual advances over a four- to five-week period:

- While Chamberlin was riding to a job site with Zsofka in his truck, he told her she had a good body, adding, "If you worked out, you'd have a great body." Chamberlin, feeling very uncomfortable, made no response, but changed the subject of conversation.
- Two weeks later, while visiting a construction site, Zsofka moved very close to Chamberlin until they were nearly touching, and said, "You look good in tight jeans. It shows off your butt." Chamberlin said nothing, but turned around and walked to the other side of the building.
- On a visit to another building site, Zsofka again told her she looked good in jeans. Chamberlin pretended she had not heard him, hoping he would cease making such comments.
- While having lunch, Zsofka took Chamberlin's hands and said, "I like my women with good looks and brains." Chamberlin immediately removed her hands, and began discussing business matters.
- At a subsequent luncheon, Zsofka again took Chamberlin's hands and said, "My women are special. I like to put them on a pedestal." Chamberlin once again removed her hands and changed the subject.

Although Zsofka at first was pleased with Chamberlin's performance, after these incidents he began to find fault with her work, and about two months later, he fired her on grounds of inexperience, incompetence, and disloyalty. Chamberlin then sued for quid pro quo sexual harassment, claiming Zsofka terminated her employment only because she had not responded positively to his sexual advances.

Chamberlin did not directly confront Zsofka with his acts of harassment and, not surprisingly, he later placed the welcomeness of his conduct in issue. The court, however, ruled in Chamberlin's favor, observing she had endeavored to communicate to Zsofka that his sexual advances were not welcome. On the two occasions that he grasped her hands, she immediately withdrew them and changed the subject of conversation. Similarly, when he remarked that her jeans highlighted her buttocks, she immediately left his presence, and on the occasions of his other advances, she diverted his attention by turning to another topic of discussion. These actions were sufficient to apprise Zsofka that his behavior was unwelcome. Having received the message, he should have altered his behavior.

In evaluating a woman's response to sexual overtures, the court should take into account all the circumstances the victim confronted at the time of the harassment, as those circumstances often dictate the woman's method of coping with aberrant behavior. Chamberlin muted her responses to Zsofka's advances because he was the owner of the company for whom she worked, and more emphatic means of communicating her unwelcomeness could conceivably have prompted him to order her immediate discharge. In this case, an enlightened court, clearly alert to the difficulties that confront victims of sexual harassment, viewed the welcomeness issue from a woman's perspective, thus allowing Chamberlin to prosecute her claim.[5]

Employers raise the welcomeness issue in all types of circumstances, even when little hope exists they will succeed in effecting the dismissal of a woman's claim. Elizabeth Morton sued her employer, Steven Ford-Mercury, claiming she was forced to work in an offensive and hostile working environment, centering her complaint on sexual comments made in her presence by co-workers and supervisors. The company claimed that Morton welcomed conversations of a sexual nature, as she commonly discussed such topics as nude sunbathing and topless fishing. But according to Morton, she engaged in such conversations only with a female co-worker, and these exchanges became more widely known among company employees only because a male co-worker eavesdropped on them. The company also argued that Morton encouraged sexual commentary by bringing to work copies of a Victoria's Secret catalog and a Cosmopolitan magazine. But her male co-workers became aware of the contents of those publications only after the eavesdropping co-worker covertly removed them from Morton's desk and showed them to other male workers. The court found the company's argument unpersuasive, as neither event suggested that Morton welcomed talk of a sexual nature with male co-workers.

The company also argued that Morton must have welcomed the sexual commentary; otherwise she would have directly confronted those who engaged in it. Morton claimed she tried to ignore the sex talk, hoping it would cease. But, in addition, when she found herself in the center of such commentary, she expressed heightened emotional responses in the form of exasperation and anger, suggesting that this type of commentary was undesirable, and, indeed, some of her fellow employees were aware these conversations upset her. Again, the court found the company's position unpersuasive.[6]

Suppose, contrary to the circumstances of the *Morton* case, a female worker claims her working environment was replete with sex-related conversations, but the evidence shows she engaged in such commentary with male co-workers. Will the welcomeness issue lead to the defeat of her sexual harassment claim? In one case, a female worker regularly used vulgar language at work, initiated sexually oriented conversations with male co-workers, and asked them about their marital sex lives and whether they engaged in extramarital affairs. She showed no reluctance to discussing her own marital sexual relationship, making it a regular topic of office conversation, while volunteering intimate details of her premarital sex encounters with her husband. Although the court noted that the working environment was very distasteful—which under other circumstances could very well support the sexual harassment charges of the type advanced—the evidence showed that the complainant actively contributed to those working conditions, and she welcomed—and even encouraged—the harassing conduct she later complained of. Her own profane and sexually suggestive conduct fostered the work environment offensiveness she alleged as the basis of her sexual harassment claim. The court dismissed her case.[7]

The courts generally rule that a woman's willing and frequent involvement in sexually oriented conduct in the workplace provides a strong indicator she considers such conduct neither unwelcome nor hostile. This does not mean a woman's participation in actions of a sexual or vulgar nature completely undermines her claim. For example, if at some point she alters her stance and makes her co-workers and supervisors aware she no longer welcomes such conduct, and thereafter declines to participate in it as she had in the past, a continuation of conduct of that nature may serve as a basis for a sexual harassment claim.[8] Simply withdrawing from continued participation, however, is insufficient to show such activity is no longer welcome. Rather, she must unambiguously inform her co-workers and supervisors she no longer considers sexually oriented behavior to be acceptable.[9]

Suppose a female worker appears to welcome some but not all workplace sexual conduct. What are her rights under those circumstances? In one case, a number of office workers, including the plaintiff, used foul language and circulated dirty jokes. If the plaintiff's sexual harassment claim had been based solely on foul language and dirty jokes, her claim would have been dismissed, since her participation in that type of activity demonstrated she was not offended by it. However, when a supervisor solicited her for oral sex and inappropriately touched her, she made it clear that she was highly offended. The employer contended that since she participated without objection in the general office sex-banter, her supervisor's request for oral sex and the touching incident must have been welcome to her. The court rejected that position. Her participation in less offensive types of sexual behavior did not constitute a waiver of her Title VII protections against highly offensive acts of sexual harassment.[10]

In another case, an alleged harasser, accused of having used foul language in the plaintiff's presence, argued in defense that she normally engaged in similar language with other workers. But, at the time he used foul language in her presence, he was unaware of the nature of her conversations with others. Therefore, he could not have been under the impression that foul language was welcome to her. In fact, she told him not to use such language in her presence. Under these circumstances, it would be inappropriate for the court to consider plaintiff's conduct with other workers as evidence of her welcomeness to the harasser's conduct.[11]

Even in circumstances where the complainant is shown to have participated in conduct similar to that which she alleges to have been harassing, the harasser's conduct may nonetheless have been unwelcome. Mary Carr worked for Allison Gas Turbine, a division of General Motors, as a tinsmith apprentice, the first woman to work for Allison in that capacity. Her male co-workers were not pleased with the assignment of a woman to the tinsmith shop, and they made her the target of derogatory comments of a sexual character and played various sex-and gender-related pranks on her. Eventually, their conduct crossed the line separating the merely vulgar and mildly offensive from the deeply offensive and sexually harassing conduct. But the trial judge who heard her sexual harassment suit ruled she had invited the co-workers' conduct:

> She was not merely the recipient of crude behavior and crude language—she also dished it out . . . [and] contributed just as much abusive language and crude behavior as did the male tinners, and therefore was just as responsible for any hostile sexual environment that consequently arose. . . . The tinners' conduct, to the extent it may have constituted sexual harassment, was not unwelcome.

The appellate court that later reviewed this decision characterized the lower court's ruling as one that relied on a finding that Carr had provoked the misconduct of her co-workers. In effect, the judge sitting in the lower court was saying that, "Had she been more ladylike . . . they would have left her alone." The appellate court, however, pointed out that Carr's conduct was not comparable to that of her male co-workers. Even if the court were to ignore the question why "unladylike" behavior necessarily constituted evidence of welcomeness, and even if it were to discount Carr's testimony that she talked and acted as she did in an effort to be "one of the boys," her words and conduct could not be compared to those of her male co-workers:

> The asymmetry of positions must be considered. She was one woman; they were many men. . . . We have trouble *imagining* a situation in which male factory workers sexually harass a lone woman *in self-defense* as it were; yet that at root is General Motor's characterization of what happened here. It is incredible on the admitted facts. [Emphasis in the original]

Although Carr talked and acted as she did in an effort to be "one of the boys," her language and conduct did not signal welcomeness to the grossly offensive behavior of her co-workers. In fact, she complained bitterly about that conduct, and thus they could not have been acting under any illusion that their behavior was acceptable or welcome to her.[12]

Turning to another issue, suppose an employer wishes to offer evidence of the complainant's sexual activities outside of the workplace as proof of her welcomeness of offensive conduct occurring in the workplace. Is this type of evidence relevant to the welcomeness issue?

Lisa Ann Burns worked for McGregor Electronics Industries. The evidence admitted in her sexual harassment suit against McGregor painted a picture an appellate court later described as a "grisly and shocking [example] of unwelcome sexual harassment." The owner of the company continuously barraged Burns with sexual propositions, asked her to attend pornographic movies with him, suggested oral sex, and stalked her at work. The trial court, however, questioned whether Burns considered any of the owner's behavior offensive or unwelcome, as she had previously posed nude for two national motorcycle magazines. The trial court reasoned that a woman who would allow her nude photograph to be distributed nationally would not be offended by the type of conduct engaged in by the company's owner, thus concluding she had exaggerated its effect on her. Even though the court explicitly found Burns had not solicited or invited the owner's behavior, it ruled that due to the nature of her conduct engaged in outside of work, the sexual advances of her employer occurring within the workplace could not have been offensive to her and must therefore be considered as welcome.

An appellate court viewed the case differently. Burns's decision to pose nude outside of work hours was a choice she made that was totally separate and apart from anything that took place at work. It was not as if she had posed in a provocative and suggestive way while on the job. A woman's private life outside of the workplace, even if one were to find it reprehensible, cannot justify unwanted sexual advances in the workplace. A woman's private life cannot be used to demonstrate her welcomeness to sexual advances in the office. Activities engaged in outside of the workplace are simply irrelevant to the welcomeness issue.[13]

Women are often concerned that the welcomeness issue will open their sex lives to public examination. The possibility of the public disclosure of the intimate aspects of a woman's private life will at times discourage complainants from prosecuting lawsuits against their harassers. These fears do not pass unnoticed by unscrupulous employers, who at times use an investigation of a sexual harassment complaint as a means of sending a message to their female workers that the personal costs of pursuing a harassment claim may be too high. One writer described this tactic as a "two-for-one special of hammering the plaintiff . . . while sending out a clear message to all others."[14]

During the course of one employer's investigation of harassment charges alleged against one of its male employees, it interviewed twenty-six employees and other persons, but only five of those interviews related to the harassment charges, while the other twenty-one focused on the complainant's past conduct and background, including a failed marriage with her first husband. The scope of the investigation was designed, not only to discredit the complainant, but also to humiliate and embarrass her.[15]

The courts have expressed concern that an employer-initiated investigation of past sexual conduct may intimidate prospective Title VII claimants, and they look askance at employer tactics requiring inquiry into matters entirely personal to the plaintiff. The privacy rights of a victim of sexual harassment have been protected by most courts through the exclusion of any proffered evidence of past sexual conduct with anyone other than the person alleged to have committed acts of sexual harassment against her. Although the "welcomeness" issue will open the door to inquiries concerning any sort of sexual relationship between the harasser and the victim, other inquiries into the past sexual conduct of the plaintiff with persons outside the workplace are barred, even—as we have seen—when an employer claims the plaintiff's sexual conduct outside the workplace is relevant to her claim of unwelcomeness within the workplace.

In one case, a female police officer lodged a hostile environment sexual harassment claim based primarily on the presence of pornographic posters, videos, and magazines in the police station. The police department defended against her claim by offering evidence that she attended parties outside of work where pornographic videos were exhibited, arguing she therefore could not have been offended by the presence of pornographic materials in the police station. The court rejected this evidence on the ground that whether a woman perceives her work environment to be sexually offensive does not turn on her private sexual behavior, "because a woman's expectations about her work environment cannot be said to change depending upon her sexual sophistication." A woman's outlook on sexual matters outside of work generally differs materially from her views of sexual conduct at work. Even if a woman's outside-of-work sexual experiences were such that she could perhaps be expected to suffer less harm from viewing run-of-the-mill pornographic images displayed at her work site, the presence of the pornography could still alter her work status.[16] Inasmuch as women generally view sexual conduct at work through a lens different from the one they use to view sexual conduct outside of work, the courts should respect this difference in view.

An employer sought to make an issue of a complainant's sexual history by painting her as sexually insatiable, as a woman who was engaged in multiple affairs with married men, as a lesbian, as one suffering from a sexually transmitted disease, and as a woman freely exhibiting flirtatious behavior. The court allowed only the submission of evidence purporting to show she flirted with the alleged harasser, barring the employer's offer of all other evidence relating to the complainant's moral character and alleged promiscuity. None of the evidence the court accepted deterred it from ruling in the complainant's favor.[17]

Since it is not at all unusual for an employer accused of sexual harassment to endeavor to rake up instances of the plaintiff's past sexual conduct—anything that might possibly prejudice a jury against her—Congress, in 1994, amended the Federal Rules of Evidence to bar the misuse of a complainant's sexual history in harassment and other cases involving sexual misconduct. With certain limited exceptions, these rules bar the admission of evidence offered to prove a claimant's sexual predisposition or that she engaged in sexual behavior outside the workplace. Thus federal evidentiary rules, together with court decisions, now constitute major barriers for an employer bent on introducing a plaintiff's sexual history to public view.[18]

The Federal Rules of Evidence, however, do not bar the admission of evidence relating to a complainant's behavior with respect to the man she claims to be her harasser. This type of evidence always is relevant to the welcomeness issue, and since employers, as the cases we have reviewed clearly establish, very often claim the alleged harassing conduct was welcomed by the plaintiff, a complainant must be prepared to respond to inquiries regarding her reactions and responses to the harasser's conduct. One area of inquiry is her mode of dress. An employer may attempt to show the complainant dressed provocatively, thus evidencing welcomeness to the attentions of the harasser. But is this form of evidence admissible in a sexual harassment case?

In Mechelle Vinson's case, the Supreme Court ruled that the welcomeness issue may require a court to consider whether the plaintiff dressed provocatively while at work.[19] However, the amendments to the Federal Rules of Evidence, enacted after the *Vinson* case, exclude "evidence offered to prove any alleged victim's sexual disposition."[20] The Supreme Court has yet to revisit the issue since the federal rules were amended, and thus the law remains open to interpretation in this respect. Moreover, when the court considered the issue in the Vinson case, it failed explicitly to define "provocative dress." As one writer put it, "provocation, like beauty, is in the eye of the beholder."[21] Is a short skirt an invitation to a sexual advance? Are tight sweaters provocation for offensive conduct? One legal scholar has posed the query whether men are "legally entitled to treat women whose clothes fit snugly with less respect than women whose clothes fit loosely," adding that "by accepting the notion of 'sexually provocative' clothing, the Court effectively denies women the right to dress as they wish."[22]

Allegations that a claimant dressed provocatively opens up the proverbial "can of worms"—what is judged as provocative by some may be considered good taste by others. Thus it behooves a woman who has been subjected to sexually harassing behavior to exercise caution in the selection of her wardrobe.

The welcomeness issue may also arise when a worker involved in a consensual sexual relationship decides to end it. Feelings of betrayal may elicit unsubstantiated charges of harassment on the one hand, or acts of actual harassment on the other. Shayne Kahn worked for Objective Solutions International as a senior executive recruiter and had a consensual sexual relationship with Steven Wolfe, the company's owner and president. Soon after Kahn's second anniversary with the company, Wolfe told her that because of his wife's objections, he was terminating their relationship, and he told her that if he could not be intimate with her, he no longer wanted her present in the office. He then fired Kahn.

Kahn sued Wolfe and the company for sexual harassment, but the court dismissed her claim. In view of the fact that her relationship with Wolfe had been consensual and had not constituted a condition of her employment, her involvement with him could not be said to have been "unwelcome." Nor could she claim her termination of employment arose out of a refusal on her part to submit to sexual requests. Rather, she could only allege she was discharged in the wake of Wolfe's decision to terminate their sexual relationship. As observed by the court, these facts cannot support a claim of quid pro quo harassment.

Kahn also pleaded a hostile work environment but was unable to offer any evidence of harassing conduct that occurred as a consequence of her sexual relationship with Wolfe. Participation in a consensual office affair does not amount to sexual harassment merely because the end of the employment relationship coincides with the end of the affair. Wolfe's decision to simultaneously terminate the sexual and the employment relationships may have been unchivalrous behavior, but it was not sexually harassing conduct.[23]

A woman who has a consensual affair with her supervisor, but later terminates it, is not barred by the welcomeness doctrine from claiming the supervisor's sexual advances, made after the conclusion of the affair, were no longer welcome. Even though his sexual advances may have been welcomed in the past, once he learns they are no longer considered as acceptable conduct, he may be guilty of sexually harassing conduct if he persists in failing to alter his conduct.

Some legal scholars and commentators would relieve a claimant from the need to establish the unwelcomeness of the alleged harasser's conduct. They argue that when sexual advances are welcome, a woman does not sue for sexual harassment. Since she sues only when the advances are unwelcome to her, welcomeness should be a nonissue. They also maintain that since the welcomeness issue requires consideration of evidence pertaining to the plaintiff's behavior in response to the harasser's conduct, the court tends to focus its attention on the woman's conduct rather than on the harasser's. This attention is contrary to the spirit of Title VII.

But is there an alternative? The elimination of the concept of welcomeness would require a court to assume that all sexual advances that are the subject of a sexual harassment claim are inappropriate. But what about those sexual advances, later alleged to be harassing, that occur in a consensual romantic relationship between co-workers? In those circumstances, a court would be justified in assuming inappropriateness only if sexual advances have no place whatsoever in a work environment. This, obviously, is not the case.[24]

As long as workers continue to consider co-workers as potential sex or marriage partners, the welcomeness issue will remain the standard distinguishing acceptable from unacceptable behavior.

CHAPTER FOUR

Severe or Pervasive Conduct

The Supreme Court ruled in Mechelle Vinson's sexual harassment case against Meritor Savings Bank (discussed in chapter 1) that harassing conduct violates Title VII only if it is sufficiently "severe or pervasive" to alter the terms and conditions of the victim's employment, thus creating an abusive and hostile working environment.[1] From a victim's perspective, the most significant word in the court's ruling is "or"—severe *or* pervasive, not severe *and* pervasive. When an individual act of harassment is severe, the working environment is generally rendered hostile long before the harassment becomes pervasive. Conversely, harassing conduct may pervade the workplace even though each individual act of harassment may not be severe. A plaintiff sustains her burden of proof by establishing either element.

The Supreme Court emphasized in its *Vinson* ruling that not every working environment having sexualized overtones may be characterized as one barred by the statute. Rather, the work environment must be one a reasonable person finds hostile and one the victim herself also perceives to be so. If the workplace is not thus viewed, the conditions of the victim's employment cannot be said to have been altered by reason of working in that environment, and the complained-of behavior is not actionable under Title VII.[2]

In deciding whether the complained-of conduct is sufficiently severe or pervasive to alter the conditions of a victim's employment, the courts consider all factors—commonly referred to as the "totality of the circumstances"—of a woman's working environment. The very fact that harassment exists in a specified "environment" requires the court to consider all aspects of that environment as a whole, rather than considering each aspect in isolation. The courts consider the frequency of the harassing conduct, its duration, whether it is psychologically threatening or humiliating, the extent of its interference with the victim's employment, whether it is physically or verbally harassing or both, the degree of its offensiveness, and all other factors that may bear on the level of the severity or pervasiveness of the harasser's conduct. Except in incidents of intimate physical touching—almost always considered severe or pervasive—the courts do not have at hand a "mathematically precise test" to assess severity or pervasiveness.[3] As a consequence, varied judicial perspectives, as we shall see in the cases about to be reviewed, reflect the absence of a precise standard.

Although the Supreme Court has established "totality of the circumstances" as the relevant criterion to be applied in deciding whether harassing conduct is severe or pervasive, for our purposes, a separate analysis of various elements of harassing conduct is useful in learning to recognize the forms of conduct that are material to that determination. While acknowledging that no single factor may be determinative, we will proceed to segregate and analyze separately the various components that constitute the totality of the circumstances, but we use this approach merely as a tool to gain an understanding of the significance of each factor to the overall determination. We must remain mindful, however, that ultimately the totality of the circumstances is the proper criterion to be applied.

Physical Acts of Sexual Harassment

As noted, the touching of an intimate portion of a woman's body is almost always characterized as severe and pervasive behavior. A single instance of such touching may be sufficient for purposes of establishing a sexual harassment claim. When Lynn Fall worked for the South Bend branch of Indiana University, the chancellor of the university put his arms around her, started kissing her, and forced his hands down her blouse and groped her breasts (see chapter 2). Although Fall alleged only this one incident of sexual harassment, the court ruled that a single harassing act involving physical assault, such as Fall experienced, was sufficiently severe to alter the conditions of her employment.[4] In another case, the touching of a woman's breast for several seconds was held to be sufficiently severe to support the victim's sexual harassment claim.[5] The

Equal Employment Opportunity Commission (EEOC) has adopted the position that a single, offensive physical event can "seriously poison" a victim's working environment, and if an employer advances the position that such a physical touching was not sufficiently severe to create a hostile work environment, then the burden of proving the adequacy of that position shifts to that employer—a rare instance where the burden of proof is allocated to a defendant employer.[6]

The mere threat of physical force may be sufficient to constitute conduct sufficiently severe or pervasive to alter a woman's working conditions.[7] Thus her working conditions may be altered even without an actual physical encounter or any other harassing incident.

Verbal Acts of Sexual Harassment

Verbal acts of sexual harassment generally are considered less severe or pervasive than physical acts of harassment. It would be a rare case indeed for a court to consider a single incident of verbal harassment as sufficiently severe or pervasive to alter the conditions of a victim's employment.

The point at which acts of verbal harassment pass over the line separating merely obnoxious conduct from that considered sufficiently severe or pervasive to alter the conditions of a woman's employment is an issue much contested in the courts. Susan McKenzie, an employee of the Illinois Department of Transportation, was responsible for training one of her co-workers, Donald Croft, in the use of a computerized inventory system. On one occasion during a training session, McKenzie became ill and vomited. At the time, Croft remarked to her that she had "screwed around" so much with one of her supervisors she probably was pregnant. Several weeks later, Croft telephoned McKenzie and said he had heard that coffee induces sexual arousal, and since he was about to come to her office, he wanted to know if she was drinking coffee. Shortly after, when another worker mentioned to Croft that he had to collect some money from McKenzie for her participation in a baseball betting pool, Croft suggested he "take it out in trade."

Croft's remarks were made over a three-month period. When McKenzie sued for sexual harassment, the court held that a reasonable person would not perceive her work environment to be hostile or abusive:

> Title VII is not directed against unpleasantness per se but only . . . against discrimination in the conditions of employment. . . . Although Croft's

comments were most certainly offensive, we cannot hold that the frequency or severity of the comments rose to the level of unreasonably interfering with Ms. McKenzie's working environment.

Accordingly, the court dismissed McKenzie's claim.[8] A complainant requires more than three isolated instances of moderately offensive behavior to establish an alteration in the terms and conditions of her employment.

The court that ruled on Valerie Baskerville's sexual harassment claim against Culligan International Company attempted to establish the line separating severe or pervasive conduct from that which is merely vulgar or mildly offensive. Culligan hired Baskerville as a secretary in its marketing department and assigned her to work for Michael Hall, a regional sales manager, also newly hired. Baskerville later claimed that over a period of seven months, Hall committed a number of verbal offensive acts:

- He was accustomed to calling her a pretty girl.
- He made a grunting sound when she wore a leather skirt to the office.
- On one occasion when she commented on how hot his office was, he said, "Not until you stepped your foot in here."
- When the office public address system announced, "May I have your attention please," he commented to Baskerville, "You know what that means, don't you? All pretty girls run around naked."
- He told her his wife had advised him "to clean up his act" and that he had better view Baskerville as another Anita Hill.
- He told her he had left the office Christmas party early because with so many pretty girls present, he "didn't want to lose control."
- When Baskerville complained that his office was smoky, he responded, "Oh really? Were we dancing, like in a nightclub?"
- On one occasion, when he spoke to Baskerville about his wife's absence from the city, he made a gesture as if he had engaged in masturbation.

The court noted, in ruling that these incidents did not add up to sexual harassment, that the "concept of sexual harassment is designed to protect working women from the kind of male attentions that can make the workplace hellish for women. . . . It is not designed to purge the workplace of vulgarity." The court proceeded to draw a line between sexual harassment and vulgarity, between a hostile or deeply repugnant working environment and merely an unpleasant workplace:

On one side lie sexual assaults; other physical contact, whether amorous or hostile, for which there is no consent express or implied; uninvited sexual solicitations; intimidating words or acts; obscene language or gestures; pornographic pictures. . . . On the other side lies the occasional vulgar banter, tinged with sexual innuendo, of coarse or boorish workers.

In the court's view, Hall's conduct fell on the side of vulgarity, rather than on the side of harassment. Baskerville's work environment was unpleasant, but not "hellish." "Hall, whatever his qualities as a sales manager, is not a man of refinement; but neither is he a sexual harasser."[9]

Workplace socializing and flirting, even if unseemly or boorish, fail to rise to the level of sexual harassment, since those types of conduct usually fall short of being severe or pervasive. Sheri Bishop failed to recognize this when she mistakenly labeled her supervisor's attentions to her as sexual harassing. She testified that her supervisor asked her out on a date, but she rejected his offer. On another occasion, he followed her around the workplace, and on another, asked her why she did not wear looser clothing. He once asked her if she was involved with anyone and inquired as to why not. Although one of his responsibilities as Bishop's supervisor was to observe her work performance, she complained that he watched her working while he was in his office, with the lights turned off. When Bishop sued for sexual harassment, the court categorized the supervisor's conduct as ordinary workplace socializing and flirtation, conduct that should not be confused with sexual harassment that breeds discriminatory conditions of employment.[10] His conduct was neither pervasive nor sufficiently severe to create a hostile work environment.

Having reviewed cases where the complained-of conduct was determined not to be harassing, we turn to a case where the harasser's offensive behavior was described by a court as tending "toward the lower end of the spectrum" of sexually harassing conduct. Brenda Borello worked as a bookkeeper for A. Sam & Sons Produce Company. Charles Sam, son of the president of the company, served as the company's vice-president. Borello's job required her to have intermittent contact with Sam, such as at times when she forwarded telephone messages and obtained delivery authorizations. Five months into her employment, Borello left a delivery slip on Sam's desk for his signature. The following morning, she found the slip on her desk with Sam's notation, "Whore, what is the amount?" Later that day, Borello overheard a loud argument in the office in which Sam shouted that all the women in the office were "whores and all [they] knew how to do [was] fuck." In the following week, while walking near Borello's office, Sam remarked, "nothing but a whore, nothing but a little whore, just a whore." A week later, while Borello was waiting to punch her time card, Sam said as he passed by, "Why don't you stare at the time clock a little bit more, ya whore." About a week later, when Borello called Sam to advise him he had telephone messages, he shouted "go fuck yourself" and slammed down the receiver.

When Borello sued the company for sexual harassment, the company centered its defense on the argument that since the incidents of Sam's conduct were both sporadic and isolated they were neither sufficiently severe nor pervasive to create a hostile environment. The court, however, ruled otherwise. A female worker need not be subjected to an extended period of demeaning and degrading treatment before becoming entitled to the protections of Title VII. The offensiveness of the behavior complained of also is a factor to be considered, and the greater the degree of offensiveness, the fewer the number of incidents needed for it to be characterized as severe or pervasive. The court concluded that Sam's obnoxious commentary was indeed severe and pervasive.[11]

The setting in which verbal comments are made may be a factor in determining their severity. Debbie Smith worked as an accounts service representative for Norwest Financial Acceptance in Casper, Wyoming, the only female full-time employee in the five-person office. The employees shared a small open office space without partitions, affording them little if any privacy. Smith claimed her supervisor uttered six offensive and sexually harassing comments over the two years of her employment. On one occasion he advised Smith to "get a little this weekend" so she would "come back in a better mood." Another time he remarked that Smith "would be the worst piece of ass that I ever had," and later commented that Smith "must be a sad piece of ass [who] can't keep a man."

Because of the open setting of the office, Smith's co-workers heard these remarks. The open and public nature of the work environment only increased the severity of the comments and Smith's resulting humiliation. The court ruled that the supervisor's conduct was sufficiently severe to create a hostile work environment for Smith.[12]

Shelby Scott was only fifteen years old when she started working at a Taco Bell restaurant in Maryland. She alleged that the restaurant manager, Edwin Wheeler, continuously told sexual jokes, frequently discussed sexual positions and experiences, and commented on the size of her buttocks and breasts. When Scott sued, claiming sexual harassment, the court ruled the severity of Wheeler's sexual misconduct was compounded by the context in which it took place:

Throughout his campaign of torment, Wheeler was an adult male in a supervisory position over young women barely half his age. And he is alleged
to have engaged in a systematic effort to cripple the self-esteem of the
teenagers who assisted him at the store. This eclipses the threshold of
severity.[13]

A comparison of Debbie Smith's and Shelby Scott's cases with the
other reviewed cases of verbal harassment demonstrates the significance
of the totality of the circumstances approach. The pivotal point in
Smith's case was the public setting in which the harassment occurred and
the resulting public humiliation Smith suffered. If the court had limited
its analysis to the number of harassing incidents or the degree of their offensiveness, its decision may have differed. Similarly, if the court had ignored Scott's young age, it may have looked less critically on her manager's behavior.

The significance of the totality of the circumstances approach also is illustrated in the contrasting circumstances confronted by Debbie Smith
and those encountered by Lynn Fall. The court considered the harassing
conduct of Smith's supervisor as severe primarily because it occurred in
an open office area, enabling Smith's co-workers to witness it, thus
adding to her humiliation. Lynn Fall, on the other hand, was harassed
within the confines of the university chancellor's office, outside the view
of fellow workers, but in her case the isolated nature of the harassing
conduct only added to its severity.

The Frequency of the Harassing Conduct

Two elementary schoolteachers received several anonymous letters
containing sexual content. It was later determined that the sender of the
letters was the school principal. When the two teachers sued the school
district for sexual harassment, the court had to determine whether the receipt of the letters was sufficiently pervasive to create a hostile workplace. Although the court recognized that an occasional anonymous letter may be a frightening experience for a woman, it ruled that the receipt
of four letters over a two-and-a-half-year period failed to evince a sufficient modicum of hostility to support the teachers' claims. The court
commented that the "frequency factor affords [the teachers] little or no
support."[14]

The frequency factor in Donna Hurley's sexual harassment claim
against the Atlantic City Police Department culminated in a different

outcome. Hurley, the first female graduate of the city's police academy, alleged she had been subjected to acts of sexual harassment as early as her training period at the academy. She also testified that after her assignment to police duties, her sergeant harassed her by making sexually derogatory comments during roll call, by disturbing her while she was changing clothes in the drill room, and by speaking to her in condescending tones. Even after Hurley was promoted to sergeant, her supervisors and co-workers continuously harassed her. Among the more egregious acts of harassment she was forced to endure was the placement of sexually explicit graffiti and drawings of herself at three separate locations. In fact, she was required to attend roll call in the presence of a life-size drawing of herself performing oral sex. Other female employees of the department testified to similar treatment.

The unrelenting vulgarities encountered by Hurley and other women working in the police department were more than sufficient to establish the severity and pervasiveness of the harassing behavior of department officials and co-workers. The frequency factor, in contrast to the elementary schoolteachers case, strongly supported Hurley's claims of harassment.[15] Of course, when the totality of the circumstances of this case is considered, the gross offensiveness of the harassing conduct tended to reduce the significance of the frequency factor. The degree of offensiveness and the frequency factors generally stand in an inverse relationship, with the courts attaching less significance to the frequency of the harassing acts when the heightened degree of their offensiveness is clearly present.

One female worker alleged ten incidents of harassment committed by her supervisor over the course of a two-year period, including the touching of her waist, brushing his backside against hers, looking at her chest, and touching her hand on one occasion and her arm on another. The court ruled that some of these occurrences may have been nothing more than incidental physical contact. In any event, they could not be categorized as severe since they were not physically threatening or intimidating and they could not be considered pervasive since only ten incidents occurred over a course of two years.[16] If the supervisor's acts of physical conduct had been more offensive, the severity and pervasiveness factors may have been satisfied, despite the relative infrequency of harassing acts.

The Length of Time the Victim Is Forced to Endure the Harassment

A woman need not subject herself to an extended period of demeaning and offensive conduct before becoming entitled to legal relief. In determining the severity or pervasiveness of harassing conduct, the courts are more likely to examine the offensiveness of the harassing conduct, rather than how long it endures. Even though a single act of touching may be sufficient to trigger a harassment claim, on occasion the length of time the offensive conduct continues becomes a pivotal factor. In one case, a woman's harassment claim centered on lewd graffiti, directed specifically at her, that her co-workers placed on workplace walls. Although she complained to her supervisors, they undertook no action to remove the graffiti, and there it remained for more than two years. The court held that the presence of the graffiti poisoned the environment that the worker was forced to endure for the "privilege" of working for her employer.[17] If her supervisors had ordered the graffiti removed when she first complained, her sexual harassment claim would have less likely succeeded.

In some instances, the duration of the offensive conduct may be a factor favoring the employer's position, since the very fact the conduct persisted over an extended period without complaint suggests that the plaintiff considered it as insignificant. On the other hand, a claimant must show more than the occurrence of a few minor, isolated harassing incidents if she expects to convince a court that she was compelled to work in a hostile environment. It must be again emphasized that Title VII does not create a basis for a claim of sexual harassment for each and every crude joke or sexually explicit remark made on the job. Accordingly, a sexual harassment claim is more likely to succeed if the evidence demonstrates the presence of a continuing pattern of harassing behavior persisting over an extended period of time.

The Offensiveness of the Harassing Conduct

Teresa Harris worked as a manager for Forklift Systems, an equipment rental company. Throughout the course of Harris's two years of employment, Charles Hardy, the company's president, made insulting gender and sexist remarks in Harris's presence and made her the target of a running sexual commentary. When Harris sued for sexual harassment, a lower court rejected her claim on the ground that Hardy's conduct was not so severe as to seriously affect Harris's psychological well-being. The lower court reasoned that since Harris had not been psychologically damaged, it could not be said that Hardy's conduct was sufficiently offensive to interfere with her employment. His conduct had failed to create a working environment "so poisoned as to be intimidating or abusive to Harris."

Ultimately, Harris's case reached the Supreme Court, which had to decide whether a woman could validly assert a hostile environment sexual harassment claim even though the harassment she complained of had not caused her to suffer psychological injury. The court rejected the lower court's rationale, ruling that "Title VII comes into play before the harassing conduct leads to a nervous breakdown":

> A discriminatorily abusive work environment, even one that does not seriously affect employees' psychological well-being, can and often will detract from employees' job performance, discourage employees from remaining on the job, or keep them from advancing in their careers.

The court permitted Harris to pursue her claim, even though she could not prove Hardy's conduct was so offensive as to cause her psychological injury.[18]

As we have observed, a sexual harassment claimant must show the conduct alleged to be harassing was offensive, not only to her, but also to any reasonable person encountering those circumstances. Although she does not have to prove the conduct was so offensive as to cause her psychological problems, evidence that she did suffer that type of injury may nonetheless be a factor a court considers in deciding whether the offensive behavior indeed was severe or pervasive. The greater the severity of the offensive conduct, the more likely it will cause psychological injury. Thus the claimant's mental state may be a relevant factor in assessing the severity of the harasser's behavior.

Obviously, not all sexually offensive conduct rises to the severe or pervasive level. Shirley Breeden was responsible for screening job applicants, and as part of her job, she reviewed reports of sexually explicit comments made by applicants. On one occasion, her male supervisor met with her and another male employee to review the psychological evaluation reports of four job applicants. The report for one of the applicants disclosed he had once commented to a co-worker, "I hear making love to you is like making love to the Grand Canyon." After reading the comment aloud, the supervisor said to Breeden, "I don't know what that means." The other male employee then commented, "Well, I'll tell you later," and both men laughed. Breeden sued for sexual harassment, and when her suit reached the Supreme Court, it held no reasonable person could have believed this single incident was so offensive as to violate Title VII standards.[19]

When Marcia Taylor sued her employer for sexual harassment, she encountered problems similar to those confronted by Shirley Breeden. Taylor was working as a processing technician for Regeneration Technologies when the company appointed Ed Anderson, also a processing technician, to the position of weekend shift leader. Taylor and Anderson at times worked the same weekend shift, and on those occasions, Anderson made inappropriate sexual comments. Taylor at first did not believe that the offensiveness of these comments rose to the level of sexual harassment, but on one weekend Anderson told her he was aware she knew of his affairs with two other female employees. When Taylor told him she thought his behavior was disgusting, Anderson responded, "I just wanted to ask you one thing. If it was you and me would you spit or would you swallow?" Of course, Anderson's remark was highly offensive, but was this single comment severe enough to alter the terms of Taylor's employment? The court answered in the negative, stating that offhand comments and isolated incidents will ordinarily not result in an adverse change in the terms and conditions of the victim's employment, and Anderson's comment was not so serious as to achieve that end. The court dismissed Taylor's case.[20]

Although a single, isolated comment is not likely to be viewed as equivalent to a single act of physical harassment, the unabated offensiveness of some acts of verbal harassment may rise nearly to that level. Some readers may feel, as I do, that Anderson's offensive remark achieved that level. Anderson was Taylor's shift leader. His remark, coming from the mouth of one having supervisory authority, may very well have altered the conditions of Taylor's employment. But the court ruled that "despite the offensiveness of this single comment, Anderson's conduct viewed as a whole, was not severe and pervasive enough to alter the terms and conditions of . . . Taylor's employment," and it dismissed Taylor's harassment claim.

Instead of dismissing her claim, the court should have granted Taylor the opportunity to prove, before a jury of her peers, that the conditions of her employment were in fact altered. Given the offensiveness of Anderson's remark, she may very well have succeeded in sustaining that burden of proof. A shortsighted court, undoubtedly viewing the circumstances from the perspective of a man rather than a woman, declined to give her that opportunity.

Suppose offensive comments are accompanied by physical touching. Red Mendoza worked in the accounting department of the Miami facility of Borden's Dairy. Daniel Page was the controller of the Miami office and, as the highest-ranking employee in the office, had supervisory authority over Mendoza. Mendoza claimed Page harassed her, that he constantly stared at her and followed her around the office. "He would look me up and down . . . in a very obvious fashion." He never said anything when he was looking her up and down, but on two occasions when he looked down, he stopped at her groin area and "made a sniffing motion." Another time, Page made a sexual remark. On another occasion, as he walked past her, their hips rubbed together, and at the same time he touched her shoulder and smiled at her. This was the only physical contact Mendoza had with Page during the eleven months she worked for him. The court held that the conduct alleged by Mendoza was not so offensive as to alter the conditions of her employment.[21]

> Considering the following and staring described by Mendoza with and in the context of the sniffs, one verbal statement, and one slight touching as Page walked by . . . , we find Mendoza's claim still falls far short of actionable hostile environment sexual harassment.

If the physical contact had been more offensive, undoubtedly the court would have viewed Mendoza's claim more favorably.

Socializing and Flirting

Title VII was never intended to become a "general civility code" for the workplace. The Supreme Court has emphasized that Title VII does not prohibit "genuine but innocuous differences in the ways men and women routinely interact with members of the . . . opposite sex:"

> The prohibition of harassment on the basis of sex requires neither asexuality nor androgyny in the workplace; it forbids only behavior so objectively offensive as to alter the "conditions" of the victim's employment. Conduct that is not severe or pervasive enough to create an objectively hostile or abusive work environment . . . is beyond Title VII's purview. . . . We have always regarded that requirement as crucial, and as sufficient to ensure that courts and juries do not mistake ordinary socializing in the workplace . . . for discriminatory conditions of employment.[22]

Generally, the courts have ruled that the sporadic use of abusive language, gender-related jokes, and sex-oriented teasing and flirting are insufficiently serious to violate Title VII. Nonetheless, these same courts have often found it difficult to establish a clear dividing line between conduct it labels as workplace socialization and conduct it considers sufficiently offensive to alter a female worker's conditions of employment. When does flirting cross the line and become intrusion? The courts have often failed to handle issues of this sort with any consistency. The cases that follow bear witness to the difficulties courts have experienced in this area.

A female worker alleged her supervisor repeatedly winked at her, and whenever she asked him for assistance, he habitually responded, "What will I get for it?" Co-workers slapped her buttocks and commented she probably moaned and groaned during sex. The court dismissed the worker's case since it did not consider her work environment sufficiently hostile to support a sexual harassment claim.[23] This may have been a borderline case, but the evidence seems to indicate the court may have placed itself on the wrong side of the border.

A teacher claimed school administrators subjected her to hostile working conditions when they forced her to work with a male teacher who continuously harassed her. Over the course of a year, she alleged her fellow teacher

- stared at her while she was teaching,
- touched her knee five times when he bent down to talk to her,
- touched her shoulder ten times to get her attention,
- frequently stood too close to her, thus invading her "private space,"
- questioned her about her weekend, and
- fondled her at a private party.

The court ruled that the allegations of harassment were insufficiently severe or pervasive to support her sexual harassment claim, and it dismissed her suit.[24] In the court's view, the severity of the co-worker's conduct was at most borderline harassment. But the court may have erred in not ruling that the complained-of behavior was pervasive. In its overly restrictive view, the court appears not to have given sufficient consideration to how a woman feels and reacts to circumstances in which she is compelled to endure her co-worker's unwanted, constant attention for extended periods of time. The court might very well have found that this attention adversely altered the teacher's working conditions.

A female employee of the Chicago Police Department alleged she was continuously harassed by several members of the department over a period of ten months. She claimed that

- her immediate supervisor and another department worker made sexual remarks in her presence,

- a fellow police officer told her she should not wave at squad cars in front of the police station as people would assume she was a prostitute,
- at least three police officers stared at her breasts on a number of occasions, and
- one of the officers poked her in the buttocks.

The court noted that the most salient feature of the alleged harassment was its lack of severity, that the conduct complained of fell into the category of simple teasing. Offhand comments and other isolated incidents that the claimant alleged were harassing failed to culminate in discriminatory changes in the terms and conditions of her employment. The most serious misconduct, the touching of the complainant's buttock, "took the relatively mild form of a poke and occurred only once." In the court's view, the alleged acts of harassment were "too tepid," intermittent, or equivocal to constitute a violation of Title VII.[25]

The courts have refused to lower the bar in considering whether defendants may be held liable under Title VII for bothersome or mildly offensive conduct. Improper or distasteful conduct causing transitory embarrassment fails to affect the conditions of employment in a manner giving rise to Title VII liability.[26] Unless the harasser's conduct is clearly severe or pervasive, a prospective complainant is well advised to think long and hard before proceeding to litigation. Unless she is able to establish that the harassing conduct was sufficiently severe or pervasive to have caused an adverse change in her working conditions, the court will most likely reject her claim. To avoid dismissal of her claim, the complainant must prove the acts of harassment were sufficiently serious to corrupt her workplace, thus making it more difficult for her to perform her job functions, take pride in her work, or desire to remain in her position.[27]

Borderline cases generally are dismissed. Cases involving genuinely offensive behavior normally proceed to judgment in favor of the complainant. Many of the cases reviewed in the chapters that follow fall into the latter category. In contrast to some of the cases just reviewed, they involve severe and pervasive acts of offensive conduct that clearly alter the working conditions of the women subjected to such conduct.

CHAPTER FIVE

A Woman's Rights When Other Women Are Sexually Harassed

When a supervisor engages in a sexual relationship with a subordinate female employee and favors her with preferential treatment in the form of salary increases and promotions, questions arise regarding the rights of other subordinate female workers, denied similar raises and promotions, to assert sexual harassment claims.

A supervisor's grant of preferential treatment in favor of a female employee with whom he has a consensual sexual relationship may disadvantage other female workers, but it also disadvantages male workers working under his supervision. Sexual harassment, we must remember, is a form of sex discrimination. A female employee denied an employment benefit as a consequence of such favoritism is not treated less favorably because she is a woman. Since women in these circumstances are treated as well—or as poorly—as their male co-workers, the supervisor's conduct, though notably unfair, cannot be said to be discriminatory. Thus a female worker may not assert a valid claim of sexual harassment in this type of setting.

That is not the case, however, where the relationship between supervisor and the subordinate female employee is not consensual. When a supervisor induces a female employee, through promises of favored treatment, to enter into a sexual relationship with him, or withholds employment benefits unless she submits to his sexual demands, he makes sex a condition of her employment. This is a condition of employment not required of a male employee. Thus the supervisor's imposition of this condition of employment in these circumstances is discriminatory, not only against the woman who submits to his demands, but also against other women working under his supervision. Even though the other women are not directly subjected to the same conditions of employment, they are nonetheless denied employment benefits, and thus are entitled to pursue a Title VII sexual harassment claim. A claim of this nature is substantially the same as a quid pro quo harassment claim—a claim that sexual favors are implicitly or explicitly demanded in return for job benefits.

The testimony elicited in a sexual harassment claim asserted by a coffee shop waitress disclosed that another waitress had submitted to the sexual advances of the shop owner, that he then provided her with preferential job assignments, and later permitted her to continue her employment despite her substandard work performance and rudeness to customers. The evidence also disclosed that other waitresses who tolerated the owner's sexual behavior were granted preferential job assignments. The court ruled that evidence of this type was sufficient to permit the complaining waitress to establish a Title VII claim for sexual harassment:

> Title VII is . . . violated when an employer affords preferential treatment to female employees who submit to his sexual advances or other conduct of a sexual nature, or when by his conduct or statements, implies that job benefits will be conditioned on an employee's good-natured endurance of his sexually charged conduct of sexual advances.

The complaining waitress established a Title VII violation by showing that waitresses who acceded to the owner's sexual demands were granted job preferences denied to her. The conditions of her employment were altered even though she was not the object of his sexual demands.[1]

Margaret Toscano was one of a number of applicants for promotion to an administrative position at a Veterans Administration Hospital in Delaware. The applicant eventually selected for that promotion was at the time engaged in a sexual affair with the supervisor responsible for making the selection. When Toscano sued the supervisor and the Veterans Administration for sexual harassment, she submitted evidence showing that the supervisor demonstrated a total inability to separate his work life from his private life outside the hospital. He described himself as a "lifetime womanizer" and made little or no attempt to suppress that aspect of his character while working at the hospital. He made harassing telephone calls to female employees at their homes, engaged in suggestive behavior at work, and habitually telephoned female employees working the night shifts to describe his supposed sexual encounters with female

workers under his supervision. Although no evidence was offered showing he explicitly made acquiescence to his sexual advances a condition
for the promotion to the administrative position, that condition was
implicit in his general behavior.

The circumstances confronting Toscano were essentially the same as
those confronting any female whose supervisor demands sexual favors as
a quid pro quo for receipt of job benefits. By implicitly making acquiescence to sexual demands a condition for promotion, the supervisor was
guilty of sexually harassing each of the female candidates who sought
that promotion.[2]

The EEOC's position on this issue is clear. When a woman is coerced
into submitting to unwelcome sexual advances of her supervisor in
return for favored treatment, other women working under his supervision may claim that sex was a condition for receipt of those benefits. In
order for these women to be made recipients of the favored treatment
they would have had to accede to that condition. Sex is thus made a condition of employment for the woman who submits to the supervisor's
demands as well as for those women who do not submit.[3]

Let us now suppose that preferential treatment is extended to a number of female workers, each of whom freely engages in a sexual relationship with her supervisor. Suppose further that other female workers,
although they are neither the subject of sexual advances nor directly
affected by the preferential treatment extended to the women involved in
sexual relationships with their supervisors, view this type of work environment as wholly offensive. Do they have valid sexual harassment
claims? These were the circumstances encountered by Catherine
Broderick, an employee of the U.S. Securities and Exchange Commission
(see chapter 2).

In Broderick's department at the SEC, three supervisors had ongoing
sexual relationships with women working in the department. Each of
these women was favored with salary increases, promotions, commendations, bonus awards, and other favored treatment. Broderick was grossly
offended by the nature of the environment in which she was required to
work, and eventually these circumstances adversely affected her performance. Where sexual harassment is widespread, supervisory and management employees implicitly convey the message that they view women as
"sexual playthings," thereby creating a working environment demeaning
to all female workers. A court ruled that Broderick and other women
forced to work in such an environment may rely on Title VII for appropriate relief.[4]

Now suppose a woman claims she has been subjected to sexually harassing behavior and other women working with her also have been sexually harassed. Is evidence of the harassment of other women admissible to bolster her claim that she was required to work in a hostile and offensive environment? We look to Kim Hirase-Doi's sexual harassment case asserted against U.S. West Communications for the answer.

Hirase-Doi worked for U.S. West as a directory assistance operator. During the course of her employment, the company hired Kenneth Coleman for a directory assistance operator position. Coleman was first assigned to a training program where he made sexually offensive remarks to two women in the program. He asked them about their sex lives and persistently requested sex with them. He made open-ended invitations to all female employees to satisfy his sexual desires. His training supervisor warned him his conduct was inappropriate, but Coleman was not deterred, and he continued to engage in sexually offensive behavior toward numerous women working in his area.

Coleman did not exclude Doi from his objectionable behavior. Doi was present when Coleman approached other women, and she was generally aware of his sex-oriented behavior. Ultimately, Coleman propositioned Doi and attempted to touch her breasts and her legs. When Doi reported these incidents, U.S. West suspended Coleman and he immediately resigned. Doi then commenced a legal action against the company, alleging she had been forced to work in a hostile environment.

U.S. West argued that the court should bar the admission of all evidence in Doi's case that related to Coleman's harassment of other women, and inasmuch as Doi's hostile work environment claim would fail without that evidence, her claim should be dismissed. In effect, U.S. West maintained that Doi's claim had to stand on its own—that evidence of the harassment of other women was irrelevant to her hostile environment claim. The court ruled, however, that evidence of Coleman's harassment of the other women was admissible in evaluating Doi's claim, but the admissibility of this type of evidence was limited. Unless Doi was aware of Coleman's behavior toward other women, she could not have perceived that this behavior was an element of her working environment. On the other hand, knowledge of his harassing behavior toward other women would make it an element of her working environment. Thus Doi's allegations that she was aware of Coleman's harassment of other women, along with allegations of harassing acts directed at her, if proved, would provide the court with a reasonable basis on which to rule that Doi was subjected to hostile work environment sexual harassment. The court, therefore, denied U.S. West's motion to dismiss Doi's claim.[5]

Diane Leibovitz attempted to take this type of hostile environment claim one step further. Leibovitz, one of forty deputy superintendents employed by the New York City Transit Authority, had been placed in charge of repairing subway cars. While assigned to that position, she learned from a female worker that a woman employed as a subway car cleaner had complained that her supervisor, Russell Woodley, sexually harassed her. The worker also told Leibovitz that Woodley was engaged in a pattern of harassing other female workers. Leibovitz was neither present at nor did she witness any of the acts of harassment allegedly committed by Woodley, and was unaware of any of this harassment as it was occurring.

After the car cleaner complained to management that she was being harassed, the Transit Authority investigated Woodley's conduct. The outcome of the investigation, however, was inconclusive. Leibovitz later claimed management had proceeded with the investigation of the harassment charges without any sense of urgency. She sued the Transit Authority for sexual harassment, claiming she had suffered a major depressive disorder flowing from her frustration in unsuccessfully attempting to secure a remedy for the women who were harassed by Woodley.

Leibovitz, a highly regarded member of middle management, was never the object of inappropriate conduct. Her claim for sexual harassment rested solely on occurrences of supervisory harassing conduct directed at other women employed by the Transit Authority, conduct she claimed was the cause of her emotional distress. She admitted she was not present at any of the incidents of alleged harassment by Woodley and she learned of them only after their occurrence. The court was required to determine whether Woodley's acts of harassment, committed against other female workers, created a hostile work environment in which Leibovitz was required to work.

Leibovitz's allegations of a hostile working environment centered on her claim that the Transit Authority had been deliberately indifferent to the existence of sexual harassment in its workplace, and as a result, her work environment was replete with sex-oriented conduct sufficiently severe or pervasive to alter the conditions of her employment. The trial court ruled in Leibovitz's favor, relying on evidence showing that:

- Leibovitz was repeatedly apprised of instances of the sexual harassment of other women working for the Transit Authority.

- When Leibovitz complained about this harassment, management responded in a passive and unconcerned manner.
- Although several additional incidents of harassment were reported to management, timely remedial action was not taken.
- An underlying belief existed among female workers that sexual harassment complaints would result in retaliation against those complaining.

The trial court ruled this evidence was sufficient to prove that Leibovitz's work environment was so permeated with instances of sexual harassment that a reasonable person would find her working conditions hostile.[6] The Transit Authority immediately appealed the court's ruling.

The appellate court began its analysis of the lower court ruling by reviewing the general principles applicable to a sexual harassment case. For a hostile environment harassment case to succeed, the alleged acts of harassment must be sufficiently severe or pervasive to alter the terms and conditions of the victim's employment and create a hostile or abusive environment. The sufficiency of the claim is subject to both subjective and objective measurement—the plaintiff must demonstrate that she personally considered the environment hostile and her work environment rose to an objective level of hostility. "Conduct that is not severe or pervasive enough to create an objectively hostile or abusive work environment—an environment a reasonable person would find hostile or abusive—is beyond Title VII's purview."

With these principles in mind, the court focused on the trial evidence indisputably showing that the alleged harassment did not occur in Leibovitz's immediate vicinity and that her knowledge of these events was second-or even thirdhand. The experiences of the harassed women came to Leibovitz's attention only through hearsay, inasmuch as the women who were allegedly harassed were working in another area, out of Leibovitz's sight and ordinary orbit of activity. The court stated that

> In terms of the objective impact of the harassment alleged, the harassment might as well as have been going on in a nearby office or another firm, or been the subject of an infuriating newspaper article, or been a false rumor of a kind that would be upsetting if true.

In these circumstances, Leibovitz could not demonstrate she suffered either in subjective or objective terms, or that the harassment of the other women adversely affected her working conditions.

The appellate court further observed that the only way it could characterize Leibovitz's work environment as hostile would be to expand the concept of "work environment" to include areas in which she did not work. "Such a characterization would open the door to limitless employer liability, and allow a recovery by any employee made distraught by office gossip, rumor or innuendo." Leibovitz neither presented evidence that her *own* working environment was hostile nor that the harassment of other women adversely affected the terms and conditions of her *own* employment.

Although Leibovitz's claim failed, the court recognized that in other circumstances evidence of sexual harassment directed against co-workers may be relevant to a complainant's own claim for harassment. It was only because Leibovitz had not witnessed the harassment of the other women, having learned of it only indirectly and through hearsay, that it remained irrelevant to her harassment claim. Her claim also was flawed in that it was based on a contention that her working environment was hostile, but that hostility arose solely as a consequence of acts of harassment committed against her co-workers, as Leibovitz herself was not at any time the object of sexually harassing conduct.[7]

This decision does not undermine the rationale of the cases discussed earlier in this chapter. Toscano was directly affected by her supervisor's decision to promote a woman with whom he was having an affair, rather than promoting her. Broderick's work performance was undermined by the offensive nature of the sex-oriented conditions existing in her office, and thus her working conditions were altered. Doi was permitted to offer evidence of the harassment of other women because the same person who harassed other women in similar circumstances harassed her. Because the focus of a court's inquiry centers on the nature of a plaintiff's work environment "as a whole," a woman who herself experiences acts of sexual harassment may assert in support of her claim evidence of incidents of harassment suffered by other women working in that environment. But evidence of acts of harassment committed against other women may not be offered to bolster a claim asserted by a woman who is unable to prove she was the object of harassment or that she suffered any adverse change in the terms and conditions of her employment.

Arguments favoring the admission of evidence of co-worker harassment generally are based on the following line of reasoning:

- A claimant may assert a valid hostile work environment claim only by showing acts of sexual harassment sufficiently severe or pervasive to alter the conditions of her employment.

- In assessing the severity or pervasiveness of acts of harassment, the court must consider the totality of the claimant's circumstances, including all aspects of her work environment.
- Thus instances of harassing conduct—that the claimant was aware of—directed against other women working in her environment may be relevant to an evaluation of the level of hostility to which the plaintiff is subjected.

This evidence may also disclose the attitude of the harasser toward women in general, as well as the nature of his treatment of them as employees, and it may in turn substantiate the plaintiff's allegations pertaining to the harasser's attitude toward her and his treatment of her as an employee.

The courts, in some instances, have placed more restrictive conditions on the admissibility of evidence of co-worker harassment. This was the case in Sheila Garvey's sexual harassment claim against Dickinson College. Garvey, a professor of drama at the college, claimed her immediate supervisor had sexually harassed her. During the course of ensuing litigation, the college asked the court to exclude any evidence that Garvey's supervisor had harassed other female staff members. In analyzing the issue, the court compared evidence of co-worker harassment with evidence offered in other types of employment discrimination cases where evidence that a defendant made disparaging remarks about the class of persons of which the plaintiff was a member may be introduced to show that the defendant harbored a prejudice toward that group. Thus in a race discrimination case, the use of racially offensive language by a person in a supervisory capacity is relevant to issues relating to whether racial animus underlay decisions made with respect to an African American employee. Similarly, evidence that Garvey's supervisor harassed other women was relevant to her claim that he harassed her, since it tended to show his attitude toward women generally and his treatment of them at the college.

The court, however, also placed a limitation on the admissibility of evidence of this type. It excluded testimony of incidents "too remote in time or too attenuated from plaintiff's situation." It restricted the admissibility of evidence of incidents of harassment of other women to those incidents involving women who worked with Garvey in the college's drama department, and excluded evidence of harassment of women in all other departments at the college. The court also excluded evidence of the harassment of women employed in the drama department prior to Garvey's appointment to a position in that department.

In a small institution such as Dickinson, a woman's working environment could be considered as extending throughout the college, but the court limited Garvey's work environment to the drama department. It limited the admissibility of evidence of co-worker harassment to a specified place and a particular time.[8]

The *Garvey* and the other cases just reviewed establish the rule that evidence of offensive conduct directed against other female employees, relevant in time and place to allegations of harassment directed against the plaintiff, is admissible in connection with issues relating to the severity or pervasiveness of sexually harassing conduct experienced by the plaintiff. This evidence oftentimes is crucial to the prosecution of a sexual harassment claim, and thus this rule provides complainants with a powerful weapon. But the courts have provided complainants with still other weapons, and one of those is described in a case involving Yvette Cruz and her employer, Coach Stores.

Cruz, a Hispanic, held a secretarial position with Coach before claiming the company was guilty of sexual and racial harassment. She alleged that Coach's human resources manager, Rick Bloom, was notorious for his discriminatory attitudes toward minorities, particularly Hispanics, an attitude he expressed through racial and ethnic slurs. He frequently referred to Hispanics as "spics," stating they were "only capable of sweeping the floors at McDonalds." In her presence and in the presence of others, Bloom also made racist remarks about African Americans, referring to them as "niggers." Moreover, he made sexist remarks, such as "women should be barefoot and pregnant."

Cruz alleged that Bloom sexually harassed her, testifying he was accustomed to stand very close when conversing with her, making her feel uncomfortable. She often found herself pressed up against a wall with Bloom looming over her as he spoke to her. When Cruz informed Bloom that she objected to this behavior, he merely laughed or ignored her.

The court made short work of Coach's argument that Bloom's sexually harassing conduct was neither severe nor pervasive. "We find . . . that the physically threatening nature of Bloom's behavior, which repeatedly ended with him backing Cruz into the wall . . . brings this case over the line separating merely offensive or boorish conduct from actionable sexual harassment."

The court ruled in favor of the admissibility of evidence of Bloom's racial remarks made in the presence of other employees, even those comments that were made when Cruz was neither present nor the target of the remarks. Bloom's offensive racial comments were relevant to Cruz's sexual harassment claim as they tended to show that Bloom's conduct created an overall hostile or abusive working environment. In the interplay between his racial-based and sex-based harassment, Bloom's offensive comments that tended to disparage employees other than Cruz, exacerbated the effect of his sexual harassing behavior directed at Cruz:

> Given the evidence of both race-based and sex-based hostility, a jury could find that Bloom's racial harassment exacerbated the effect of his sexually threatening behavior and vice versa. . . . Based on the evidence Cruz presented of both racial and sexual harassment, therefore, a jury reasonably could conclude that Bloom's behavior [altered] the conditions of [her] employment based on her race and/or her gender.[9]

In effect, the court permitted Cruz to strengthen her sexual hostile environment claim through the submission of evidence of racial harassment.

The *Cruz* decision has been widely praised by attorneys representing those claiming sexual harassment, as it allows a worker to submit evidence of other forms of harassment directed against other workers to bolster her sexual harassment claim. By combining evidence of sexually harassing behavior with other forms of harassing conduct, the workplace is more readily recognizable as hostile.[10]

Evidence pertaining to the working conditions of other female coworkers may be relevant to a plaintiff's sexual harassment case in still another type of situation. As we have seen, in order to prove a case of sexual harassment under Title VII, it is necessary to show that gender was a substantial factor underlying the treatment afforded female employees. In other words, if they had been men, they would not have been similarly treated. But the offensive conduct complained of need not necessarily include overtly sexual overtones. Intimidating and hostile treatment of women, merely because they are women, may result from conduct other than that which takes the form of explicit sexual advances. For example, the pervasive use of derogatory and insulting language relating to women in general may serve as evidence of a hostile working environment.[11] In cases of this character, complainants often rely on the testimony of hostile and abusive treatment of co-workers to prove the existence of workplace hostility (see chapter 7).

A woman contemplating sexual harassment litigation against her employer must remain alert to every type of hostile and discriminatory conduct that appears in her workplace. Evidence of sexually harassing conduct directed against her female co-workers may constitute strong support for the existence of hostility in her work environment. Occurrences of racial or ethnic discriminatory conduct as well as gender-related workplace behavior also may serve to materially strengthen her case.

CHAPTER SIX

Sexual Harassment in Other Settings

Sexual harassment differs from setting to setting. In a blue-collar workplace, sexual harassing behavior tends to be far more direct, offensive, and vulgar than in a white-collar environment. As we learned in chapter 2, sexual harassment in a blue-collar work environment also tends to occur among larger numbers of workers, and it is not uncommon for a woman to be subjected to the harassing acts of several co-workers or even a group of them.

Male workers increasingly use the internet and e-mail as a means of approaching female co-workers with sexual solicitations. Other workers use fax communications. Most harassing conduct takes place in the workplace, but under certain conditions, the occurrence of harassing behavior at places outside what is normally considered as the workplace are considered as conduct barred by Title VII.

In this chapter, we will further examine sexually harassing conduct as it often appears in blue-collar work environments. We will also review cases of internet, e-mail, and fax communication harassment, as well as cases involving off-premise sexually harassing acts.

Sexual Harassment in a Blue-Collar Setting

Courts that first decided cases of sexual harassment in the 1970s and the 1980s often ruled that a woman must accept the work environment as she finds it. If a woman freely consents to working in an environment replete with crude, vulgar, and sexually oriented behavior, then she must not have considered that environment offensive or hostile, else in the first instance she would have refused to accept employment there. A court adopting that judicial attitude requires a woman to suffer a far greater degree of harassment before it considers her work environment as hostile. Vivienne Rabidue encountered such a judicial perspective in a sexual harassment case alleged against her employer.

Rabidue began her career at Osceola Refining Company as an executive secretary. The company later promoted her to administrative assistant and assigned her duties normally performed by its credit and office managers. Occasionally, her duties intersected with those of Douglas Henry, described by the court as "vulgar and crude." Henry habitually used offensive language in the office, openly referring to female employees as "cunt," "pussy," and "tits," and on one occasion he called Rabidue a "fat ass." A number of other Osceola male workers were accustomed to displaying pictures of nude or partially dressed women in their offices and in work areas frequented by Rabidue and other female workers.

The court was required to determine whether Rabidue's work environment, in circumstances such as these, was hostile. The court purported to rely on EEOC guidelines defining sexual harassment as conduct that "has the purpose or effect of *unreasonably* interfering with an individual's work performance or creating an intimidating, hostile or offensive working environment."[1] But when does a worker's conduct "unreasonably" interfere with another's work performance? Does the "unreasonableness" of the worker's conduct depend on the character of the work environment? The court proceeded to answer these questions in such a way as to undermine Title VII.

In the court's view, use of the word *unreasonably* required it to consider the particular characteristics of the work environment in which the complainant was harassed. It reasoned that the character of a woman's work environment determines her expectations regarding the type of conduct she will experience while laboring in a workplace of that sort. Under this approach, a determination that a male worker's conduct is hostile or offensive is dependent on the particular setting in which he works. Consequently, the court must evaluate allegations of hostile and offensive behavior in light of the character of that workplace.

The court noted that in some work environments humor and conversation, rough-hewn and vulgar, are common. If they are common, can they be said to be offensive and hostile? In the court's view, although sexually oriented conversations and pictures of nude women may have abounded in Rabidue's work environment, "Title VII was not meant to—or can—change," the character of the working environment and it cannot effect "a magical transformation in the social mores of American workers." A woman must accept the workplace as she finds it. The court ruled, therefore, that Rabidue had failed to sustain her burden of proving the conduct to which she was subjected created an intimidating, hostile, or offensive work environment.[2]

This form of judicial analysis was commonly applied to blue-collar sexual harassment cases. One example is Patricia Gross's sexual harassment case against Burggraf Construction Company. Gross worked as a truck driver. She claimed her supervisor repeatedly used vulgar language and profanity when conversing with her, embarrassing and humiliating her in the presence of other Burggraf workers. Adopting the rationale of the *Rabidue* case, the court ruled that Gross's harassment claim had to be viewed in the context of a blue-collar environment where crude language is common. "Speech that might be offensive or unacceptable in a prep school faculty meeting, or on the floor of Congress, is tolerated in other work environments." The criteria for evaluating workplace hostility differs with the work environment. In a road construction environment, profanity and vulgarity are not considered hostile—at least as the court perceived it—thus requiring the court to rule that Gross had failed to prove her working conditions were sufficiently severe or pervasive to alter the terms of her employment.[3]

The court made a number of assumptions that have since been rejected. First, it assumed profanity and vulgarity are not considered offensive or hostile in a road construction company type of work environment. That may have been the case when a construction company's workforce was entirely male, but with the arrival of female workers at company work sites, that assumption ceased to have any validity. Second, the court assumed women like Gross freely entered such a work environment, thus consenting to endure its negative aspects. But the selection of a particular job by a woman may not have been freely made, as no other options may have been available to her at the time. A woman's particular circumstances, or those of her family, may have compelled her to accept employment in that position and, surely in those circumstances, it cannot be said she freely agreed to labor in offensive and hostile conditions. Third, the court assumed, as did the *Rabidue* court, that Title VII was not designed to transform the social mores of the American worker. Although not thus designed, the vigorous enforcement of Title VII has succeeded, at least in part, in changing commonly held perceptions of acceptable conduct in the workplace. The courts cannot simply disregard this.

In deciding whether worker conduct violated Title VII, the courts in both the *Rabidue* and *Gross* cases first examined the type and mode of the workplace in which the complainant worked, and in both cases proceeded to analyze issues relating to the level of severity and pervasiveness of the offensive conduct in light of the character of that work environment. Under this approach, women working in a rough, male-oriented, blue-collar environment are required to establish a higher level of harassment than women working in other work environments. Women who elect, or who are compelled to work, under those more hostile and offensive conditions are more apt to be denied the protections of Title VII.[4]

More enlightened courts have rejected the approach of the *Rabidue* and *Gross* courts. Marilyn Williams sued General Motors Corporation, her employer of more than thirty years, alleging that several workers had sexually harassed her. Over the years she had worked in various departments at GM and ultimately was assigned to a warehouse position on the midnight shift. It was while working in that position, in a male-dominated work environment, that she was subjected to a series of offensive acts:

- A co-worker constantly used "the F-word" in normal conversation with Williams and referred to her as a slut.
- While looking at her breasts, her general supervisor said to her, "You can rub up against me anytime." He added, "You would kill me, Marilyn. I don't know if I can handle it, but I'd die with a smile on my face."
- Another co-worker, on several occasions, made overtly sexual remarks in her presence.
- A co-worker glued a box of forms to her desk top.
- During an argument, a male co-worker threw several boxes at her, one grazing her hip.
- Williams was the only worker in her department denied a key to the office. Moreover, she was the only worker denied rest breaks.

The lower court dismissed Williams's suit on the ground the incidents of alleged sexual harassment, occurring in a warehouse setting, while offensive, were not so severe or pervasive as to create a hostile work environment.

On Williams's appeal of this decision, the appellate court approached the issues of severity and pervasiveness from the perspective of "the totality of the circumstances" that Williams encountered at work. Since one of those circumstances was the context in which the harassment occurred, the court agreed it should examine the character of the warehouse working environment. But that did not mean it would be justified in relying on the warehouse worker's long-standing hostility toward women to excuse current offensive workplace behavior. The court asked itself whether the conduct alleged in the case would be tolerated in its own courthouse. It answered in the negative:

> We do not believe that a woman who chooses to work in the male-dominated trades relinquishes her right to be free from sexual harassment; indeed, we find this reasoning to be illogical, because it means that the more hostile the environment, and the more prevalent the sexism, the more difficult it is for a Title VII plaintiff to prove that sex-based conduct is sufficiently severe or pervasive to constitute a hostile work environment. Surely women working in the trades do not deserve less protection from the law than women working in a courthouse.[5]

Title VII was intended to protect all women, not some women rather than others. The character of a woman's working environment should not affect her right to protection from sexually harassing conduct. A blue-collar, female worker, employed in a male-dominated, rough and tumble, rowdy work environment should be afforded no less protection from offensive workplace conduct than a woman employed in a workplace exhibiting civility, tactfulness, and total respect for women.

The Supreme Court has emphasized that Title VII does not stand as a "general civility code" for the American workplace, and thus ordinary workplace socialization between the sexes must be distinguished from conduct that is hostile or offensive. In making that distinction, "an appropriate sensitivity to social context" should enable the court to distinguish between less serious behavior, such as flirtation and teasing, and conduct a reasonable person in a complainant's position would find hostile or offensive.[6] Thus, in these limited circumstances, the context of the work environment may be considered in differentiating between sexual harassing conduct and ordinary workplace socialization. But the character of the work environment cannot transform offensive behavior into that which is not offensive.

Sexual Harassment through Internet, E-Mail, and Fax Communications

The use of the internet and e-mail has recently become more common as a means of sexually harassing women while at work. The dissemination of sexually explicit internet materials as well as unwelcome sexual invitations and advances made through e-mail communications have begun to appear in court cases as grounds for hostile work environment claims, and thus the courts have been required to address issues in connection with these forms of harassment of women.[7]

Susan Coniglio worked as a secretary in the legal department of the City of Berwyn, Illinois. Coniglio was aware that her supervisor frequently viewed pictures of naked women on various internet sites on his office computer. At times, these internet sites pictured women in various sexual positions with creatures resembling medieval gargoyles. She could not avoid noticing these pictures whenever she entered her supervisor's office, and since his office had a picture window, she also noticed them whenever she walked past his office. Coniglio also observed that he kept pictures of naked women, apparently obtained from various internet sites, which he then printed on glossy photographic paper and placed in binders. Other female employees also testified to having seen the supervisor viewing pictures of topless or naked women. In addition, Coniglio was subjected to other offensive actions. She received e-mail communications from an unknown source, the subject lines of which contained suggestive topics, and one included sexually oriented pictures.

When Coniglio sued the City of Berwyn for sexual harassment, she relied on the presence of the internet photos and e-mail communications to support her harassment charges. The court held that the working conditions Coniglio described were sufficient to establish grounds for a sexual harassment claim against the city. The open display of pornographic materials in the vicinity of her work station and the receipt of sexually offensive e-mail messages added to the severity and pervasiveness of the hostile working conditions she encountered while working for the city.[8]

The fax machine is another means used to harass female workers. One of my clients worked as an administrative assistant for an upper management employee of a New York City investment banking firm. One of her assigned tasks was to retrieve messages addressed to her boss from the firm's centralized fax machine. On many occasions, she had to hand-deliver to him faxed pornographic cartoons circulated by a group of his friends working in other firms. These cartoons were sexually explicit, extremely vulgar, and very upsetting to my client. Faxed pornography was part of the daily routine of harassing acts she was forced to endure while working for that man.

A number of employers have reacted to harassment claims based on the offensive content of e-mail and fax communications by adopting policies specifically barring the use of company office equipment to send or exhibit harassing messages and also prohibiting the use of company computers for the purpose of obtaining pornographic materials from internet sources.[9] The ever-expanding use of computers and other technological office equipment, however, undoubtedly will result in their increased use as a ready means of harassment of female employees.

Sexual Harassment Outside the Employer's Premises

A survey of sexual harassment cases appearing on federal court dockets between 1986 and 1995 disclosed that in 23 percent of those cases, complainants alleged that at least one act of harassment was committed outside the employer's premises, and in more than one-half of those cases, all of the alleged harassing conduct occurred outside of the workplace. A number of those cases involved company parties and other social events, such as a private drink after work, and about one-third included phone calls, letters, or visits to the claimant's home.[10]

Employers often deny liability for off-premise acts of harassment. Under what circumstances may an employer be held liable for sexual conduct committed outside of what is ordinarily considered as the workplace? Carole Tomka's sexual harassment case against her employer provides us with some insight as to how a court is likely to handle the issue.

The Seiler Corporation provided its institutional clients with management services for their cleaning staffs. After Tomka had been working for the company for eighteen months, Seiler assigned her to work with a new account in Rochester, New York. Soon after her appointment, Daniel Lucey, district manager for the company's Rochester region, asked her to have dinner with him and two male co-workers, all of whom were involved in the Rochester start-up operation. During the course of the dinner, all four consumed a large quantity of alcohol. Tomka later alleged that after the dinner, Lucey and the two co-workers raped her. When Tomka sued for sexual harassment, Seiler denied any liability for the rapes, arguing that since the dinner was not a business event, it could not be considered an element of Tomka's workplace. But the testimony elicited in the case clearly showed it was customary for Seiler employees engaged in a start-up operation to eat as a group, and they generally discussed business at their meals. Moreover, Lucey was Tomka's supervisor. In combination, those factors left little doubt the rapes were committed in an off-premise workplace environment, thus rendering Seiler liable for the conduct of its employees.[11]

In another case, a supervisor lured a female subordinate to a meeting in a local restaurant, purportedly to discuss her promotion. In a later harassment suit, the court had no difficulty in ruling that the offensive conduct committed by the supervisor at the restaurant was committed in an extension of the claimant's workplace.[12]

Suppose a supervisor is not present at the time of the off-premise conduct. Under what circumstances may a social event, attended only by the complainant and a co-worker, be considered as an off-premise work site?

Flight attendant Penny Ferris sued Delta Airlines for acts of sexual harassment allegedly committed by fellow flight attendant Michael Young, while both she and he were off-duty. Delta assigned Ferris and Young to a flight from New York's JFK International Airport to Rome. They had neither met nor heard of each other prior to that particular flight. On their arrival in Rome, the flight crew was driven in a Delta Airlines bus to a hotel where the airline had arranged for them to stay until the return trip to New York the following day. According to Ferris, Young invited her to his hotel room to taste a vintage wine he had purchased. While she was in his room, he served her the wine spiked with a "date rape" drug. When Ferris blacked out, Young removed her clothes and raped her vaginally, orally, and anally. Ferris partially regained consciousness intermittently during the multiple rapes, at one point telling Young to stop, and then she passed out again.

When Ferris later sued Delta for sexual harassment, the court began its analysis of the case with the general proposition that employers are not responsible under Title VII for hostile sexual acts resulting from non-work-related, off-duty interactions between co-workers. In this case, the threshold issue was whether Ferris's presence in Young's hotel room was sufficiently related to her employment so that the hotel room could be considered as part of her work environment. The court concluded it was not:

> In the instant case . . . the environment was not work-related. [Ferris] was not only off-duty, she voluntarily associated with [Young]—someone who had no supervisory authority over her—for purely personal reasons. No evidence linking her decision to go to his room with her employment by Delta has been presented. Had [Young] been a supervisor or had . . . supervisory authority, an inference that [Ferris] felt coerced into going to his room might present a fact question of whether the attack occurred in a "work environment." Alternatively, had [Ferris] introduced evidence that Delta had a policy or practice of encouraging flight attendants to commingle in one another's rooms, a fact question might exist as to whether the at-

tack took place in a "work environment." No such evidence has been presented.[13]

The court gave little weight to the fact that at the time of the sexual attacks, both Ferris and Young were between Delta flights and staying at a hotel under arrangements made by and paid for by Delta.

The appellate court that reviewed this decision felt different about the issue. From the appellate court's perspective, the alleged rapes could be considered as having occurred in Delta's workplace. The circumstances surrounding the lodging of the flight crew, during a brief layover in a foreign country, in a block of hotel rooms booked and paid for by Delta, are totally different from the circumstances of most workers who go home to their families at the close of their workday. Although members of the flight crew were not required to stay in the rooms reserved by Delta, they generally did, since on their arrival the airline furnished them with transportation from the airport to the hotel and back to the airport on departure. In circumstances where the crew members stayed in the same hotel in a foreign country where, in most instances, they were not conversant with the local language, it is likely they would band together to socialize and, as a matter of course, this took place in the hotel where they stayed. The appellate court ruled that in circumstances such as these, the hotel was an extension of the Delta workplace, and thus it could be held liable to Ferris for Young's conduct.[14]

A court is more likely to declare off-premise conduct as workplace harassment if the claimant's supervisor committed the alleged offensive conduct. Under those circumstances, the court finds it easier to extend the workplace beyond what is ordinarily considered as its normal boundaries. Conversely, the offensive behavior of a co-worker is less likely to achieve that result unless his conduct is extremely offensive as in the Ferris case.

In a case involving harassment by a supervisor, a woman who worked evenings was offered a ride home by one of her friends who had visited her at work. The woman's supervisor, however, ordered her to tell her friend to leave, ostensibly because of the employer's policy prohibiting employees from allowing friends to visit them during business hours. Although she told the supervisor her friend was the sole source for her ride home, he remained insensitive to her pleas except to say he would drive her home. Later, on the way to her home, the supervisor detoured to a park and sexually assaulted her. When she sued for sexual harassment, her employer argued it could not be held liable for the supervisor's behavior since the claimant had not been subjected to an act of harassment while at work. The court rejected the employer's position:

> The court cannot exclude from its consideration those allegations of sexual conduct which occurred after work hours. . . . The question, rather, is whether there are sufficient facts from which to infer a nexus between the sexual conduct and the work environment. . . . While the harassing conduct need not occur in the workplace, it must occur in a work-related context.

Two factors brought the supervisor's conduct within the ambit of the workplace. First, the assault occurred immediately after the complainant's shift ended and before she arrived at her home. Second, because of the supervisor's authority over the complainant, he was able to place himself in a position to compel the complainant to accompany him by making it more difficult for her to make other arrangements to get home. Thus a causal nexus could be inferred between the workplace and the sexual assault, thus placing the occurrence of the assault within the bounds of the complainant's work environment.[15]

Evidence of off-premise offensive behavior may become a significant factor in sexual harassment cases in which the claimant is also subjected to on-premise conduct of a similar nature. One court relied on a claimant's testimony that a management employee approached her in an offensive manner while she was socializing at a bar with another female employee, and then, a few days later, harassed her again, this time at work. Even though the initial act of harassment occurred outside the normal workplace setting, the court stated that in light of the later acts of on-site harassment, the bar incident could have contributed to the hostile nature of the claimant's work environment. Moreover, the later acts of harassment could also be viewed as a continuation of the previous conduct. Thus, in determining the severity and pervasiveness of the harassment, evidence of the off-premise incident was properly included in the totality of the circumstance considered by the court.[16]

CHAPTER SEVEN

Gender Harassment

In the cases reviewed in the last chapter, the courts cited several instances of sexually harassing conduct that appear to have nothing to do with sex. Truck driver Patricia Gross charged her supervisor with embarrassing and humiliating her in the presence of co-workers, and Marilyn Williams accused General Motors co-workers of gluing a box of forms to her desktop, throwing boxes at her, and denying her a key to the office. Absent from each of these allegations is even a hint of sexuality. They fail to reference sexual advances, unwelcome verbal or physical sexual behavior, or any other incident having sexual overtones. Are allegations of harassing behavior, wholly without sexual content, properly considered in a sexual harassment case?

Darla Hall, Patty Baxter, and Jeanette Ticknor sued their employer, Gus Construction Company, and their foreman, John Mundorf, for sexual harassment. After the court awarded judgment in favor of the three claimants, Gus Construction and Mundorf appealed. One of the principal issues presented for review by the appellate court centered on the lower court's decision to admit evidence of harassing conduct of a non-sexual nature in support of the allegations of sexual harassment asserted by the three women.

Mundorf hired the three women as traffic controllers, referred to as "flag persons," to serve at road construction sites in various localities in Iowa. A flag person was assigned to stand at one end of a section of road under construction, another at the other end of that section, and the third to drive a pilot truck leading motorists through the construction area. Each of the women was in her thirties, and Hall and Baxter were single mothers who sought this type of employment to enable them better to support their young children. No other women were assigned to the work sites at which the three women worked.

Soon after Mundorf hired the three women, male members of the construction crew began to verbally abuse them. They referred to the women as "fucking flag girls," and nicknamed Ticknor "Herpes" after she suffered a skin reaction following an extended period of exposure to the sun. On one occasion, Baxter returned to her car at the end of the day to find "Cavern Cunt" written in the dust on the driver's side of the car and "Blond Bitch" on the passenger's side, where Hall customarily sat. Crew members repeatedly asked Hall if she "wanted to fuck" and asked both Hall and Baxter to engage in oral sex with them. Mundorf was present at the time when many of these incidents occurred, and on one occasion, he in like manner referred to the women as "fucking flag girls." Each of the women told Mundorf that the verbal abuse was offensive, and although Mundorf spoke to the crew members about their conduct, the verbal abuse continued.

The harassment was not limited to verbal abuse, as crew members subjected Hall and Baxter to offensive physical touching as well. Workers would corner the two women between trucks and then reach out of the truck cab windows and rub their hands up and down the women's thighs and grope their breasts. One crew member lifted Hall up to a truck cab window so other crew members could touch her. Male crew members pulled down their pants and mooned the women while they were working, and one of them exposed himself to Hall. They flashed obscene pictures of naked couples engaged in oral sex. Even though Mundorf had observed these incidents, he did nothing to stop them.

In addition to harassing incidents of a sexual nature, crew members repeatedly harassed the women in other ways. One crew member urinated in Hall's water bottle, and several others in the gas tank of Ticknor's car, causing it to malfunction. When carbon monoxide fumes leaked into the cab of the pilot truck causing the driver to become drowsy, the crew mechanic ignored the women's complaints, and the women were forced to rotate their positions so as to limit their time in the truck. Later, when a male crew member was required to use the truck, it was immediately repaired. The women were denied transportation to a neighboring town for bathroom breaks, and thus were forced to relieve themselves in a ditch, while crew members observed them through surveying equipment.

Noting that many of the "Animal House" antics of its male workers were committed in a nonsexual context, the defendants argued that the lower court had committed error in failing to distinguish between conduct of a sexual nature and conduct lacking sexual content, that the court should have limited the admission of evidence to the former as the latter was irrelevant to allegations of sexual harassment. In support of their position, they purported to rely on EEOC regulations that defined sexual harassment as "[u]nwelcome sexual advances, requests for sexual favors, and other verbal or physical conduct of a sexual nature."[1] They contended that calling Ticknor "Herpes," although cruel, was not conduct of a sexual nature, that the urinating incidents were merely practical jokes, and the company's failure to repair the pilot truck's carbon monoxide problem was totally unrelated to the issue of sexual misconduct.

The appellate court rejected these arguments, ruling that the lower court correctly considered all incidents of harassment, whether of a non-sexual or of an explicitly sexual nature. Acts of harassment that would not have occurred but for the fact that Hall, Baxter, and Ticknor were women were relevant to their allegations of sexual harassment, since "intimidation and hostility toward women because they are women can obviously result from conduct other than explicit sexual advances." Although the three women had to prove they had been subjected to "unwelcome sexual harassment," proof of such harassment was not limited to conduct of a solely sexual nature. The offensive conduct need not have explicit sexual overtones. Rather, the women only had to prove the conduct they experienced, nonsexual or sexual, was unwelcome, in the sense that they did not solicit it and regarded it as undesirable and offensive.[2] The lower court properly considered as relevant any incident of harassment that would not have occurred but for the fact that Hall, Baxter, and Ticknor were women.

Another case in point involved Dianne Evans, a life insurance salesperson. After a long and successful career with Metropolitan Life Insurance Company, Evans was recruited by Durham Life Insurance Company, which promised her, among other things, her own office and secretary. She achieved even greater success during her first two years at Durham, significantly increasing her commission income. Another insurance company then acquired Durham, and new management arrived on the scene. From that point onward, Evans's career proceeded downhill.

At the point when new management assumed control of Durham, Evans was the only full-time female sales agent in an office of thirty agents. Male members of the new management team, apparently resenting the success that Evans, a woman, had achieved, set out to undermine her position by depriving her of the staff and other support Durham's previous management had provided her. Two members of management told Evans she failed to fit the company profile for sales agents; her clothes and shoes were too expensive, she dressed too well for the job, and "made too much money for a goddamn woman." Thereafter, Evans suffered repeated slights from members of new management. At an awards dinner, the top-selling agents were honored for having exceeded specified minimum sales. While the sales numbers of the male agents were announced, no reference was made to Evans's sales figures, even though she was the top producer in the office. She was identified only as one who had sold in excess of the required minimum. Evans felt management had deliberately humiliated her in the presence of her colleagues and her son, who had attended the dinner with his mother.

At a training session, Evans was publicly mocked on account of her speech and by reason of the manner in which she carried herself when she walked. Her supervisors refused to afford her the legal assistance she required, and as a result she lost an important account. When she tried to explain to her manager why she had lost the account, he cut her off with, "What do you know about annuities, you're only a woman." Management assigned her far more than her share of work with lapsed policies—a thankless job, generally distributed proportionately among the sales agents—thus further reducing her commission income. Her secretary was fired and not replaced, and then she was forced out of her private office and some of her critical files unexplainably disappeared. Again, Evans suffered a reduction in commission income.

In addition to incidents of nonsexual harassment, Evans was bombarded with sexist remarks and continuously subjected to crude sexual touching. After patiently enduring this type of harassing behavior for several months, Evans, concluding she no longer had a future at Durham, resigned and sued the company for sexual harassment.

After Evans succeeded in securing a favorable trial verdict, management appealed, arguing that the trial court had erred in aggregating sexual and non-sexual incidents in its ruling that Evans had worked in a hostile environment. The appellate court disagreed:

> Some of these events were apparently triggered by sexual desire, some were sexually hostile, some were non-sexual but gender based, and others were facially neutral. . . . Title VII may be applied to all of these types of conduct. . . . Title VII prohibits sex discrimination. Although "sex" has several common meanings, in Title VII it describes a personal characteristic, like race or religion. We generally presume that sexual advances of the

kind alleged in this case are sex-based whether the motivation is desire or hatred. Likewise, hostile or paternalistic acts based on perceptions about womanhood or manhood are sex-based or "gender-based."

The court ruled that management's adverse treatment of Evans, in combination with the overt sexual behavior of her supervisors, created a hostile working environment in which Evans was compelled to work, and thus Durham was liable to her for the damages she suffered as a consequence of that treatment.[3]

Guidelines pertaining to sexual harassment promulgated by the EEOC primarily address conduct that is sexual in nature, but they also provide guidance on a category of harassing conduct not involving sexual content. The guidelines affirm the premise that evidence of nonsexual harassment may be combined with evidence of harassing conduct of a sexual nature to support allegations a claimant was compelled to work in an offensive and hostile environment. "Acts of physical aggression, intimidation, hostility or unequal treatment based on sex may be combined with incidents of sexual harassment to establish the existence of discriminatory terms and conditions of employment."[4] Therefore, actions directed against women solely on account of their gender may be considered as acts of sexual harassment even if the actions lack sexual content.

A number of legal scholars and commentators justify the admission of evidence of nonsexual behavior in sexual harassment hostile work environment cases on the ground that power, not sex, lies at the root of these cases. Men holding positions of authority in the corporate hierarchy may assert their power by subjecting women to acts of sexual as well as nonsexual harassment, and the result of both forms of conduct tends to keep women in their place.[5] Harassment devalues a woman's role in the workplace by directing attention, not only to her sexuality, but also to her gender.

Irrespective of the underlying theory, it is now well established that acts of sexual harassment are not limited to those wholly sexual in nature. Courts now generally refer to nonsexual harassment as "gender harassment."[6] As one commentator has noted, the use of this term "dispenses with the problem involved in using a word like 'sexual,' which can refer both to sex as the immutable gender characteristic and to sex as describing a range of behaviors associated with libidinal gratification. And, it continues to focus on the key element: 'harassment.'"[7] Clearly, gender harassment is a form of sexual harassment.

Suppose a claimant alleges only occurrences of nonsexual conduct;

absent from the allegations of harassment are any charges the harasser was guilty of offensive sexual advances or of any other inappropriate sexual behavior. May the claimant establish a sexual harassment claim solely with evidence of acts of a nonsexual nature? This was the issue in the gender harassment case alleged by Lee Kopp against the Samaritan Health System.

Kopp worked for Samaritan for fifteen years as the lead cardiology technician in the hospital's respiratory-cardiology department. Throughout her employment, she had received "excellent" evaluations and her supervisors considered her a dedicated employee. Dr. Saadi Albaghdadi, a cardiologist with privileges at Samaritan, viewed Kopp quite differently. In fact, as Kopp alleged, she had several nasty encounters with him. On two occasions he shouted at her and on another threw his stethoscope at her. At still another time, after noticing a medical test report was missing from a patient's chart, Albaghdadi grabbed Kopp by the lapels of her jacket, pulled her close to him, shouted through gritted teeth, and shook her violently before releasing her. Kopp lodged a formal complaint against Albaghdadi and later filed a harassment suit against him and the hospital.

By the time the case reached the court for trial, a considerable volume of deposition testimony had been obtained from other Samaritan employees recounting numerous instances of Albaghdadi's shouting, swearing, and throwing objects at female employees of the hospital. This testimony also disclosed that Albaghdadi was prone to push women around and use vulgar language when referring to them, and although Albaghdadi abused male staff members as well, his abuse of women occurred far more frequently and was of a far more serious nature.

Despite the fact that Albaghdadi's harassment of Kopp was not of a sexual nature, his abusive mannerisms were as offensive as the types of unwelcome sexual conduct we have witnessed in other cases. Kopp was singled out for abusive treatment, not because she was a sexual object, but because she was a woman. Even though Albaghdadi's behavior toward Kopp was not explicitly sexual in nature, he harassed her because of her gender. The court ruled, therefore, the type of conduct she endured violated Title VII.[8]

The term *sexual harassment* may appear to be a misnomer when acts of a nonsexual nature are the subject of the allegations before the court. But as the *Evans* and *Kopp* cases make clear, the essence of a sexual harassment claim is not necessarily constructed on sexual advances or other incidents having sexual overtones. Because intimidation and hostility toward women—merely because they are women—may be as harassing as conduct involving explicit sexual advances, the courts have adopted the term "gender harassment" to distinguish "nonsexual" harassment from harassment that is sexual or erotic in nature. Both types of conduct, however, are included in the concept of sexual harassment as understood under the rubric of Title VII.

Gender harassment is not always motivated by hatred of women. However, the motivation is always some sort of bias against women. In Dianne Evans's case, the bias evolved from a perception of women that refused to allow for female success in a business world dominated by men. Evans was harassed because she failed to fit a mold conceptualized by her male peers. If she had been less successful or less productive and had earned less money, she probably would not have been subjected to harassing conduct.

A broad-based animus toward women often underlies gender harassment cases. Elizabeth Smith encountered that type of animus during her employment with the First Union National Bank. Smith initially worked for the bank as an adjuster, arranging for payments on delinquent accounts. The bank later promoted her to team leader in the consumer credit collections department where she assisted her manager in supervising sixteen adjusters. Smith reported to Ronald Scoggins who, Smith claimed, subjected her to a barrage of threats and gender-based insults. Certain of Scoggins's remarks were directed at Smith individually, while others reflected Scoggins's hostile view of women in general.

During Smith's first few weeks in her new position, Scoggins informed her, on at least thirty occasions, he would have preferred a man in the team leader position because men are "natural leaders" and women are not. Scoggins also told her he felt it unwise to assign women to management positions because they are "too emotional to handle a managerial role." Whenever one of his female subordinates became upset about some matter, Scoggins customarily would remark to Smith that the worker must be menstruating or "needed a good banging."

Scoggins also demeaned the workplace successes of the bank's female employees. He openly and frequently expressed the opinion that "the only way for a woman to get ahead at First Union was to spread her legs," and he wished he had been born a woman so he could "whore his way through life." He also expressed his animus toward women through the reiterated recitation of the cliché that "women should be barefoot and pregnant," and it was his belief a woman's sole goal in life was to find a man to marry.

Other female employees reported Scoggins's antiwomen attitudes as well as his derogatory comments about Smith and other female employees of the bank. They claimed his conduct was threatening and demeaning to them as well, and one woman resigned because of his harassing remarks.

Scoggins's behavior toward Smith was often physically threatening. He habitually stood outside her cubicle barking orders at her, often concluding with the remark, "or else you'll see what will happen to you." He accused her of conspiring with his supervisor against him. On one occasion, he entered her cubicle, grabbed her chair and spun her around violently to face him and stated he could "see why a man would slit a woman's throat." Fearing for her safety, Smith then asked the bank to remove her from Scoggins's supervision.

When Smith later sued the bank, claiming sexual harassment, the trial court, relying on a rule of law already rejected by almost all courts, dismissed her case, placing great emphasis on the fact Smith had not claimed Scoggins had inappropriately touched her, ogled her, or invited her, explicitly or by implication, to have sex with him, and it thus concluded that she could not have been sexually harassed. After Smith appealed the dismissal of her claim, the appellate court ruled that the trial court had erred in failing to recognize that a woman's work environment may be hostile even if she is not subjected to sexual advances or propositions:

> An employer violates Title VII when the workplace is permeated with discriminatory intimidation, ridicule, and insult, that is sufficiently severe or pervasive to alter the conditions of the victim's employment and create an abusive working environment. . . . A [workplace] consumed by remarks that intimidate, ridicule, and maliciously demean the status of women can create an environment that is as hostile as an environment that contains unwanted sexual advances.[9]

Title VII prohibits gender-based harassment that rises to the severe or pervasive level of hostility and offensiveness. Intimidating, ridiculing, and demeaning behavior directed not only against Smith but also against other women working in the bank marked her work environment. The antiwomen animus, repeatedly expressed by Scoggins, was sufficiently severe and pervasive to corrupt the bank's work environment, thus placing the bank in the position of being held liable for Scoggins's harassing behavior.

An antiwomen animus may arise from a number of sources. In some instances, a man in a position of authority feels threatened by his female subordinates. Apprehensive, he responds to the perceived threats by lashing out at the women he believes are undermining or threatening his position. The result is a hostile environment for the women working under his supervision. These were the circumstances existent at the time Virginia Delgado filed her sexual harassment suit against the U.S. Navy.

Delgado was an equal employment opportunity officer assigned to the Naval Facilities Engineering Command in Alexandria, Virginia. The head of the EEO office was John Joseph, Delgado's boss. The EEO office employed three others, all women, and they were unanimous in charging Joseph with having created an extremely hostile work environment, replete with acts of antiwomen animus and abuse toward women.

Joseph deliberately interfered with Delgado's performance of her duties. He barred her from his office although it housed materials she needed to perform her job tasks. He deliberately delayed the delivery of mail to her desk, thus inhibiting her ability to perform her assigned job responsibilities in a timely fashion. He refused to give her guidance in the performance of her duties, and then criticized her when she sought help outside the office. He screamed at and threatened her. He habitually used abusive language and referred to her as "babe." On one occasion, he kicked open Delgado's office door, and on another, he prevented her from leaving her office. On still another, he blew cigar smoke into her face, although he was fully aware she detested cigars.

Joseph was equally abusive of the other women assigned to the EEO office. He shouted at one woman, insulted her, and berated her in office meetings and called her stupid. On the day following a screaming incident, the woman who had been the target of his display of anger refused to acknowledge him when he said "good morning." In response, he screamed at her "good morning," "good morning," "good morning" over and over again. When another woman complained about his conduct, he told her that since she and her female co-workers "behaved like children, they would be treated like children." He complained to his own supervisor that he had "dumb females working for him who couldn't read or write."

Joseph also had difficulties with women other than those working in the EEO office. At times, he treated women as if they were not present, customarily ignoring what they said, rudely interrupting them, and using derogatory terms when referring to them. He never treated men in this fashion.

When Delgado sued the Navy claiming sexual harassment, the court had little difficulty in concluding that Joseph had created a hostile environment for women working in the EEO office. It attributed Joseph's derogatory attitude toward women to his view that they threatened his position. He verbally attacked women as a way of protecting his turf. As the court noted, it was ironic that the harassment of these women took place in the EEO office, whose head was charged with the responsibility of preventing harassment.[10] For a person exhibiting this type of anti-women animus, Joseph held the wrong position. Irrespective of his position, his conduct was sexually harassing.

Of course, every instance of animosity expressed by a male supervisor toward a female employee does not rise to the level of an act of sexual harassment. The courts carefully distinguish between acts of harassment and acts merely expressing dislike of a female employee. Rochelle Galloway, a packer in the parts department of General Motors, sued GM for failing to protect her from the behavior of a co-worker named Bullock. Galloway and Bullock had previously had a romantic relationship, but it soured, and thereafter, Bullock repeatedly referred to Galloway as a "sick bitch," the "sick" an apparent allusion to Galloway's previous hospitalization for a psychiatric disorder. He also verbally abused her in other ways, but the court that ruled on Galloway's sexual harassment claim did not equate Bullock's abusive verbal conduct with acts of sexual harassment. Bullock's "sick bitch" comments, even if repeatedly made over an extended period of time, were made in the context of a failed sexual relationship. They were not intended to be coercive or otherwise sexually harassing. The repetition of the remark, together with other verbal animosities reflected an aborted personal and intimate relationship, rather than a belief that women do not belong in the workplace or are in some way inferior to men. It was not an expression of animosity toward women in general.

The court noted that if Bullock had called Galloway "loonie," or "nut case," or "whacko," those terms could not be considered as sexually harassing since they did not relate to Galloway as a woman. Similarly, Bullock's use of the term "bitch" did not necessarily connote a specific female characteristic; it failed to draw attention to Galloway's sexual, maternal, or other female characteristics. In these circumstances, no inference could be drawn from Bullock's behavior that Galloway worked in a hostile environment. Galloway, by virtue of her womanhood, was not disadvantaged in relation to her male co-workers. The court dismissed her sexual harassment claim.[11]

The courts also distinguish between behavior that is offensive solely to women and behavior offensive to both men and women. In one case, a complainant alleged her male supervisor remarked to her, "I have no time for you or your fucking menopausal bitches." A court ruled that this comment was offensive to men as well as women, and thus the supervisor had not discriminatorily targeted women. Consequently, the evidence was insufficient to show the working environment was hostile because of the claimant's gender:

> This court is faced with a plaintiff who concludes from her experiences with an employer that she was the target of gender-based harassment. The record shows evidence of poor treatment by her supervisor, but it shows no basis on which this court or any reasonable jury could conclude that this treatment was discriminatorily targeted toward women. In the absence of such evidence, this Court must conclude that there was no hostile working environment based on gender.[12]

One may quarrel with the court's view in this instance, but the principle it relied on is clear; gender harassment does not exist unless it can be shown that the conduct found objectionable by the claimant affected women only.

There is one exception. Even in those instances where both male and female workers find a supervisor's conduct offensive, a woman may successfully plead a gender harassment claim if she is able to demonstrate the harassing conduct disproportionately affected women. In such a case, her success rests on a showing that the harsh treatment to which she was subjected exceeded—qualitatively and quantitatively—the treatment afforded her male co-workers.[13]

CHAPTER EIGHT

The Reasonable Person and Reasonable Woman Standards

Harassing conduct violates Title VII only if that conduct is unwelcome and is sufficiently severe or pervasive to alter the conditions of a woman's employment, thus creating an abusive environment in which she is compelled to work. Whose perspective—that of the harasser or that of the victim of his harassment—should prevail in assessing the welcomeness of his conduct? What standard should a court rely on in determining whether the alleged conduct is sufficiently severe or pervasive to create an abusive working environment? Should the harasser's conduct be evaluated from the viewpoint of a "reasonable person" or that of a "reasonable woman?"

The reasonable person standard combines the perceptions of a reasonable man with those of a reasonable woman, but the reasonable woman standard depends solely on a woman's view of workplace issues. Since men and women view workplace sexuality from entirely different perspectives, the outcome of a sexual harassment case may very well turn on which of these two standards the court applies. Thus the appropriate standard to be used in evaluating sexual harassment issues has itself become a major issue.

The resolution of a sexual harassment case may be dependent on a determination that the sexual advances of a male worker were innocent or offensive. A male supervisor, for example, may believe it wholly acceptable to tell a female subordinate she has a great figure or nice legs, but she may find comments of this nature uttered in the workplace to be offensive.[1] Male workplace behavior, viewed as offensive or threatening by women, is commonly perceived by men as harmless or even complimentary of female workers.

An exhaustive study of sex in the workplace conducted by Barbara Gutek revealed that while women are more likely to view workplace sexual encounters as inappropriate and undesirable, men are more disposed to perceive them as entirely proper and mutually desirable. Men are less likely to view their behavior as harassing and more apt to consider it merely a reflection of a woman's physical or personal attributes. That which women consider as sexual encounters, men view as normal work-related interchanges. Women are more apt to attribute the source of a male worker's sexual advances to his need for power or desire to dominate, and women often express the view that men frequently treat them as sex objects rather than as individuals.[2] Men reject both views as totally unrealistic.

Rosemary Agonito, who has written extensively on workplace gender issues, observes that when a man is confronted by sexual behavior at work he does not see himself as vulnerable in the same way a woman does:

> Since men view their sexuality as a kind of prowess, indeed the prized essence of manhood, having someone call attention to it results in enhancing his image in many situations. Having his sexuality recognized in no way diminishes a man's persona—his talents, intelligence, authority and experience remain intact in the eyes of all observers. Not so with a woman who must continually "prove" she is something more than a sexual creature. Calling attention to her sexuality reinforces the stereotype and reminds everyone that she exists as a sex object, diminishing her talents, intelligence, authority and experience to a peripheral status. So what is sexual harassment to a woman is, in many instances, a compliment to a man.[3]

A woman's view of sexual conduct in the workplace is conditioned by her general attitudes concerning sex. As Cornell professor of law Kathryn Abrams has suggested, a woman's vulnerability to sexual coercion may make her wary of any kind of sexual encounter, inside or outside the workplace, and thus she tends to hold a more restrictive view with regard to the circumstances and types of relationships in which she views sexual conduct to be appropriate. "Because of the inequality and coercion with which it is so frequently associated in the minds of women, the appearance of sexuality in an unexpected context or a setting of ostensible equality can be an anguishing experience."[4] Catharine

MacKinnon, in her work referred to in chapter 1, states that if men were to perceive their actions as women see them, a transformation in consciousness would be achieved, and then "only clinically sick men would sexually harass women and it would be relatively rare."[5]

Since women and men experience workplace behavior differently, it comes as no surprise that a court's selection of the reasonable person standard rather than the reasonable woman standard less likely culminates in a determination of sexual harassment issues in favor of the victim of the harassment. This clearly was the situation in the *Rabidue* case, reviewed in chapter 6.

Vivienne Rabidue, an employee of the Osceola Refining Company, was the only female employee working in a management position. She and other female employees were daily exposed to pictorial displays of nude and partially nude women exhibited throughout Osceola's workplace. One of these pictures showed a supine woman with a golf ball on a bared breast, while a man holding a golf club stood over her, yelling "fore." One of the company's supervisors regularly spewed antifemale obscenities, routinely referring to women as "whores," "cunt," "pussy," and "tits."

In dismissing Rabidue's sexual harassment complaint, the court applied the reasonable person standard. Under that standard, the court determined that the sexually oriented pictures and posters had a "de minimis" effect on Rabidue's working environment, and the supervisor's obscenities, although annoying, were not so startling as to have seriously affected her psyche or that of any of the other female employees. Thus, the court ruled, Rabidue's work environment could not be considered hostile or offensive.

The decision was affirmed on appeal, but one of the appellate judges, dissenting from the court's ruling, viewed the circumstances of the case from a different perspective. In his view, the reasonable person standard clearly failed to take into account the wide divergence that exists between a woman's viewpoint of appropriate workplace sexual conduct and that of a man. Thus he would have had the court apply a reasonable woman standard, thus allowing the court to consider sociological differences between men and women and their views of appropriate workplace behavior. As he pointed out, unless the perspective of a reasonable woman were adopted, employers would be permitted to continue to rely on "ingrained notions of reasonable behavior fashioned by the offenders," that is, on notions of the appropriateness of workplace behavior fashioned solely by men.[6]

As noted in chapter 6, the *Rabidue* court's approach to the particular issues of that case leaves much to be desired. All aspects of their decision have been severely criticized by other courts. The dissenting opinion, moreover, demonstrated that the application of the reasonable woman standard would have produced a different result—a decision in Rabidue's favor instead of a dismissal of her case. Many courts, including the court that considered Kerry Ellison's sexual harassment claims, found this difficult, if not impossible, to ignore.

Kerry Ellison worked as a revenue agent in the Internal Revenue Service office in San Mateo, California. One of her co-workers, Sterling Gray, worked at a desk situated close to Ellison's. IRS agents working in the San Mateo office often lunched in groups, and on one occasion Ellison lunched with a group of co-workers that included Gray. Ellison later claimed that thereafter Gray pestered her with silly questions and dawdled around her desk. About two months later, Gray asked her out for a drink after work, an invitation Ellison declined. A week later, Gray, uncharacteristically dressed in a three-piece suit, asked her to lunch, but Ellison again was unwilling to accept his invitation. A few days later, Gray handed her a handwritten note: "I cried over you last night and I'm totally drained today. I have never been in such constant term oil [*sic*]. Thank you for talking with me. I could not stand to feel your hatred for another day."

Ellison was so shocked and frightened by the tone of the note that she rose from her desk and ran from the office. Gray followed her into the hallway and demanded she talk to him, but she fled the building. Ellison later reported Gray's behavior to her supervisor, who agreed Gray was engaging in sexually harassing conduct. Rather than file a formal complaint of harassment, however, Ellison decided to handle the matter herself. She asked a male co-worker to speak to Gray and inform him she was not interested in him and he should leave her alone.

The following week, after Ellison had started a four-week training session in St. Louis, Gray sent her a three-page love letter that Ellison described as "twenty times, a hundred times weirder" than the prior note:

> I know that you are worth knowing with or without sex. . . . Leaving aside the hassles and disasters of recent weeks, I have enjoyed you so much over these past few months. Watching you. Experiencing you from O so far away. Admiring your style and elan. . . . Don't you think it odd that two people who have never even talked together, alone, are striking off such intense sparks. . . . I will [write] another letter in the near future.

Ellison later testified to her reaction to the letter: "I just thought he was crazy. I thought he was nuts. I didn't know what he would do next. I was frightened."

Ellison notified her supervisor she was frightened and upset and requested that either she or Gray be transferred to another office. The supervisor immediately confronted Gray and directed him to cease all contact with Ellison. Subsequently, the IRS transferred Gray to its office in San Francisco, but after he filed a union grievance, he was ordered transferred back to San Mateo. Before returning, Gray wrote another letter to Ellison, intimating they had some sort of relationship. Ellison was "frantic." In order to avoid Gray on his return to the San Mateo office, Ellison asked to be transferred, and she followed her request with the filing of a formal complaint alleging sexual harassment.

The court that considered Ellison's harassment case was required to decide whether Gray's conduct was sufficiently severe or pervasive to have altered the conditions of her employment. The court rejected the reasonable person approach, noting that if the court were to limit its examination solely to the question whether a reasonable person would have engaged in conduct similar to Gray's, it would run the risk of reinforcing prevailing levels of workplace behavior, thus enabling harassers to continue to harass only because their behavior conformed with offensive conduct that to that point had been common to the workplace. Rather, the court emphasized, the victim's view of allegedly offensive conduct must first be considered and fully understood:

> We therefore prefer to analyze harassment from the victim's perspective. A complete understanding of the victim's view requires, among other things, an analysis of the different perspectives of men and women. Conduct that many men consider unobjectionable may offend many women. . . . [M]any women share common concerns which men do not necessarily share.

Men and women do not share the same perspective with regard to rape and sexual assault. Since women are far more often victims of criminal sexual assault, they are much more concerned with any form of aberrant or aggressive male sexual behavior. Even when confronted with a mild form of sexual harassment, a woman may be concerned that a harasser's conduct is merely a prelude to a violent assault. A man, on the other hand, who probably has never been the subject of a sexual assault, may view the same conduct without a full appreciation of the underlying threat of violence a woman perceives. Based on this rationale, the court rejected the reasonable person standard and concluded the severity and pervasiveness of Gray's actions should be viewed from the perspective of a "reasonable woman." This approach was necessary, the court added, because "a sex-blind reasonable person standard tends to be male-biased and tends to systematically ignore the experiences of women."

Analyzing the facts of this case from Gray's point of view, one can conclude that he was only trying to woo Ellison. There was no evidence he harbored any ill will toward her, and thus from his vantage, his actions were nonthreatening. Ellison, however, was offended, shocked, and frightened by Gray's conduct. Inasmuch as women share concerns of sexual assault, her reaction cannot be described as at all unusual for a woman. The court agreed that a reasonable woman would have similarly reacted and would have considered Gray's behavior to be sufficiently severe and pervasive to alter the conditions of her employment, thus creating a hostile working environment.[7] The court's adoption of the reasonable woman standard in judging the type of behavior exhibited by Gray led it to conclude his conduct violated Title VII. It appears apparent that the court would not have arrived at that result had it rejected the reasonable woman approach and had applied the reasonable person approach instead.

With the *Ellison* decision, the reasonable woman standard arose as a major issue for the courts to ponder in sexual harassment cases. Should a court rely on the reasonable person or the reasonable woman standard? Arguments abound favoring and opposing both sides of the issue.

Critics of the reasonable person approach point to some rather bizarre results that have flowed from its use. The acts of harassment suffered by six women working at the Lamar Truck Plaza in Colorado—harassing behavior the court failed to recognize as severe and pervasive—point up the limitations of the reasonable person approach. The women, restaurant workers employed by the truck plaza, claimed that management employees regularly used vulgar language and repeatedly touched them offensively, thus creating a hostile and offensive working environment. Each of the women testified to specific instances of vulgarity and to the touching of their breasts and buttocks.

Unbelievably, the trial court ruled that the plaintiffs failed to establish that management's antics were based on sex. Moreover, it expressed the viewpoint that the working environment at the truck plaza failed to exhibit the sort of hostility Title VII was intended to prevent. The vulgar language complained of by the women was typical of that heard in the restaurant business and, in any event, "Congress did not intend for Title VII to obliterate the use of foul language in the American workplace." As for the illicit touching, the court described those episodes as quite "sparse." Based on these findings, the court ruled that the plaintiffs had failed to establish the existence of a pervasive, sexually hostile work environment.[8]

What did the court mean by "sparse"? The EEOC and several courts have ruled that a single instance of offensive physical touching of a woman's body is sufficient to create a hostile working environment.[9] The evidence in this case disclosed six incidents of breast and buttocks touching over a period of approximately one year. Nevertheless, the court viewed their occurrence as "sparse."

The women appealed, but to no avail, as the appellate court relied on the rationale of the *Rabidue* court, specifically referring to that court's holding that Title VII was not intended to cover workplace language that was "rough-hewn and vulgar," nor was it intended "to bring about a magical transformation in the social mores of American workers." The appellate court declared that the conduct of the truck plaza management was acceptable, since a reasonable person would not find the women's work environment to be offensive.[10] Neither the trial court nor the appellate court viewed the conduct of the management employees from the perspective of a woman.

In another case, a supervisor forcibly kissed a female subordinate on two occasions and touched her thigh. Even though she made it clear to him that his conduct was offensive to her, he told her off-color jokes and asked her to dinner on several occasions. The court, adopting the perspective of a reasonable person, held that the total effect of the supervisor's actions was not such as to interfere with a reasonable person's work performance. Case dismissed.[11] Again, if the court had viewed these harassing incidents from the perspective of a reasonable woman, undoubtedly it would have arrived at a far different result.

The reasonable woman approach is not without its critics. The *Ellison* court itself noted that use of the reasonable woman standard may at times classify conduct as violative of Title VII even though the harasser may fail to realize his behavior is unlawful. Thus, well-intentioned compliments of co-workers or supervisors may form the basis of a sexual harassment claim if a reasonable woman were to consider the compliments to be offensive. But others argue that the use of the reasonable woman approach is nevertheless justified because liability for sexually harassing behavior is not based on fault. Rather, the focus of Title VII is directed at the consequences of particular workplace conduct and is less concerned with the motivation of the harasser. In order to mitigate the difficulties that well-intentioned male workers may encounter, an employer may be required to educate and sensitize its workforce so as to eliminate conduct reasonable women consider objectionable. In any event, these critics argue that prevention is the best tool for the elimination of sexual harassment from the workplace.[12]

While a few courts have adopted the reasonable woman standard, others continue to rely on the reasonable person approach. The Supreme Court had the opportunity to resolve these conflicting positions when Teresa Harris's sexual harassment case against Forklift Systems appeared on its docket (see chapter 4). Throughout Harris's employment as a rental manager, the company's president, Charles Hardy, insulted her and made her the target of sexual commentary. On several occasions, in the presence of other employees, Hardy said to her, "You're a woman, what do you know," and "We need a man as the rental manager," and referred to her as a "dumb ass woman." He suggested that the two of them "go to the Holiday Inn to negotiate [her] raise." He frequently asked Harris and other female employees to retrieve coins from his front pants pockets, and threw objects on the floor and asked them to pick them up. When Harris was in the process of negotiating a rental transaction with a customer, Hardy asked her, again in the presence of others, "What did you do, promise the guy . . . some [sex] Saturday night?" At that point, Harris quit.

In deciding the *Harris* case, the Supreme Court resolved several sexual harassment issues (discussed in later chapters), including the standard the courts should use in judging the severity and pervasiveness of harassing conduct. Without even mentioning or referring in any way to the reasonable woman approach, the court—almost in passing—approved the reasonable person approach: "Conduct that is not severe or pervasive enough to create an objectively hostile or abusive environment—an environment that a reasonable person would find hostile or abusive—is beyond Title VII's purview."

Although the court ignored the perspective of a reasonable woman, it did not specifically reject it. In fact, nothing in the opinion indicates the court even considered the issue or was aware a conflict of views existed in the lower courts. It simply did not address the issue or acknowledge the conflicting views.[13]

For those who advocate the reasonable woman approach, the *Harris* case failed to put the issue to rest; indeed, the court—perhaps inadvertently—left an opening for further consideration of the issue, and the EEOC was quick to take advantage of that opening. The EEOC noted that while in its Enforcement Guidance Notices it also used the term *reasonable person*, it has always emphasized that the reasonable person standard "should consider the victim's perspective and not stereotyped notions of acceptable behavior." Consideration of the victim's perspective is inappropriate, however, if she is a "hypersensitive" person. In other words, the victim's perspective is relevant only if it is that of a reasonable woman. Since the Supreme Court did not elaborate on its definition of a "reasonable person," the EEOC believes the position it had previously promulgated is consistent with the *Harris* decision.

The EEOC continues to analyze sexual harassment issues under the rubric of a reasonable person standard that also reflects the views of the victim of the harassment, so long as that victim is a reasonable woman.[14] The EEOC has directed its investigators to consider all charges of sexually harassing behavior "from the standpoint of the reasonable person in [the charging party's] circumstances." Thus, according to EEOC procedures, the welcomeness issue and the degree of severity and pervasiveness of sexually harassing conduct cannot properly be evaluated unless the perspective of the victim of the harassment is fully considered. The EEOC guidelines insist that reliance on reasonable person standard is inappropriate unless the perspective of the woman who suffered the harassment is also considered as an element of that standard.[15]

The EEOC appears to have given new life to the reasonable woman standard. As noted earlier, the dissenting judge in the *Rabidue* case stated in his view that the reasonable person standard fails to account for the wide divergence between women's perspective of appropriate workplace sexual conduct and the viewpoint of men, and unless the point of view of a reasonable woman were adopted, "ingrained notions of reasonable behavior"—notions fashioned by the very people accused of sexual harassment—would continue to unduly influence evaluations of sexually harassing behavior.[16] These fears largely evaporate when the reasonable person standard is modified to include the perspective of the victim of the harassment, which, as the EEOC has made clear, is considered only if it is the perspective of a "reasonable" woman.

Subsequent to the *Harris* decision, the *Ellison* appellate court, which had strongly supported the reasonable woman approach in its ruling in favor of the position espoused by Kerry Ellison and opposed by the IRS, restated its position on the issue. It announced that in future sexual harassment cases it would rely on the perspective of a reasonable person who possesses the defining aspects of the victim of the harassment. One of those defining aspects, of course, is gender.[17] Although the *Ellison* court may have appeared to have modified its view, in reality, its position seems to parallel that adopted by the EEOC. In fact, if the *Ellison* court had applied the EEOC standard to the facts of the case, its decision probably would not have been different.[18]

Other courts have adopted variations on that theme. One court stated that in determining whether alleged sexually harassing conduct is sufficiently severe or pervasive to create a hostile work environment, it would consider the actual effect of the harasser's conduct on his victim and also the effect similar conduct would have on a "reasonable person in the plaintiff's position."[19] Another court put it this way: "The court must consider both the victim's subjective impressions of [the alleged acts of harassment] and whether the alleged actions would constitute unlawful sexual harassment from the perspective of a reasonable victim."[20]

The courts appear determined to rely on the reasonable woman standard, in one form or another. Unless the Supreme Court decides to again address the issue, it is likely the courts will continue to circumvent—if not subvert—the rationale of the *Harris* decision, thus allowing a more nuanced examination of sexual harassment issues.

Professor Abrams, however, has offered a simpler solution. She advances a reasonable person standard "interpreted to mean not the average person, but the person enlightened concerning the barriers to women's equality in the workplace."[21] Such a person would surely qualify both as a representative of the views of a reasonable person as well as those of a reasonable woman.

CHAPTER NINE

Employer Liability for Workplace Sexual Harassment

Incredibly, harassers are not liable under Title VII, no matter how egregious their conduct. Although acts of sexual harassment are committed by human beings, the courts have consistently ruled only employers are liable for damages suffered by victims of sexually harassing conduct.

Relying on that provision of Title VII that specifies it is unlawful for an *employer* to discriminate against a woman because of her sex, the courts have insulated harassers from liability for their conduct.[1] Although Congress may not have specifically intended to relieve individual harassers from paying a price for their offensive behavior, its allocation of liability to their employers has had that effect. Thus a woman's sexual harassment claims alleged against a male worker will come to naught, unless she works in a state where she may rely on the law of that particular state to hold an individual transgressor liable. Only in those circumstances is a woman entitled to recover damages directly from her harasser. Since, in all other instances, a victim's damages are recoverable from employers, the question of employer liability for the harassing conduct of its employees has become a major issue in sexual harassment cases.

Concomitant with the growth and development of federal law barring sexual harassment, courts have expanded employers' liability for harassment found in their workplaces. They have held an employer liable for harassing actions committed by nonsupervisory workers in those circumstances where the employer knew, or it can be demonstrated that it should have known, of the occurrence of the acts of harassment. Courts also have held an employer liable for acts of sexual harassment committed by nonemployees, such as customers or clients, if it knew or should have known of the harassing conduct and either acquiesced in its continuance or failed to undertake sufficient measures to eliminate it. That has left for consideration the question of employer liability for acts of sexual harassment committed by its supervisors. Under what conditions will an employer be held liable for the sexually harassing conduct of one of its supervisors? For a complainant alleging acts of sexual harassment committed by her supervisor, that is a question of significant import, because, as we shall see, under certain circumstances, a sexually harassed victim may be barred from recovering damages or securing any other relief from her employer, even though she may have been cruelly victimized by her supervisor.

Kimberly Ellerth worked in the Chicago office of Burlington Industries, initially as a merchandising assistant and later as a sales representative. After about a year on the job, Ellerth alleged that throughout her employment she had been subjected to the sexually harassing behavior of one of her supervisors. She claimed that beginning with her preemployment interview, Theodore Slowik, a mid-level manager, asked her sexually suggestive questions and stared at her breasts and legs. Once hired, Ellerth had only intermittent contact with Slowik, but on those occasions he told her offensive, off-color jokes and made other sexually inappropriate comments. While on a business trip, Slowik invited Ellerth to the hotel lounge, an invitation Ellerth felt compelled to accept since Slowik was her boss. During their ensuing conversation, after Ellerth failed to respond to Slowik's remarks about her breasts, he told her to "loosen up" and warned her he "could make [her] life very hard or very easy at Burlington."

Burlington management later considered Ellerth for promotion. During her promotion interview, Slowik expressed reservations concerning her prospects for attaining a higher position in the company, commenting she was not "loose enough." At that point he reached over and rubbed her knee. When Slowik later phoned her to announce the promotion had been authorized, he said, "You're gonna be out there with men who work in factories, and they certainly like women with pretty butts/legs." During a subsequent telephone call, Slowik said, "I don't have time for you right now, Kim—unless you want to tell me what you're wearing." On another call, he asked if she was "wearing shorter skirts yet" as it "would make [her] job a whole heck of a lot easier."

Although Ellerth knew Burlington had a sexual harassment policy in place, she did not report any of Slowik's behavior, purportedly out of fear her position would be placed in jeopardy. Ultimately, after another supervisor criticized her performance, Ellerth resigned. She later informed the company she had quit because of Slowik's behavior.

Ellerth sued Burlington Industries for sexual harassment. When her case reached the Supreme Court in 1998, the court was required to determine the circumstances under which an employer may be held liable for the sexually harassing behavior of one of its supervisors. At the outset of its analysis, the court reaffirmed a major distinction between a workplace act of sexual harassment culminating in a "tangible employment action" and one that does not. As defined by the court, a "tangible employment action" is one that causes a significant change in the employment status of the victim of the harassment. As a general proposition, only a supervisor, acting with the authority of his employer, possesses the power to effect a tangible employment action. A nonsupervisory employee may cause physical or psychological harm to a co-worker as readily as a supervisor, but a nonsupervisory employee is not empowered to hire or fire, promote or demote, or increase or reduce another worker's pay. Tangible employment actions fall within the special province of one with supervisory power and authority, one who has been empowered by his employer to make employment decisions affecting the status of workers working under his control:

> Tangible employment actions are the means by which the supervisor brings the official power of the enterprise to bear on subordinates. A tangible employment decision requires an official act of the enterprise, a company act. . . . For these reasons, a tangible employment action taken by the supervisor becomes for Title VII purposes the act of the employer.

Thus, when a supervisor's harassment of a subordinate female employee culminates in an employment action materially affecting her employment status—that is, a tangible employment action—the employer is liable for the supervisor's conduct.

Ellerth, however, had not been subjected to a tangible employment action as a consequence of Slowik's behavior. In fact, she had been promoted, and she later resigned from the company without ever having complained of Slowik's harassment. Under these circumstances, could Burlington Industries nevertheless be held liable to Ellerth for Slowik's harassing conduct? The Supreme Court answered in the affirmative, but also provided Burlington with a defense that could insulate itself from liability. To establish this defense, Burlington would have to prove:

1. It had exercised reasonable care to prevent and promptly correct sexually harassing behavior occurring in its workplace, and
2. Ellerth unreasonably failed to take advantage of preventive or corrective opportunities provided by Burlington to avoid harm from sexual harassment, such as failing to report the harassment in accordance with Burlington's sexual harassment policy.

The court emphasized that this defense is available to employers only in circumstances where no tangible employment action has been taken by the supervisor during the course of his harassment. Conversely, if the victim of harassment has been subjected to a tangible employment action, and the employer does not have a nondiscriminatory explanation for such action, it always is liable.

Because this ruling essentially constituted a new statement of the law, the court remanded the case for further proceedings, thus providing Ellerth with another opportunity to establish Burlington's liability and affording Burlington the opportunity to plead and prove the newly fashioned defense.[2]

The court's decision clarified, for workers and employers alike, the circumstances under which an employer may be held vicariously liable for the sexually harassing conduct of its supervisors. It also provided a warning for employers. If they wished to remain on the right side of Title VII, they should establish policies and procedures formulated to prevent sexually harassing conduct from appearing in their workplaces, and if it does appear, they should have in place policies and procedures designed to correct it. Employers also should provide an adequate means for their employees to report acts of supervisory harassment.

In summary, the Supreme Court's ruling affirmed an old standard of liability and established a new one as well. It reaffirmed an employer's liability for a supervisor's acts of sexual harassment that culminate in a tangible employment action affecting the victim's employment status. Unless the employer is able to furnish the court with a nondiscriminatory explanation for the tangible employment action, it will be held liable for the damages suffered by the victim of the harassment. The court also ruled an employer may remain responsible for a supervisor's conduct even if the harassment does not result in a tangible employment action, but in those circumstances the employer must be given the opportunity to es-

Table 9.1

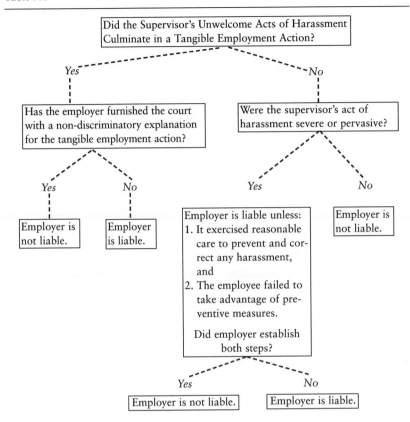

tablish a defense that, if proven, would relieve it of liability for the behavior of its supervisor. The court, however, placed the burden of proving the essential elements of the new defense squarely on the employer. Under the law, this type of defense is commonly referred to as an "affirmative defense."

The procedural measures outlined by the Supreme Court are set forth in Table 9.1.

The Supreme Court proceeded at some length in explaining why a tangible employment action justifies holding an employer liable for supervisory harassment. In his supervisory capacity, a supervisor normally acts on behalf of the company. Thus a supervisor's decision that affects the status of a harassed worker is a decision that would not have been made absent the agency relationship existing between supervisor and employer:

A tangible employment action in most cases inflicts direct economic harm. As a general proposition, only a supervisor, or other person acting with the authority of the company can cause this sort of injury. A co-worker can break a co-worker's arm as easily as a supervisor, and anyone who has regular contact with an employee can inflict psychological injuries by his or her offensive conduct . . . . But one co-worker . . . cannot dock another's pay, nor can one co-worker demote another. Tangible employment actions fall within the special province of the supervisor. The supervisor has been empowered by the company as a distinct class of agent to make economic decisions affecting other employees under his or her control.

Tangible employment actions are the means by which the supervisor brings the official power of the enterprise to bear on subordinates. A tangible employment decision requires an official act of the enterprise, a company act. . . .

For these reasons, a tangible employment action taken by a supervisor becomes for Title VII purposes the act of the employer.[3]

In addition to the reasons cited by the Supreme Court, employer liability for the misuse of supervisory authority is justified because employers have a greater opportunity to guard against misconduct by their supervisors, as they have the opportunity as well as incentive to screen supervisors, train them, and monitor their performance.[4]

Issues relating to an employer's vicarious liability for supervisory workplace behavior have become significantly more important as the courts have struggled with the application of the principles enunciated in the *Ellerth* case, and undoubtedly they will continue to play a major role in future sexual harassment litigation. Who qualifies as a supervisor is one of those issues.

A supervisor's authority to influence, adversely or beneficially, an employee's status and daily work life enhances his ease and ability to harass a female employee. A supervisor generally exercises control over subordinate employees by ordering or withholding tangible employment benefits, and thus his actions and decisions draw on his superior position over those who report to him. Accordingly, a supervisor generally is defined as one who has immediate or successively higher authority over a worker and who is authorized to make decisions regarding employment actions affecting that worker. Even if someone in a position of higher authority must approve his decisions, and he is thus limited to making recommendations for employment action, he meets the definition of a supervisor as long as those who make the final decision give his recommendations substantial weight.[5]

An individual authorized to direct or regulate a subordinate's day-today activities, even if unauthorized to order or recommend other employment decisions, may also qualify as a supervisor. Because his ability to commit harassment is enhanced by his authority to increase a worker's workload or to assign her difficult or undesirable tasks, it is appropriate, in deciding whether the employer is vicariously liable for his behavior, to consider him as occupying a supervisory role.[6]

Thus the essence of supervisory status is the authority to significantly affect, in one way or another, the terms and conditions of employment of a subordinate employee.[7] The manager of a human resources department has the authority to set the terms and conditions of employment. Does his status render his employer liable for his conduct? The issue arose in Betty Sowers's sexual harassment case against Kemira, Inc.

Although Sowers had not earned a college degree, her extensive work experience was considered equivalent to a two-year degree in industrial engineering, and one of her career goals was to secure an engineering position. When Kemira offered Sowers an inventory control clerk position, Jack Skinner, Kemira's manager of human resources, told her that if she accepted the position "she would have her foot in the door . . . to advance to the engineering department if a vacancy arose."

During her tenure as an inventory control clerk, Sowers remained intent on obtaining an industrial engineering position, and ultimately the company elevated her, on a six-month trial basis, to the position of industrial engineer aide, with the understanding that if she performed acceptably, the promotion would be made permanent. Her direct supervisor, pleased with her performance, later recommended that her promotion to the engineering aide position be made permanent. Sowers then met with Skinner to discuss the aide position and an increase in salary. According to Sowers, Skinner was more interested in discussing personal matters. He told her she was pretty and sexy, invited her to lunch and for drinks after work, and asked to "make out with him." On another occasion, he was more specific; he invited her to go to the company store and have sex. About a month later, when Sowers again met with Skinner about making her promotion permanent, Skinner expressed his disappointment she had not acceded to his request to have sex in the company store, and indicated that if she "played his game" she would achieve permanent status.

When Sowers sued Kemira for sexual harassment, the company argued that Skinner had no authority to prevent the aide position from being made permanent, nor did he possess the authority to block Sowers's salary increase. His involvement in these matters, according to

Kemira officials, related only to the preparation of the required paper-work. But the court was not persuaded. Skinner had the power to delay implementation of decisions affecting Sowers's position in the company, and through delay he hoped Sowers would accede to his sexual advances. Although not the ultimate decision maker, Skinner had a great amount of influence over plaintiff's awaited promotion and increase in salary, and he also was charged with carrying out the various bureaucratic steps necessary to finalize them. Thus, while Skinner was not Sowers's direct supervisor, he had sufficient authority over personnel decisions affecting her status as to render Kemira liable for his conduct.[8]

Suppose a victim of harassment believes her position to be subject to the supervisory authority of the person harassing her, but because her employer has not clearly established a chain of supervisory command, she is mistaken, and her harasser does not actually possess such authority. Is her employer nevertheless liable for the harasser's conduct? The EEOC has taken the position that if the victim of the harassment "reasonably believed" the harasser had the power to affect the terms and conditions of her employment, then the employer is strictly liable for the acts of harassment committed against her.[9]

Another issue often arising in these cases relates to whether an employment action ordered by the alleged harasser actually rises to the level of a tangible employment action. As discussed above, if the harassing supervisor's actions culminate in a tangible employment action affecting the victim of the harassment, the new affirmative defense is not available to the employer, and it will be held liable for its supervisor's conduct. Thus, as you might very well suspect, whether a particular employment action is determined to be or not to be a tangible employment action has become a much-litigated issue.

The Supreme Court defined a "tangible employment action" as a "significant change in employment status, such as hiring, firing, failing to promote, reassignment with significantly different responsibilities, or a decision causing a significant change in benefits."[10] The EEOC's definition, however, is somewhat more expansive, as it also includes in its definition any significant change in a worker's duties, with or without a change in salary or benefits. As an example, under the EEOC definition a change in duties blocking an opportunity for promotion would qualify as a tangible employment action. But a change in job title probably would not, unless the title modification signaled a demotion or other downward change in status.[11]

The employment actions taken against Dianne Evans, giving rise to her sexual harassment case against Durham Life Insurance Company (discussed in chapter 7), included the nonreplacement of her dismissed secretary, the loss of her private office, the unexplained disappearance of files critical to her work, and her assignment of a disproportionate share of work that earned low commission income. None of the four actions falls within any one of those specified in the Supreme Court definition of a tangible employment action, but in combination, they caused a significant change in Evans's employment status, and thus the court held the affirmative defense was not available to Durham.[12]

The resolution of the employment issues Lisetta Molnar encountered at the East Chicago Community School illustrates the flexibility courts have adopted when considering controversies related to tangible employment actions. Hired as an intern to teach art, Molnar hoped to qualify at the conclusion of her internship for a license as a full-fledged art teacher. Beginning with her first day at the school, her principal, Lloyd Booth, made sexual advances she found offensive. Booth told her he could secure various benefits for her, such as a permanent art room and additional art supplies, benefits other interns had not been granted. Molnar perceived these offers as sex-related, making her very uncomfortable. During succeeding weeks, Molnar rejected all of Booth's advances, and after Molnar had spurned him, Booth ordered the return of all art supplies previously furnished her, and all discussion of a permanent art room ceased. At the end of the school year, Booth gave Molnar a negative performance evaluation, making it less likely she would be granted a license to teach art.

When Molnar sued for sexual harassment, the court ruled the affirmative defense was unavailable to the school because Booth had subjected Molnar to tangible employment actions. The most significant, in the court's estimation, was his confiscation of art supplies she required to perform her functions as an art teacher. The negative performance evaluation also fell into that category of employment action. Even though the school board later reversed Booth's negative evaluation, the fact that Molnar's career had been temporarily derailed was sufficient to render the original evaluation a tangible employment action. With the affirmative defense unavailable to the school, a jury rendered its verdict in Molnar's favor.[13]

Employment decisions tending to undermine a worker's opportunities for future advancement are frequently relied on as a basis for denying the affirmative defense to an employer. Emily Bryson, a tenured full professor at Chicago State University, claimed she was the victim of sexual harassment inflicted by the university's provost, but her case was dismissed after a lower court ruled she had failed to demonstrate she had suffered a tangible employment action.

Bryson had joined the Chicago State faculty as a bibliographic instruction librarian. After she was awarded tenure, Bryson was assigned the "in-house title" of Special Assistant to the Dean, and in that capacity performed various administrative duties. In-house titles, such as that given to Bryson, were important for professional advancement at the university. In addition to her duties as an assistant to the dean, Bryson served on several committees, including the Budget Committee, which made financial recommendations for the entire university. Service on committees allowed a faculty member to gain the credentials and qualifications requisite for career advancement. After Bryson rejected the sexual advances of the provost, he deprived her of the in-house title, failed to reappoint her to the university's administrative committees, including the Budget Committee, and ignored her requests to serve on other committees. Bryson filed a sexual harassment claim against the university.

In ruling that Bryson had not suffered a tangible employment action, the court was unimpressed with her loss of the in-house title, as it had only "speculative value," and rejected the view that the committee assignments were essential to her academic career. It might have ruled otherwise, the court said, if Bryson had applied for a promotion and had been unsuccessful, but the mere possibility of future promotion denials did not rise to the level of a tangible employment action.

When Bryson appealed, the appellate court rejected the lower court's reasoning, asserting it had erred in assuming, merely because Bryson had not applied for promotion, that her employment status had not been altered when she lost her in-house title and committee assignments. "Depriving someone of the building blocks for [promotion] is just as serious as depriving her of the job itself." The appellate court reversed the lower court decision and held that Bryson had indeed been the subject of tangible employment actions, thus rendering the university liable for the provost's acts of harassment.[14]

As noted earlier, a change in job title ordinarily does not qualify as a tangible employment action, unless the change is accompanied by a diminution in salary, benefits, or duties. On the other hand, if a significant change in the status of a worker's position occurs because the new title is less prestigious than the previous title, it will be considered a tangible employment action.[15] Bryson's loss of her in-house title clearly fell into that category of change in job status.

In one case an employer removed two sales accounts from those assigned to a female employee who had alleged her supervisor had sexually harassed her. Because the loss of the two sales accounts had a tangible effect on her earnings, the court ruled the affirmative defense to her sexual harassment charges was not available to her employer:

> As sales positions [have] greater financial rewards because of either a bonus or commission structure, the loss of plaintiff's . . . accounts could have had a very real tangible effect on her earnings. This is exactly the type of tangible employment action envisioned by the Supreme Court as an exception to the affirmative defense.[16]

The affirmative defense is unavailable to the employer even if a subordinate female employee accedes to the demands of her supervisor and as a result obtains a tangible employment benefit. In chapter 2 we reviewed the case of Terri Nichols who, because she was deaf and mute, could communicate with her supervisor only through sign language. When Nichols encountered serious personal problems at home, she asked her supervisor for a leave of absence, and he granted her request only after she agreed to perform oral sex for him.[17] In commenting on this case, the EEOC noted it would be perverse policy indeed to grant an employer an affirmative defense for its supervisor's conduct because the victim of his harassment was afforded a job benefit—a job benefit granted only after she submitted to his unwelcome sexual demands. Whether she acquiesced in his demands is irrelevant. In either case, she was subjected to a tangible employment action.[18]

A worker's compliance with the unwelcome sexual demands of her supervisor, under threat of a tangible employment action, even though the threat is not carried out, may itself constitute a tangible employment action. Min Jin worked for Metropolitan Life Insurance Company as an insurance sales agent at its Broadway branch in Manhattan. Gregory Morabito, Jin's supervisor, engaged in a pattern of egregious conduct toward Jin that included (1) crude sexual remarks; (2) offensive touching of Jin's buttocks, breasts, and legs; and (3) requiring her to attend once a week private meetings in his office during which he kissed and fondled her, attempted to undress her, and forced her to fondle him until he ejaculated on her. He repeatedly threatened to fire Jin if she did not acquiesce to his sexual demands.

In her subsequent sexual harassment case against MetLife, Jin argued that when Morabito threatened to fire her if she declined to submit to his weekly private office meetings and the ensuing sexual activity, he engaged in a tangible employment action—an action that significantly affected her employment status—thus rendering MetLife liable for his conduct. The court began its analysis of the case by noting that an employee forced to engage in unwanted sex acts confronts one of the "most pernicious and oppressive forms of sexual harassment that can occur in the workplace." When Morabito ordered her to submit to demeaning sexual acts, explicitly threatening to fire her if she failed to submit, he used his authority as Jin's supervisor to impose on her an additional job requirement—a requirement she submit to weekly sexual abuse in order to retain her employment. The empowerment of Morabito to make decisions affecting workers under his control enabled him to compel Jin to submit to his sexual advances, and thus Morabito's use of his supervisory authority to require Jin's submission constituted an act of his employer, MetLife. Under threat of a tangible employment action, a worker's acquiescence to a supervisor's acts of sexual abuse is itself a tangible employment action.[19]

In each of the cases just reviewed, the plaintiff presented evidence clearly demonstrating a material deterioration in her employment status, occurring directly as a consequence of the sexual harassment inflicted on her by her supervisor. In each case, the plaintiff clearly experienced a tangible employment action. In some cases, however, the evidence is not as clear. Kathryn Reinhold's claim against her employer is a case in point.

Reinhold, a school psychologist assigned to the diagnostic department of the Virginia School for the Deaf and Blind, worked as a member of a treatment and diagnostic team consisting of several multidisciplinary professionals. She counseled children, performed psychological testing, and worked with other team members whenever student behavioral problems surfaced. Reinhold alleged that during the course of her employment, Dennis Martin, her immediate supervisor, subjected her to unwelcome sexual advances. The primary issue in the trial of her sexual harassment suit against the school was whether Martin's harassment culminated in a tangible employment action, thus rendering the school vicariously liable for his conduct.

In his role as supervisor of the diagnostic department, Martin was responsible for approving leave schedules, convening departmental meetings to discuss work plans and projected work assignments, and for developing the departmental budget. He also evaluated staff members' job performance, conducted departmental workshops, and was vested with the responsibility of ensuring performance of job tasks of department members.

When Reinhold made it clear to Martin his sexual advances were un-welcome, he threatened her with the loss of her job. He then began to as-sign her extra work that fell outside her job description. As an example, he assigned her the task of counseling, disciplining, and monitoring an-other member of the department who was not performing to Martin's satisfaction. Reinhold objected, arguing that although one of her func-tions was to counsel students, it was inappropriate for her to counsel a professional co-worker. Martin also ordered her to train a fellow teacher in diagnostic testing, a subject it had taken Reinhold two years to master. Since the designated teacher had no training in this area, Reinhold protested that she could not possibly fulfill her regular duties while en-gaged in a long-term training assignment. Nevertheless, Martin insisted she assume this additional responsibility.

Martin then refused to authorize Reinhold's attendance at a profes-sional conference, a conference she very much wanted to attend since one of the subject matters scheduled for discussion related directly to a problem suffered by one of the students she was counseling.

Even though the evidence was clear that once Reinhold rejected Martin's advances, he increased her workload, required her to counsel a co-worker, assigned her other undesirable assignments, and denied her the opportunity to attend a professional conference, the court still ruled Reinhold had not been subjected to a tangible employment action. The court's ruling followed on its conclusion that Reinhold had not "experi-enced a change in her employment status akin to a demotion or a reas-signment entailing significantly different job responsibilities."[20]

The court's reasoning is difficult to fathom, and the EEOC later regis-tered its disagreement with the court's rationale. While the EEOC recog-nized that minor changes in work assignments may not rise to the level of a tangible job action, Martin's actions were sufficient to materially alter Reinhold's employment status. That being the case, the EEOC concluded Reinhold had been subjected to tangible employment actions, and thus the school should have been held liable for Martin's conduct.[21] Subsequently, in a similar case, a court ruled that the assignment of extra and less desirable work tasks may be considered a tangible employment action akin to a demotion or a reassignment that entails significantly dif-ferent job responsibilities.[22]

In general, plaintiffs have been unsuccessful in convincing the courts to view a change in work schedule, as distinguished from a change in work tasks, as a tangible employment action. In one case, the plaintiff worked as a produce clerk in a super market. When she complained to management that her supervisor was harassing her, her work schedule was altered to such an extent she was forced to give up a second job she had held until that time. The court, without even considering the effect the change in work schedule held for the plaintiff, simply stated that a change in work schedule is not a change in work status.[23]

In summary, if a plaintiff proves that the harassing conduct of her supervisor caused her to suffer a tangible employment action, and the employer cannot offer a nondiscriminatory basis for that action, all questions pertaining to the employer's liability for its supervisor's sexual harassing conduct are resolved at that point. The employer is liable. If, on the other hand, the plaintiff fails to show she suffered a tangible employment action, further proceedings are required to determine whether the employer will be held liable. We now turn to those proceedings.

CHAPTER TEN

The Employer's Duty to Prevent and Promptly Correct Acts of Sexual Harassment

Before a woman proceeds to formally charge her employer with sexually harassing acts committed by one of its supervisors, she should closely examine the program her employer has put in place to prevent and correct harassing conduct in its workplace. This examination is essential, lest the prospective claimant advance a cause with little chance of success, since her claim will be subject to dismissal if the employer is able to establish the *Ellerth* affirmative defense, thus relieving it of liability for the harassing conduct of its supervisor. The employer may assert the defense if the sexually harassing behavior of its supervisor did not result in a tangible employment action altering the terms and conditions of the woman's employment. This defense requires proof that the employer exercised reasonable care in preventing and promptly correcting any harassment in its workplace and that the victim of the harassment failed to take advantage of preventive or corrective opportunities provided by the employer to avoid the harassment. Thus if an employer is able to prove that:

(1) it discharged its duty of exercising reasonable care in preventing acts of sexual harassment from occurring in its workplace,

(2) the complainant refrained from reporting the harassment as required by the employer's sexual harassment complaint procedures, and

(3) when it learned of the harassment, it exercised reasonable care in promptly acting to correct it and to prevent any further harassing conduct from occurring,

it may avoid all liability for the supervisor's harassment. Conversely, if the employer is unable to establish any one of these elements, it may be held liable for the sexually harassing behavior of its supervisor.

After the Supreme Court gave birth to this affirmative defense in its 1998 *Ellerth* ruling, federal courts across the country struggled, in hundreds of reported cases, to mark the limits, with some degree of specificity, an employer's duty to exercise reasonable care in preventing and correcting acts of sexual harassment. In general terms, most courts have ruled that an employer exercises reasonable care only if it provides persuasive evidence it adopted, distributed, and enforced an antiharassment policy—a policy calculated to encourage victims of sexual harassment to come forward with complaints of unwelcome workplace sexual conduct—and once notified that a female employee was harassed, it promptly undertook measures to correct such conduct and to prevent it from reoccurring. The application of these precepts has given rise to a number of subsidiary issues, each raising questions the prospective claimant must resolve before proceeding with a sexual harassment claim.

Has the Employer Instituted an Adequate Antiharassment Policy?

EEOC Guidelines suggest that, at a minimum, an adequate antiharassment policy will contain the following elements:

1. A clear description of prohibited conduct.
2. The prohibition of sexual harassment covers everyone in the workplace—supervisors, co-workers, and nonemployees.
3. Employees are encouraged to report harassment before it becomes severe or pervasive.
4. Assurance that employees who report acts of harassment, or provide information relating to such complaints, will be protected from any form of retaliation.
5. Clearly described reporting procedures, providing accessible and, where necessary, alternate avenues of complaint for the harassed worker.
6. Assurance that the employer, to the extent possible, will provide confidentiality for the complainant.
7. A complaint process providing for a prompt, thorough, and impartial investigation.
8. Assurance that the employer will take appropriate corrective action once it determines harassment has in fact occurred in its workplace.[1]

The courts have consistently found an employer's efforts to combat sexual harassment inadequate where it fails to include one or more of these elements in its antiharassment policy. For example, one employer defined sexual harassment as "any unwelcome offensive sexual advances, requests for sexual favors, and other verbal or physical conduct of a sexual nature." On first examination, this description may appear adequate, but when a company employee charged her supervisor with "gender harassment" (see chapter 7)—that is, harassment of a non-erotic nature—she justified her failure to report his acts of harassment on the ground she did not recognize her supervisor's behavior as barred by the company's antiharassment policy. The definition made it appear as if a sexual advance or some other explicitly sexual act was required to activate the policy's procedures. The court agreed with her. The policy in that respect was misleading, and the court refused to rule that the company's antiharassment policy was sufficient to prevent or correct all forms of sexual harassment.[2]

In Mechelle Vinson's harassment case alleged against the Meritor Savings Bank (see chapters 1 and 3), the Supreme Court noted that a general prohibition against sex-based discrimination would not necessarily be understood by the ordinary worker to encompass acts of sexual harassment.[3] When a harassment victim is uncertain the conduct she experiences falls within the employer's antiharassment prohibitions, she may be reluctant to complain, thus rendering the policy ineffective. An employer, therefore, should spell out in sufficient detail the types of conduct banned by its antiharassment policy. The failure to do so will open the gates for victims of sexual harassment to advance their claims.

An employer's failure to assure its employees that it will refrain from subjecting them to retaliatory measures once they report sexually harassing conduct may undermine the company's efforts to prove it established an adequate antiharassment policy. In one case, the employer's antiharassment policy did not contain any express antiretaliation language, although it did state all complaints "will be handled with confidentiality and promptly investigated by our Human Resources staff." The court held this provision was "woefully inadequate" in assuring an employee she would not encounter retaliation or punishment for reporting acts of sexual harassment.[4]

A court also may find an antiharassment policy inadequate if the reporting requirements are not clearly specified. Courts also routinely reject reporting procedures that fail to provide alternate avenues of complaint. If the policy requires the complainant to report acts of harassment to her supervisor, and the supervisor is the source of her harassment, the policy obviously fails to provide an effective means of complaint. An adequate reporting procedure allows the complainant in these circumstances to bypass her supervisor by filing her complaint with a higher-ranking management employee or with a member of the human resources department. The EEOC recommends that an antiharassment policy permit a complaining employee to circumvent her supervisor's chain of command entirely, thus providing her with additional assurance her complaint will not be processed by company personnel who might be more likely to believe the supervisor's version of events.[5]

To the extent possible, an employer's antiharassment policy should afford the complainant with confidentiality. However, if the commitment to confidentially interferes with or impedes a complete investigation of the harassment charges, the commitment must yield to the investigation. Regardless of the victim's desire for confidentiality, an employer, placed on notice of the occurrence of sexually harassing conduct in its workplace, risks being held liable for its supervisor's harassing behavior if it fails to undertake an adequate investigation of that conduct.[6] A complainant cannot reasonably expect to be afforded confidentiality if an investigation of her harassment charge may not be adequately conducted without disclosure of the details of her charge, especially in those circumstances where it may be necessary to disclose them to other workers who may have witnessed the acts of harassment and be in a position to provide corroborating testimony.

An antiharassment policy will be deemed adequate only to the extent it is duly implemented and enforced. As later cases disclose, the best-formulated policy will afford a female worker little or no protection from supervisory harassment unless the employer is committed to enforcement of that policy. Adoption of an antiharassment policy without a commitment to adequate enforcement is pointless. The prospective claimant need not be concerned with the affirmative defense if her employer fails to adequately enforce its sexual harassment policy.

Has the Employer Taken Adequate Measures to Disseminate Its Antiharassment Policy?

The low priority some employers assign to their efforts to combat sexual harassment is illustrated by the circumstances one of my clients encountered after her supervisor began to harass her. Contrary to her employer's repeated claims that each of its newly hired employees were furnished with a copy of its sexual harassment policy, my client was neither given a copy when she was hired, nor was she ever informed that the company had such a policy. When management personnel were later questioned about the details of their endeavors to disseminate copies of the company policy, they were unable to identify the person supposedly responsible for distributing copies to newly hired workers. Although my client discussed the particulars of her supervisor's harassment with the president of the company, the office manager, and the director of operations, none of them at any time made any reference to a sexual harassment policy. She also spoke to several co-workers about her supervisor's behavior, but none of them mentioned a sexual harassment policy and apparently none was aware such a policy existed. In fact, my client did not see a copy of this policy until after she commenced her sexual harrassment suit against the company and I, as her attorney, was furnished a copy by the law firm representing the company. Obviously, company implementation of its antiharassment policy was nonexistent. Its policy played an insignificant role in protecting employees from harassing behavior.[7]

At the same time the Supreme Court issued its *Ellerth* ruling, it ruled in another sexual harassment case that an employer may not rely on the affirmative defense to relieve itself of liability for the harassing conduct of its supervisors if it is unable to establish that its antiharassment policy was effectively communicated to its employees. In that case, Beth Ann Faragher, after resigning her lifeguard position with the City of Boca Raton, sued the city, alleging that her supervisors created a sexually hostile work environment, repeatedly subjecting her and other female lifeguards to "uninvited and offensive touching" and lewd and highly offensive remarks. Since the city had made no attempt to monitor the conduct of its supervisory staff and, moreover, had failed to disseminate its antiharassment policy among its beach employees, the court ruled the city could not have exercised reasonable care in preventing the supervisors' harassing conduct. The court held the city was barred from asserting the affirmative defense:

> Unlike the employer of a small workforce, who might expect that sufficient care to prevent [harassing conduct of its supervisors] could be exercised informally, those responsible for city operations could not reasonably have thought that precautions against hostile environments in any one of many departments in far-flung locations could be effective without communicating some formal policy against harassment, with a sensible complaint procedure.[8]

Some courts, however, have passed to the opposite extreme, ruling that the dissemination of an adequate antiharassment policy may be sufficient to demonstrate an employer's exercise of reasonable care in preventing sexually harassing behavior. One court went so far as to hold that "distribution of an anti-harassment policy provides 'compelling proof' that the company exercised reasonable care in preventing and promptly correcting sexual harassment."[9] These courts simply ignore circumstances where an employer issues an antiharassment policy to its employees but then fails to undertake measures to enforce it. And that brings us to another issue that frequently occurs in harassment cases, thus demanding the attention of the prospective claimant.

Has the Employer Taken Adequate Measures to Enforce Its Antiharassment Policy?

To satisfy its duty of exercising reasonable care, an employer must also undertake reasonable steps to assure adequate enforcement of its sexual harassment policy. In one case an employer disseminated an Employee Handbook, setting forth its antiharassment policy and the procedures employees were to follow when reporting acts of harassment. A worker, alleging she had been sexually harassed, admitted she knew of the company's policy, but also was aware that the company failed to implement or enforce the policy. She offered evidence that company officials apparently had never bothered to read the policy or have occasion to resort to it. One supervisor testified he had not been advised that the policy existed and had never received any training or instruction as to how to identify sexual harassment, and that he was unfamiliar with the procedures he was expected to follow in the event an employee reported sexually harassing conduct to him. Another supervisor testified he was never apprised of the steps he was expected to take if acts of harassment occurred in his work area. Since it was clear the employer had failed to expend any effort in training those of its employees placed in charge of enforcement of its antiharassment policy, and had made little if any other effort to implement the policy, the affirmative defense was unavailable to it. The employer was liable for its supervisor's acts of harassment.[10]

Other courts have viewed the extent of the training provided to employees designated to enforce a company's antiharassment policy as an indication of the importance—or lack of importance—of that policy to the employer's efforts to bar harassment from its workplace. The failure to provide such training loomed large in Patricia Baty's harassment case against her employer. Throughout the course of her employment with Willamette Industries, Baty complained to supervisors and other management personnel that she was the target of sexually harassing conduct of a number of co-workers and supervisors. When her case was tried before a jury, she submitted evidence of Willamette's indifferent attitude toward the presence of harassment in its workplace, thus demonstrating management's acquiescence in the existence of a hostile working environment. In affirming a jury verdict in Baty's favor, an appellate court noted that in light of the severity of the harassing conduct experienced by Baty, and given the minuscule amount of sexual harassment training provided Willamette workers, it was reasonable to conclude this training was wholly inadequate for the purpose of protecting Baty. Willamette was held liable for its supervisors' unlawful behavior.[11]

Has the Employer Undertaken Adequate Measures to Investigate the Alleged Acts of Harassment?

Although Baty had complained to management of multiple acts of harassment, company investigators concluded that no harassment had taken place in the company's plant. The court labeled the investigation a "sham." When an employer conducts a thorough investigation of allegations of harassment, it declares to its employees that it takes all harassment charges seriously and will not tolerate such conduct in its workplace. When it fails to conduct a thorough investigation, it signals just the opposite. Elizabeth Smith's case, involving sexual harassment charges against her supervisor (see chapter 7), illustrates how an employer may fall short in fulfilling its duty to investigate charges of sexual harassment.

Smith worked for the First Union National Bank as a team leader in its consumer credit collections department, reporting to her supervisor, Ronald Scoggins. Smith charged Scoggins with having subjected her to a barrage of threats, sexually obnoxious comments, and gender-based insults. Certain of Scoggins's remarks were directed at Smith individually, while others reflected Scoggins's hostile view of women in general. His behavior toward Smith was often threatening. On one occasion he remarked he could "see why a man would slit a woman's throat." Other female employees apprised management of Scoggins's antifemale bias, reported his derogatory comments about Smith, and described his conduct as threatening and demeaning.

After Smith complained of Scoggins's conduct, the bank assigned Marc Hutto, an employee in its human resources department, to conduct an investigation. Hutto, who had never previously been involved in the investigation of a sexual harassment claim, focused his attention on Scoggins's management style rather than on the allegations of harassment. He failed to question Scoggins about any of the harassing remarks, even though Scoggins freely admitted to other employees he had made them. Of greater consequence, Hutto failed to query Scoggins about the "slit a woman's throat" remark.

Scoggins's boss, George Andrews, worked with Hutto to investigate Smith's harassment charge. Although Andrews quickly learned of Scoggins's sexually harassing remarks, and that another female worker had resigned from the bank because of Scoggins's verbal harassment, he failed to characterize any of these occurrences as harassing. Further, he failed to follow up on his discovery that still another female employee had resigned on account of Scoggins's offensive behavior. Even though Andrews admitted that Scoggins should have been fired if he had made the "slit a woman's throat" remark, he never asked Scoggins whether he in fact had uttered it, nor did he ask his fellow investigator, Hutto, whether he had concluded Scoggins had been guilty of the remark.

Following the investigation, the bank decided to permit Scoggins to remain in his position as supervisor of the collections department. Instead of terminating him, the bank placed him on probation and counseled him to improve his management style and suggested he "smile more." The report recording the decision to place Scoggins on probation failed to mention any of his sexually harassing conduct. The court ruled that the bank's investigation clearly was inadequate.[12]

The nature and extent of an investigation of a sexual harassment charge are factors the courts regularly consider in determining whether an employer fulfilled its duty of exercising reasonable care in preventing and promptly correcting acts of sexual harassment. It is difficult to conceive how an employer, following an investigation as inadequate and as incompetent as that performed by the bank in the *Smith* case, could possibly prove it exercised reasonable care. Indeed, employer investigations exhibiting a higher degree of competency and thoroughness have failed to pass that test.

An employer's investigation of harassment charges may lend support to a worker's case in ways unanticipated. A case in point is Lynn Fall's harassment case against Indiana University (see chapter 2). Fall worked for the South Bend branch of Indiana University, and David Cohen served as its chancellor. Not long after Fall was hired, Cohen sent her an e-mail message requesting a meeting in his office to discuss university matters. On the day of their meeting, Cohen told her the e-mail message was merely a ruse to get her into his office. According to Fall, Cohen then put his arms around her, started kissing her, and forced his hands down her blouse and groped her breasts. Fall then broke from Cohen's grasp and fled his office.

During the course of Fall's subsequent harassment suit against the university, the court was required to decide whether the university had exercised reasonable care in preventing acts of sexual harassment on its campus and whether it had exercised reasonable care in correcting harassing conduct once it surfaced. There was little question university officials acted promptly once Fall reported the harassment. The university had an anti–sexual harassment policy in place, and Fall asserted a harassment claim in accordance with its provisions. Immediately after receipt of her complaint, university officials launched an expansive investigation, which eventually resulted in Cohen's resignation. Whether the university had acted as vigorously in protecting its employees from harassing conduct prior to Fall's complaint was another matter.

The court first noted that the primary objective of Title VII, rather than providing redress for harassed employees, is to avoid harm to them in the first instance. Unfortunately for the university, the same investigative report, illustrating the care taken in correcting the harassment Fall experienced, also disclosed the university's failure to act with reasonable care to prevent such harassment from occurring at all. It appeared from the testimony and other evidence that prior to the incident involving Fall, Cohen had exhibited inappropriate sexual behavior toward other female employees. When Fall reported the groping incident to a university official, he noted that this was not the first time Cohen had been accused of such conduct. Another staff member, on notification of Fall's complaint, reacted, "Oh no, not again." He later testified his reaction was based on a previous incident in which a female worker had entered Cohen's office only to have Cohen close the door and kiss her. The investigative report also disclosed the identity of a number of other female employees who had been either victims of Cohen's harassment or who were aware of incidents involving other women. It was apparent from the university's own investigation that Cohen's sexual harassment of women was so pervasive and well-known on the campus that the university, in the exercise of reasonable care, should have known and dealt with it so as to prevent further harm to female employees. A jury later found the university liable for Cohen's conduct and awarded Fall substantial compensatory and punitive damages.[13]

Some employers corrupt the investigatory process by focusing the investigation on the victim of the harassment rather than on the alleged acts of harassment. A particularly egregious example of this type of investigation occurred in a case of harassment committed by a complainant's co-worker rather than by her supervisor, but the nature of the ensuing investigation was not unlike investigations that too often occur in cases of supervisory harassment.

While working in the City of Sacramento's purchasing office, Barbara Sarro was sexually and physically harassed by co-worker Michael Cooper. When Sarro reported the incident to her supervisor, the city's Internal Affairs Department initiated an investigation, interviewing twenty-six witnesses. Of the twenty-six, only five were questioned about the harassing events in issue. Twelve persons were interrogated about a previous criminal case against a dentist who Sarro, and seven other female patients, had charged with sexual assault. Investigators also interviewed Sarro's ex-husband about problems in their marriage. They checked into allegations that Sarro had an affair with a convicted criminal, ran fingerprint checks on her, and reviewed her application for employment with the city. When investigators interviewed Sarro about her charges against Cooper, they asked her about her attire at the time of the incident, including whether she was wearing underwear. They questioned her about her romantic relationships, including an alleged relationship with a police department detective who had conducted the criminal investigation of the dentist. They questioned her about her former marriage and whether her husband had been physically abusive. They also asked her whether she had done any modeling work and whether she "ever danced on a table top or a platform fully clothed or partially clothed or unclothed" or "danced while she was intoxicated for people or for money." On the other hand, they did not question any witnesses about Cooper, the alleged harasser. His credibility and version of the facts were accepted without any investigation relating to the truthfulness of his statements.

The court characterized the city's investigation as an attempt to discredit, humiliate, and embarrass Sarro and concluded that it had conducted the investigation to deter employees from reporting harassment, rather than to deter future acts of harassment. The court stated:

> Harassment is to be remedied through actions targeted at the harasser, not at the victim. . . . The victim of sexual harassment should not be punished for the conduct of the harasser. . . . Here, the City's investigation of Sarro's

complaint focused on Sarro, not Cooper. While the City was allegedly attempting to investigate Sarro's claim, it did so at the expense of delving into Sarro's past, forcing her to relive painful memories, reveal details of her private life and dispute humiliating accusations which were wholly unrelated to her claim. This is not the price that victims must pay for reporting sexual harassment in the workplace.[14]

Has the Employer Taken Any Other Steps to Prevent and Correct Sexual Harassment?

An employer's response to a sexual harassment complaint must be commensurate with the severity and pervasiveness of the alleged harassment, and the effectiveness of that response will be evaluated in light of the measures undertaken by the employer in addressing those issues and its success in subsequently deterring employees from engaging in sexually harassing behavior.

After notification of an incident of harassment, an employer must act promptly. In one case, on the same day a human resources director learned a female employee had claimed a co-worker had harassed her, he met with and questioned the complainant and later her alleged harasser. Three days later, the harasser's supervisor confronted him with evidence of his harassing behavior and issued a written and verbal warning advising him that any future conduct of a similar nature would result in his termination. The court ruled that the employer's response was prompt, adequate, and reasonably calculated to end the harassment.[15]

In another case, after a female worker filed a harassment charge, her employer, as described by the court, "sprang into action." Several supervisors and the personnel manager immediately met with her and informed her the company neither condoned nor tolerated sexual harassment in its workplace, and it would conduct a prompt investigation of her charge. Within three days, the company completed its investigation and ordered disciplinary action taken against the harasser. Given the prompt and appropriate response of the employer, the court observed that the complainant could not "plausibly" challenge a finding that her employer had acted reasonably to prevent and correct sexual harassment among its employees.[16]

Another aspect of an employer's investigation may culminate in adverse consequences for the complainant. Upon notification of an incident of sexual harassment, the employer, pending its investigation, should assign the harasser and his victim to work in different areas. The degree of separation imposed must be a function of the severity and pervasiveness of the alleged harassment; the more egregious the harassing conduct and the more substantial the evidence supporting it, the greater the effort the employer should exert to minimize further contact between harasser and victim. If, on completion of the investigation, the harassment charges are upheld, the employer may then be faced with requiring a permanent separation of the two employees. An employer, however, may not satisfy its remedial obligation by transferring the victim of the harassment to a less desirable location or position, as such a transfer would adversely affect the terms and conditions of her employment, and may itself constitute the basis for employer liability.[17] Unfortunately, employers too often appear more willing to consider the transfer of the harassed worker rather than the harassing supervisor, and this frequently redounds to the victim's disadvantage.

An employer places itself at risk if it fails to follow its own procedures when responding to a harassment complaint. A typical case involved Wal-Mart management employees who failed to follow company rules following a complaint by a female department manager that she had been sexually harassed by her store manager. Although the store manager was disciplined and demoted for his conduct, the company's personnel records indicated the demotion was based on "leadership inconsistencies." Wal-Mart's personnel policies required company officials to inform a sexual harassment offender regarding those aspects of his conduct found to be inappropriate, but management failed to apprise the store manager of any specific examples of improper behavior. As later noted by the court, management "appeared to go to great lengths to avoid even using the term 'sexual harassment.'"[18] In this respect, Wal-Mart's remedial efforts proved to be inadequate.

Whether an employer's response to a sexual harassment claim is sufficient depends on the nature and effectiveness of its remedial measures, viewed in light of the severity and persistence of the harassment. Even if an employer undertakes some measures designed to prevent and correct sexual harassment in its workplace, it may still be held liable for its supervisor's harassing behavior if the remedial actions were not reasonably calculated to halt the harassment and deter future harassing conduct.[19] A case involving the City of Wichita police department portrays an example of an employer response that passed that standard.

After a Wichita female police officer accused a lieutenant of sexually harassing her, she sued the city, claiming it was liable for the lieutenant's conduct. On reviewing the evidence, the court found, contrary to the plaintiff's position, that the city had met its duty of exercising reasonable care in preventing and correcting sexually harassing behavior. Before the occurrence of the events in the case, the city had initiated and promulgated a policy against sexual harassment, and its employees, including the plaintiff, were given training regarding the particulars of that policy. The policy's complaint reporting procedures permitted sexual harassment charges to be processed while circumventing the harassing supervisor. There was no evidence the city was deficient in enforcing the policy or that it failed to act when a harassment claim was asserted. Once the plaintiff filed her complaint, the Police Chief assured her that unwelcome sexual behavior would not be tolerated, and he immediately commenced an investigation of the lieutenant's conduct, who was suspended pending its completion. Eventually, the lieutenant was demoted three ranks, his pay was cut proportionately, and he was reassigned to a different part of the city and to a different shift, thus reducing the likelihood he and the plaintiff would meet while on duty.

The plaintiff, however, maintained that the lieutenant should have been fired, and the city's unwillingness to terminate his employment showed it had failed to adequately address harassment in its workplace. But an employer need not necessarily fire a harasser in order to show it exercised reasonable care. The very fact that harassment of the plaintiff ceased after the city took action showed that its response had been adequate.[20]

Although continued incidents of workplace sexual harassment may lend support to a claimant's position that her employer failed to act reasonably, the law does not require the employer to eliminate sexual harassment from its workplace—it only requires an employer to act reasonably to prevent and promptly correct sexual harassment. Thus, even if acts of harassment persist, highlighting the employer's failure to eliminate sexual harassment from its workplace, the employer may nevertheless be able to establish it fulfilled its duty to act reasonably.[21] If this were not the case, courts would be required to deny the availability of the affirmative defense in any case where incidents of sexual harassment continued, no matter how reasonable the employer's efforts to prevent and correct such behavior. In these circumstances, it would be next to impossible for an employer to qualify for the affirmative defense.

An employer will most likely succeed in demonstrating it fulfilled its duty of care if its actions in response to a sexual harassment claim are wholly reasonable. If it fails to follow its own procedures, or grants a higher priority to protecting rather than investigating the harasser, or treats the victim of the harassment as if she were the guilty party, it is far more likely a court or jury will hold it liable for the sexually harassing conduct of its supervisors.

CHAPTER ELEVEN

An Employee's Duty to Take Advantage of Her Employer's Preventive and Corrective Measures

Suppose an employer has adopted an antiharassment policy and has distributed copies to all of its employees. One of its female workers is sexually harassed by her supervisor, but decides not to report the harassment, thus failing to comply with the policy's complaint reporting procedures. Although she was not subjected to a tangible employment action, the worker later sues the company for sexual harassment. May the company rely on the affirmative defense in denying liability for the supervisor's sexual harassing conduct?

The second element of the affirmative defense requires the employer to prove the plaintiff employee "unreasonably failed to take advantage of preventive or corrective opportunities provided by the employer or to avoid harm otherwise."[1] This element of the affirmative defense is based on the general legal theory that a victim of tortious conduct has a duty to minimize or, as commonly referred to in tort litigation, mitigate her damages. A victim of sexually harassing conduct acts to mitigate her damages by reporting the harassing conduct to her employer and by resorting to any other means provided by her employer to avoid harm from a harassing supervisor.

When an aggrieved worker notifies her employer that her supervisor is sexually harassing her, the employer may act to stop the harassment, thus minimizing the harm suffered by the complainant.[2] But if an employee fails to report the supervisor's conduct, thus failing to mitigate her damages, the employer may rely on the affirmative defense—assuming it has proved the other elements of the defense—to relieve itself of liability for the misconduct of its supervisor. It must, however, carry the burden of proving plaintiff's failure to complain was unreasonable.[3] Identifying the circumstances under which a worker's failure to report supervisory harassing conduct is considered "unreasonable" is an issue much litigated.

Shortly after Kelly Scrivner began her teaching career at the Socorro Independent School District in Texas, her principal uttered lewd and offensive remarks in her presence. Some time later, the superintendent of the school district received an anonymous letter—not authored by Scrivner—complaining of the principal's sexual harassment of teachers, as well as his use of vulgar language in the presence of staff and students' parents. The school district immediately undertook an investigation, interviewing sixty-four teachers and staff members, three of whom confirmed the anonymous letter writer's charges that the principal had engaged in sexually harassing conduct. When Scrivner was interviewed, however, she denied the principal had sexually harassed her. Based on its investigation, the school district found insufficient evidence of sexual harassment to discipline the principal, but in a written warning, directed him to refrain from making unprofessional jokes and comments on school premises.

Six months later, the principal intensified his harassment of Scrivner. At that point, she filed a formal harassment complaint with the school district, and a second investigation ensued. Eventually, the school district concluded that the principal's conduct created the perception that a hostile environment existed at the school, and it ordered his removal from the principal's position. Scrivner then filed a legal action against the school district.

Success or failure of Scrivner's sexual harassment claim depended on whether the school district could rely on the affirmative defense to insulate it from liability for the principal's conduct. Since Scrivner had not sustained a tangible employment action as a result of the principal's harassment, the school district could escape liability for his conduct if it proved that (1) it had exercised reasonable care in preventing sexual harassment and in acting quickly and forcefully to correct such behavior when it appeared in its workplace, and (2) Scrivner unreasonably failed to take advantage of preventive or corrective opportunities provided by the school district, including its procedures for reporting acts of sexual harassment.

Relying on two exhaustive investigations of the principal's conduct, the school district easily established that it had exercised reasonable care in preventing and correcting sexual harassment in its workplace. But was the evidence sufficient to establish that Scrivner had unreasonably declined to avail herself of the school district's preventive and corrective policies? When presented with an opportunity to disclose the harassment during the first investigation, Scrivner chose to lie, refusing to confirm she had experienced harassing conduct committed by the principal. By failing, when first given the opportunity, to inform the school district of the principal's behavior, Scrivner delayed providing notice of the principal's behavior until long after she was first subjected to his harassing conduct. The court, concluding Scrivner had acted unreasonably in not reporting the harassment when she first experienced it, dismissed her case.[4]

A female worker should not be expected to complain immediately after suffering an initial incident of harassment. Generally, she may ignore the first few incidents, provided they are minor, with the hope they will cease before it becomes necessary to file a formal complaint. Then again, she may elect to resolve the issue herself by advising her harasser that his conduct is unwelcome and the harassment must cease. In either case, if the harassment persists, she must report it in accordance with her employer's sexual harassment complaint reporting procedures. Women, however, for a variety of reasons, often either delay giving notice of harassing behavior or, on occasion, decline to notify the employer.

A number of studies have been undertaken to determine why women are reluctant to report their harasser's conduct. In one survey, conducted some years ago, women who had refrained from reporting sexual harassing conduct, were asked why they had declined to notify their employers. The major reasons for their inaction included:

- If a formal complaint had been made, they felt they, rather than their harassers, would be blamed for the harassment.
- Even if they had notified their employers of the harassment, nothing would have been done to eliminate it.
- They were too embarrassed to report it.
- If the harassment were reported, someone would be harmed, either the victim or the harasser. Although angered or disgusted by a harasser's behavior, many women did not want to hurt their harassers.[5]

More recently, attorneys William Petrocelli and Barbara Kate Repa examined the reasons why women still find it difficult to report incidents of sexual harassment and concluded "there is no simple answer":

A number of feelings often combine to keep women's lips sealed: guilt, shame, embarrassment, fear of being labeled a troublemaker. . . . Upbringing or experience may make the subject of harassment seem too painful . . . for some women to come forward. Young or inexperienced workers may even assume harassment is all in a day's work. And of course, many women keep silent because they distrust the procedures for handling their harassment complaints.[6]

Women also refrain from filing harassment claims for fear of undermining their positions in the company. They do not want to be perceived as "complainers," "snitches," "troublemakers," or as unable to handle "personnel" problems encountered on the job. No matter how compelling these reasons may appear to a female worker, the failure to report an incident of sexual harassment may lead to the dismissal of a legal action subsequently filed.

We turn now to specific cases in which the complainant failed to follow the procedures established by her employer for reporting supervisory sexual harassment. In each case, the court was required to determine whether the woman acted reasonably in failing to report her supervisor's unlawful conduct.

Sonia Riffle worked for The Sports Authority in Rockville, Maryland. The sales manager of the Rockville store, Andrew Ferguson, possessed the authority to hire, promote, demote, assign tasks to, and terminate employees, and although Riffle did not report directly to Ferguson, he exercised authority over the terms and conditions of her employment. In her sexual harassment case against The Sports Authority, Riffle alleged Ferguson made repeated unwelcome sexual advances, and when she rejected these advances, he retaliated against her by disciplining her for petty faults. Subsequently, the advances intensified, with Ferguson threatening to fire Riffle if she did not succumb to his demands. Riffle alleged that ultimately Ferguson raped her on three occasions.

The Sports Authority had previously promulgated an antiharassment policy describing the company's dedication to a work environment free of harassment. The policy provided that in the event a worker was sexually harassed, she was to notify either her immediate supervisor, a member of management, or the employee relations manager. Riffle did not follow these procedures because, as she explained it, Ferguson threatened to fire her if she told anyone. Besides, she did not believe management would assist her in dealing with Ferguson's conduct. The court rejected these reasons as justification for her failure to abide by her employer's complaint procedures. A reasonable person, the court held, would have used the complaint procedures to prevent Ferguson's harassment from becoming severe or pervasive, thus avoiding the abusive work environment she ultimately experienced. The court dismissed her complaint.[7]

Regardless of her fear of Ferguson or concern for her job, Riffle should have reported the acts of harassment. What possibly could have deterred her after the first rape? Generalized fears of retaliation, or of failure on the part of the employer to implement its antiharassment policy, generally do not constitute reasonable grounds for an employee's failure to assert a complaint of harassment in accordance with her employer's antiharassment policy.[8]

Disclosure of the harasser's conduct redounds to the benefit of the victim by allowing the company to prevent additional acts of harassment. It also may benefit other female workers who in the future may be subjected to the harassing behavior of the same individual. It benefits the company by alerting it to the disruptive misconduct of a member of its supervisory staff. The reporting requirement, therefore, serves the primary objective of Title VII, which places greater emphasis on avoiding harm to employees rather than on providing them with a means of redress. When a worker advances a speculative fear of employer retaliation as an excuse for remaining silent and for not reporting the harassment, she undermines the primary objectives of Title VII. Her inaction may result in more, not less, sexual harassment.[9] As one court expressed it, the law against sexual harassment is not self-enforcing. An employer cannot be expected to correct harassment unless the harassed employee makes an effort to inform it a problem exists.[10]

Eminently reasonable as this rule may appear, its application on occasion may produce an inequitable result. Jamie Lynn Alberter alleged that while employed at a McDonald's franchise in Nevada she was sexually harassed by her supervisor. Alberter was fifteen years old at the time and did not have any previous employment experience. Alberter quit her job and later told her friend about the harassing incidents. Her friend in turn told Alberter's father, who then confronted the McDonald's franchise manager.

The franchise owner had an antiharassment policy in place, and copies were regularly distributed to all employees. The policy allowed employees to bring complaints of harassment to any of its managers:

Employees who feel subjected to discrimination or harassment should immediately report it to management, including their personnel representative, their immediate supervisor, their supervisor's supervisor, or the Owner/Operator. We encourage employees to freely report these incidents and [we] prohibit retaliation for making or being a witness to such a report. We will thoroughly investigate discrimination and harassment reports and will do so confidentially. If the report is determined to be true, disciplinary action will be taken against the offender, ranging from a warning to termination, depending on the severity of the misconduct.

Alberter did not disclose her supervisor's conduct to anyone until several weeks after she had resigned. She testified she was too embarrassed to report it to someone in a management position and also was apprehensive about her supervisor's reaction if she disclosed his harassment. Although the court was mindful of Alberter's youth and recognized that her relative unfamiliarity with the adult workplace, as well as the fact that her harasser was an older man, may have contributed to her reluctance to talk about the harassment, the court held that these factors did not excuse Alberter for her failure to bring the matter to the attention of one of the managers:

> If all employees who were too embarrassed to bring complaints of sexual harassment to the attention of their employers were excused from their responsibilities, the primary goals of [Title VII] would be severely undercut. Discussing inappropriate sexual behavior with managers or employers will cause some degree of discomfort in almost all cases. Many victims of sexual harassment fear reprisals or negative reaction. Yet the [Supreme Court] has stated that it is, at least in part, the duty of the victim of sexual harassment to take action. The objecting employee must make use of those preventive or remedial measures available, as far as is reasonable.

The court ruled that since Alberter had failed to take advantage of the measures made available to her, and she had not advanced a compelling reason for her failure to do so, her case should be dismissed.[11] For the court, Alberter's young age did not justify an exception to the application of the rule. Youth and inexperience were not "compelling" reasons justifying her failure to report the harassment.

In another case, a female worker argued she should be excused for having failed to report her supervisor's acts of harassment because she had needed time to collect evidence against him so company officials would believe her rather than her supervisor. The court, however, reminded her that the Supreme Court in the *Faragher* and *Ellerth* cases commanded a victim of sexual harassment to report the misconduct, not investigate, gather evidence, and then report. As this complainant recognized, sexual harassment cases often pit the word of the harasser against the word of the victim, and thus her desire to gather evidence in support of her position was understandable. Nonetheless, the court faulted her for not reporting the harassment in accordance with the employer's anti-harassment policy and it dismissed her complaint.[12]

Under certain circumstances, some courts have been a bit more willing to grant complainants a degree of flexibility. For example, some courts have ruled that notice of the harassment does not necessarily need to come from the victim of the harassment, since no significance lies in the fact that a co-worker rather than the victim herself reports harassing conduct. The source of the report of harassment is not relevant.[13] Along the same line, one court ruled that the filing of a union grievance may serve the same purpose of providing notice to the employer as the filing of a formal complaint in accordance with its antiharassment policy.[14] A majority of the courts, however, have held complainants to the duty of strictly abiding by the provisions of their employer's antiharassment policy.

The courts seem to be more tractable in cases where an aggrieved worker, rather than failing to give any notice, eventually gives delayed notice of the harassment. A lengthy delay, however, is equivalent to no notice at all. As an example, a court held that an employer established the second element of the affirmative defense when it showed the complainant waited two years after the harassment began before complaining to her employer.[15] In another case, a supervisor harassed a female worker for a period of approximately seven months. On at least ten instances, she told him to stop harassing her, but still she waited seven months before availing herself of her employer's complaint procedures. The court ruled that her neglect in following these procedures for that length of time, when the harassment was escalating and her own efforts to halt the harassment were proving inadequate, constituted an unreasonable failure on her part to take advantage of her employer's corrective procedures.[16]

Disgusted with her boss's highly offensive remarks, Louise Hill, an African American, sued her employer, American General Finance, for sexual and racial harassment. Hill had begun her employment with AGF in its Alton, Illinois, office in September 1994, working as a lending/collection administrator in an office with eight other employees, including her supervisor, Darin Brandt. Within a month of Hill's arrival in the office, Brandt subjected her to offensive sexual and racial comments. In February 1995, four months after Brandt's objectionable behavior began, Hill wrote a letter to AGF's chief executive officer complaining of Brandt's behavior, but she used a fictitious name, not identifying herself as an employee of the Alton office. A few days later, she wrote a second letter, signing it as "a very worried and frightened employee." AGF's human resources department then undertook an investigation of the Alton office. Hill was interviewed, and although the investigators suspected she had written the letters, she failed to acknowledge that she had. None of the other employees confirmed any of the harassing events allegedly committed by Brandt, but they informed the investigators that conversations of a sexual nature were common in the office. Brandt was then issued a warning notice, primarily because he had allowed sex-oriented conversations to pervade the office. In April 1995, Hill again wrote a letter setting out specific instances of harassment, and this time she signed her own name. A follow-up investigation culminated in Brandt's demotion and transfer to another office.

A court later ruled that the two February letters were not reasonable efforts at notification, as Hill neither signed them nor acknowledged having written them when questioned by human resources personnel during their investigation. In fact, Hill began her April letter by apologizing: "Please accept my apology for not being completely honest during the interview with you." Hill took reasonable steps in April to avail herself of AGF's preventive and corrective harassment provisions, but the same cannot be said for her actions in February.

The court dismissed Hill's case.[17] If she had identified herself as an AGF employee and had signed the two February letters, she probably would have been happier with the outcome of her case. But perhaps not, for in another case, a court ruled that even a four-month delay was unreasonable.[18] If that rationale were applied to Hill's case, her two earlier letters would not have been delivered soon enough to provide AGF with adequate notice of Brandt's harassment.

What about a delay of six weeks? Luria Greene, a twenty-two-year-old graduate student, worked for the Navy as a temporary engineering technician. According to Greene, from the first day of her employment and on virtually every day thereafter, her immediate supervisor subjected her to "unwelcome discussions concerning sexual matters." He also made amorous advances that culminated on the tenth day of her employment with his raping her. Six weeks after the date of her hiring and the initial act of harassment, Greene reported the harassment and rape.

Seeking to avoid all liability for the supervisor's rape and harassment, the Navy asked the court to dismiss Greene's case. It argued it could establish each element of the affirmative defense, including the fact that Greene had failed to take advantage of its antiharassment preventive and corrective measures by failing to promptly report her supervisor's conduct. The court ruled that to avoid liability the Navy had to prove Greene "inexcusably delayed" the report of the rape and the other harassing behavior of her supervisor. Based on the evidence before the court, it could not rule, as a matter of law, that a person in Greene's position would have reported her supervisor's conduct earlier than she did. The court concluded, therefore, that the question of the timeliness of Greene's report was an issue that should be decided by a jury, and thus it rejected the Navy's position that the suit be summarily dismissed at that point in the litigation.[19]

Greene's suit was later resolved, and thus the issue never reached a jury for determination. If the case had proceeded to trial, a jury would have been required to decide whether Greene acted with sufficient promptness to hold the Navy liable for the sexually harassing conduct she endured. The Navy, obviously, would have argued it was unreasonable for a woman not to report her rape immediately after its occurrence. Greene, on the other hand, undoubtedly would have maintained, traumatized by the occurrence of the rape, she was unable to discuss the matter with anyone, much less become involved in an investigation of the incident. Issues involving the reasonableness of a woman's decision to delay notice of her supervisor's harassing behavior can be complex.

A court ruled that a delay in reporting a supervisor's harassing conduct was justified in the circumstances confronting Becky Corcoran, employed at a Shoney's restaurant in Virginia. Shortly after Shoney hired Corcoran, the restaurant's assistant manager made numerous sexual remarks in her presence and in the presence of other female employees. Although Corcoran did not report his behavior, the assistant manager subsequently ceased making these remarks and refrained from any improper conduct. Eight months later, however, he exposed himself to Corcoran, and she immediately reported this incident to management.

The issues before the court in Corcoran's subsequent sexual harassment case against Shoney's centered on her failure to notify management of the initial incidents of harassment. Was Corcoran's failure to report the first acts of harassment unreasonable on her part? Since it is far from uncommon for women to tend to ignore sexual remarks when they first experience them, the court stated it could not rule, as a matter of law, that it was unreasonable for Corcoran to remain silent after the initial incidents. This was especially the case given the fact the objectionable conduct ceased shortly after it started. When the assistant manager's sexually harassing behavior became virtually impossible to ignore, however, Corcoran took immediate action. The affirmative defense, therefore, was not available to Shoney's and it was held liable for the harassing conduct of its assistant manager.[20]

The *Corcoran* case ruling is consistent with the generally accepted rule that female workers are not expected to complain immediately following an initial incident of harassment. As previously noted, a woman may ignore the first few harassing incidents—provided they are minor—before she is required to file a formal complaint with her employer. If the harassment persists, however, she must report it in accordance with the employer's sexual harassment complaint reporting procedure. The failure to act at that time may lead to the downfall of any subsequently filed sexual harassment claim.

A claimant's responsibility to avail herself of the preventive or corrective opportunities provided by her employer to avoid harm from acts of sexual harassment does not end with notification to the employer of the occurrence of the harassing conduct. If an investigation ensues, she must cooperate with those named to investigate to make certain they gain a complete and truthful portrayal of the harassing conduct. If she refuses to provide that assistance, the court may rule she failed to take advantage of the company's preventive and corrective measures, thus making the affirmative defense available to the employer.[21]

As we saw earlier, Kelly Scrivner unreasonably declined to avail herself of her school district's established procedures for reporting acts of harassment. When presented with an opportunity to disclose her principal's harassment, she chose not to tell the truth, informing investigators she had not experienced any harassing conduct. The court held that she acted unreasonably by not cooperating with the investigation and it dismissed her case.[22] Another court held that a complainant's refusal to meet with company investigators was "patently unreasonable," even though she was acting in accordance with her attorney's instructions. A claimant who refuses to cooperate with her employer's investigation, thereby undermining its endeavors to prevent and correct sexually harassing behavior, may not later claim she acted reasonably.[23]

A woman must act reasonably in another respect. Wendy Jo Brown worked for the Army and Air Force Exchange Service (AAFES) of the Department of Defense. After she was on the job for about a year, her supervisors instructed her to attend a conference to be held at a hotel in Alexandria, Virginia. While at the conference, Brown was present at a social gathering hosted by William Boyd, an AAFES executive. Although Boyd was not directly involved with employment decisions relating to Brown, she was aware he could influence her career and future advancement. Later in the evening, when the other guests had left Boyd's hotel suite, Boyd made sexual advances that Brown rejected. The following day, Brown reported the incident to her supervisor, but ultimately decided not to pursue the matter further.

Six months later, AAFES held another conference at the same hotel in Alexandria, and again Boyd hosted a social gathering in his suite. Brown was reluctant to attend, but her supervisors stressed Boyd's importance to her career. When she arrived at his suite, Boyd apologized for his past conduct. As on the occasion of the first conference, Brown was the last guest at the gathering, and once again, Boyd made sexual advances. Brown again reported the incident and eventually sued AAFES.

Striving to establish the second element of the affirmative defense, AAFES claimed Brown had "unreasonably failed to take advantage of any preventive or corrective opportunities" it had provided and she had "unreasonably failed to avoid harm otherwise."[24] The court focused on Brown's obligation "to avoid harm otherwise":

> The record in the case is replete with uncontroverted evidence that Brown utterly failed to "avoid harm otherwise." Less than six months after rebuffing advances from Boyd in his hotel room late at night, Brown unnecessarily put herself in a situation that permitted repetition of precisely the same kind of advances. By her own account, Brown voluntarily decided to remain alone in Boyd's hotel room with him at night during the September conference even though the March incident was fresh in her mind. Brown not only remained alone with Boyd in his room for a second time, she also accepted Boyd's invitation to visit first a pub and then a reggae bar following the party. Finally, after the bar-hopping, Brown agreed to return to Boyd's hotel room at midnight. In light of her previous history with Boyd, no reasonable [person] could reach any conclusion other than that Brown "unreasonably failed . . . to avoid harm."

Inasmuch as AAFES had also established the first element of the affirmative defense, the court ruled it was not liable for Boyd's harassment of Brown.[25]

By focusing on an aggrieved party's duty to avoid her harasser, the court made it easier for an employer to prove a woman acted unreasonably. It is questionable that the Supreme Court intended to saddle sexual harassment complainants with a burden such as this, a burden likely in many cases to result in the employer's insulation from liability for supervisory harassment. As one commentator expressed it, the court that decided the *Brown* case does not share the sentiment that the failure to avoid harm standard is not to be used to punish the plaintiff.[26] The court punished her because she failed to anticipate Boyd would again harass her. In other words, the victim must anticipate possible additional acts of harassment and then act to avoid them. The court placed a burden on a harassment victim the Supreme Court never intended.

CHAPTER TWELVE

Other Forms of Employer Liability

Liability for the sexual harassing acts of an employee who holds a position sufficiently high in the company's hierarchy to be considered its alter ego is automatically imputed to the company. In this instance, since the actions of the harasser and the company are one and the same, the employer cannot assert the *Ellerth* affirmative defense, even if the harassment did not result in a tangible employment action for the sexually harassed victim. The type of person whose harassment will automatically be imputed to the employer includes the owner or partner of the company, its president, and its officers.[1]

An employer also may be held directly liable if the incidents of sexual harassment are attributable to its own negligence. An employer is negligent if it knew or should have known of the harassment and failed to undertake adequate measures to address it. Under this standard, an employer may be held liable for the harassing conduct of its nonsupervisory as well as its supervisory employees and, under certain conditions, for the harassing conduct of nonemployees. An employer may also be held liable to a harassed worker under various aspects of tort law, such as assault and battery and the intentional infliction of emotional distress. In this chapter, we examine each of these categories of employer liability.

Alter Ego Harassment

We previously reviewed Lisa Burns's sexual harassment case against McGregor Electronic Industries (see chapter 3). The owner of the company repeatedly subjected Burns to sexual propositions, described by the court as a "grisly and shocking [example] of unwelcome sexual harassment." McGregor Electronics was clearly liable for its owner's behavior. In harassing Burns, the owner acted as McGregor's proxy or alter ego, and thus the company's liability was not an issue in the case. Clearly, it was liable to Burns.[2]

Questions pertaining to alter ego liability generally arise in cases where it may not be clear that the harasser falls within that class of company officials considered as proxies for their employers. Jeanne Harrison's sexual harassment case against Eddy Potash is one of those cases.

Harrison worked for Potash as a miner, the only woman on a crew of approximately thirty workers. Robert Brown, an underground shift foreman and Harrison's supervisor, was responsible for delegating duties and assigning work to crew members. Brown physically and verbally harassed Harrison, and despite her protestations, the harassment continued over a period of months until she finally reported his behavior to management and later sued for sexual harassment.

Harrison alleged the company should be held liable for Brown's conduct because he exercised significant control over her conditions of employment and thus should be considered the company's alter ego. The court rejected Harrison's position, ruling that a supervisory employee, merely because he possesses a high degree of control over a subordinate, cannot be considered an alter ego of his employer.[3]

In light of the Supreme Court ruling in the *Ellerth* case, a harassed woman who has not suffered a tangible employment action might very well attempt to circumvent the *Ellerth* affirmative defense by pleading alter ego liability. On the other hand, a plaintiff who has sustained a tangible employment action will find it unnecessary to rely on the alter ego doctrine, since her employer is liable in those circumstances without regard to the affirmative defense.

Negligence as a Basis of Employer Liability for a Supervisor's Acts of Harassment

In the *Ellerth* case, the Supreme Court identified those circumstances in which an employer may be held vicariously liable for a hostile work environment that evolved from the sexually harassing conduct of its supervisors. In ruling on this issue, the court created an affirmative defense "in order to accommodate the agency principles of vicarious liability for harm caused by misuse of supervisory authority."[4] This affirmative defense is limited to those cases where the plaintiff seeks to hold the employer vicariously liable for supervisory misconduct. It is not applicable in cases where the plaintiff alleges her employer is directly liable for its supervisor's conduct.

An employer is directly liable for supervisory misconduct if a hostile work environment is a product of its own negligence. Although the affirmative defense may not be asserted in a negligence case, the employer has another advantage. Contrary to a vicarious liability claim, where the employer has the burden of establishing the affirmative defense, the plaintiff has the burden of proving her employer's negligence.[5] This is a burden of proof often difficult to sustain.

An employer may be held liable in negligence for acts of sexual harassment if it knew or should have known of the harassment in question and failed to take prompt remedial action. If an employer is aware of the harassing conduct of one of its supervisory or nonsupervisory employees and it neglects or otherwise fails to undertake reasonable action to put an end to it, then through its own inaction—or negligence—it is, in effect, a cause of the continuation of the harassment. Thus an aggrieved party may seek to hold her employer liable for sexually harassing conduct by claiming that it acted negligently—that it knew or should have known of the harassment and did nothing about it—and in those circumstances the affirmative defense fashioned by the Supreme Court plays no role in the proceedings.

To prevail under the negligence theory, a plaintiff must demonstrate her employer had either actual or constructive notice of her harassment but failed adequately to respond to that notice. In nearly all negligence cases, the primary issues relate to (1) who, if anyone, in the defendant's employ knew of the harassment, and (2) may that person's knowledge be imputed to the employer itself. A case in point is Patrice Sharp's sexual harassment suit against the City of Houston.

Sharp was one of fourteen police officers assigned to the mounted patrol, an elite unit of Houston's police department. Lieutenant Wayne Hankins, in charge of the mounted patrol, supervised two sergeants, one of whom was Edgar Bice, Sharp's immediate supervisor. The mounted patrol was stationed several miles from police headquarters situated in central Houston, and due to the unit's physical isolation, and also because its duties did not significantly overlap those of other units, Hankins exerted near absolute control over the mounted patrol operations.

Over an extended period, Hankins and Bice sexually harassed Sharp.

They made demeaning comments about her body, made her the object of lewd jokes and gestures, and generally mistreated and embarrassed her in the presence of other police officers. Apparently, sexually harassing conduct was not new to Hankins, since other female police officers had previously complained he had subjected them to vulgar and harassing remarks.

Although Sharp made it known to Hankins and Bice that she objected to their behavior, she did not formally complain to the police department's internal affairs division. She later explained she was deterred from formally complaining because she knew that any police officer who complained of the conduct of another officer inevitably suffered by it, both professionally and socially.

Hankins's and Bice's misconduct only came to light when, during the course of an internal investigation of another matter relating to the mounted patrol, Sharp disclosed to a police department investigator that she had been subjected to the harassing conduct of her supervisors. Subsequently, the police department upgraded the investigation to a full internal affairs review, and ultimately Hankins and Bice were transferred to another unit and suspended for ninety days without pay. During and after the investigation, Sharp was subjected to retaliatory conduct by fellow police officers because she had broken the "code of silence," a custom within the Houston police department designed to punish officers who complain of the misconduct of others in the department.

When Sharp sued the City of Houston for sexual harassment, she sought to hold it liable for Hankins's and Bice's acts of harassment. She alleged the city knew or should have known of the harassment and failed to act. The jury ruled in Sharp's favor, awarding her compensatory and punitive damages. The city appealed. On the appeal, the appellate court was required to determine whether the evidence introduced at the trial supported a finding that the city knew or, through the exercise of reasonable care, should have known of the harassment, but failed to take appropriate remedial action.

Until Sharp spoke to the department's internal investigators, the only persons who had knowledge of the harassment were Hankins, Bice, and the police officers assigned to the mounted patrol who had witnessed it. As a legal matter, could the knowledge of any of them be imputed to the city?

An employer has actual knowledge of harassment when it becomes known to someone in higher management or to an employee who has the power to take action to terminate the harassment. There is no actual knowledge until a person with authority to address the problem is notified. Under this standard, the city did not receive actual knowledge, since no one in higher management or anyone with remedial power knew of the harassment. But the case did not end there. The city could still be held liable if it had "constructive" knowledge of the harassment, that is, if through the exercise of reasonable care, the city *should* have known what was taking place among the members of the mounted patrol. On a court ruling that the city should have learned of Hankins's and Bice's conduct, knowledge of the harassment could then be imputed to the city, thus establishing its liability for Hankins's and Bice's unlawful behavior.

If harassing conduct is so open and pervasive that an employer should have known of its existence if it had only acted with reasonable care by opening its eyes to view it, and it was unreasonable for the employer in those circumstances not to have opened its eyes, then the employer has received constructive notice of the harassment. Hankins and Bice openly and pervasively harassed Sharp. Their harassing conduct was conspicuously displayed to those serving on the mounted patrol. But that was not enough to impute knowledge to the city. Rather, the court had to determine whether Hankins's supervisor, or someone else in the police department possessing remedial power, had constructive knowledge of the harassment.

It was noted earlier that the mounted patrol was stationed several miles from downtown Houston where police headquarters were located, and because of the unit's physical isolation, Hankins exerted near complete control over its operations. The appellate court commented it would be absurd to allow an employer to insulate itself from liability simply by isolating its work units. The city placed Sharp in an insular unit and gave unchecked operational control of that unit to one individual. The city, therefore, had a duty to exert reasonable care to ensure that its employees did not use the situation to engage in acts of sexual harassment.

The evidence showed that those persons who supervised Hankins exerted almost no supervisory authority over him or the mounted patrol, and such failure to supervise violated even internal police department procedures. Thus the appellate court held that the jury was justified in concluding that the city had breached its duty of exercising reasonable care and thus had acted negligently:

The jury also could have decided that Hankins was well known to be a "loose cannon" . . . and that he had made vulgar and harassing remarks to female officers in the past, but that [the police department], despite having been put on notice that Hankins might be a problem, had made no effort to supervise or constrain his behavior.

Furthermore, the jury could have decided that [the police department] tolerated and even fostered an attitude of fierce loyalty and protectiveness within the ranks, to the point that officers refused to address or report each other's misconduct. The jury could have surmised that [the police department's] "code of silence" prevented [Hankins's supervisor] and Sharp's fellow officers from doing anything about the harassment they saw on a daily basis.

The appellate court upheld the jury's verdict that the city, through the exercise of reasonable care, should have known of the harassment. The city had acted negligently and thus was liable to Sharp for the harassment she was compelled to endure.[6]

Sharp's case was decided before the *Ellerth* and *Faragher* rulings. Those rulings, however, did not eliminate the negligence approach from use in cases involving sexually harassing conduct of supervisors. In its *Ellerth* decision, the court stated, "An employer can be liable . . . where its own negligence is a cause of the harassment. An employer is negligent with respect to sexual harassment if it knew or should have known about the conduct but failed to stop it."[7]

The Supreme Court's provisions for vicarious liability supplements the negligence concept as a standard of employer liability. If Sharp had asserted her claim subsequent to the Supreme Court rulings in the *Ellerth* and *Faragher* cases, she and her attorneys may very well have elected to have proceeded under a vicarious liability approach, rather than alleging negligence. In that event, the city would have been confronted with proving it exercised reasonable care in preventing harassment from occurring in the mounted patrol. That it would have succeeded appears doubtful, indeed.

Tort Liability and Liability under State Antidiscrimination Laws

An exhaustive examination of the various tort remedies that may be available to a harassed employee falls outside the scope of this work. Mention should be made, however, that tort claims, such as assault and battery and the intentional infliction of emotional distress, are frequently added to a harassed woman's complaint alleging a sexual harassment claim under Title VII. Generally, these types of tort claims culminate in the recovery of damages, in addition to those recoverable under Title VII, only in certain circumstances, later discussed in chapter 18. These claims may also be useful in directing a jury's attention to particularly egregious harassing conduct, and they may create in the minds of the jurors an element of outrage that ordinarily redounds to the benefit of the plaintiff.

Claims alleging violations of state statutes barring sexual harassment in the workplace are also frequently pleaded alongside a Title VII claim. These claims may stand as vehicles for the recovery of damages not available under Title VII (see chapter 18). Unlike federal law, some state statutes provide that the harasser may be held liable in damages for his acts of harassment, a significant advantage for the plaintiff in those circumstances where the liability of the employer is in question.

Harassment by Nonsupervisory Co-Workers

Under certain conditions, employers are liable for the sexually harassing conduct of nonsupervisory employees as well as for the acts of harassment committed by supervisory employees. As in negligence cases involving harassment by supervisory employees, an employer will be held responsible for nonsupervisory co-worker acts of harassment if it knew, or should have known, of such conduct, and after receiving either actual or constructive notice of the harassment, failed to take adequate remedial or preventive measures. Generally, the primary issue under adjudication in these cases is the extent of the employer's knowledge of the co-worker's harassing behavior.

Obviously, if the victim of the harassment reports the offensive conduct to a supervisory or management level employee, the employer's knowledge will not become an issue in the case. However, as noted earlier, women often are motivated to delay disclosure of harassing acts committed against them. The failure to report the harassing conduct of a nonsupervisory co-worker, or a substantial delay in reporting it, usually proves fatal to the harassment victim's case. Where the harassment is pervasive, however, the court may assume the employer had to have known of its existence even if it had never been reported.

Brenda Lynn Franklin, a salesperson for a car dealership, was the only female member of a ten-person sales staff. Franklin alleged that several co-workers continuously harassed her. When Franklin filed suit, the car dealership asked the court to dismiss her case since she had not reported any of the alleged incidents of harassment to her supervisor, and thus management had been unaware she had been subjected to the objectionable conduct of the male members of the sales staff. In effect, management contended that the company could not be held liable for the behavior of Franklin's co-workers unless it had direct knowledge of the harassment. The court rejected this argument, observing that the acts of harassment had occurred on the dealership's showroom floor, which, by design, was "a distinctly communal employment forum." If the harassment was as pervasive as Franklin alleged, the court reasoned that it must have come to the attention of supervisory or management employees at some point in time. Accordingly, the court refused to dismiss Franklin's case.[8]

After Kim Hirase-Doi had worked for U.S. West Communications for nine years, the company hired Kenneth Coleman to work in Doi's department (see chapter 5). During Coleman's first week of employment, he made sexually offensive remarks in the presence of two female workers, who reported his conduct to their manager. The manager, who was female, met with Coleman and warned him that any further harassment could result in his dismissal. Coleman then proceeded to make sexually offensive remarks in the manager's presence.

During the ensuing three months, Coleman continued to exhibit sexually offensive behavior in the presence of numerous women, including Doi, whom he propositioned and physically harassed. Ultimately, Doi reported his conduct to management. U.S. West promptly suspended Coleman and he later resigned. Doi then sued U.S. West for neglecting to halt Coleman's harassing conduct at an earlier point in time, but U.S. West argued it should not be held liable in negligence for Coleman's conduct prior to being notified by Doi that he was harassing her.

Employer negligence is defined as a failure to take appropriate action to address hostile or offensive working conditions that the employer knew existed, or in the exercise of reasonable care, should have known existed. In the *Doi* case, the court was required to determine whether Doi, in her endeavor to establish that U.S. West knew or should have known of her harassment by Coleman, was limited to offering evidence of Coleman's behavior as it affected her, or whether she also could submit evidence of Coleman's offensive conduct toward other female employees. Could Doi, as a means of bolstering her claim that the company knew, or should have known, of Coleman's harassment of her, offer evidence that U.S. West knew, or should have known, of Coleman's harassment of other women?

The court ruled that Doi could rely on U.S. West's knowledge of

Coleman's harassment of other female employees to prove that U.S. West had constructive knowledge of Coleman's harassment of her:

> We believe that U.S. West may be put on notice if it learns that the perpetrator has practiced widespread sexual harassment in the office place, even though U.S. West may not have known that this particular plaintiff was one of the perpetrator's victims. . . . Doi may, therefore, rely on U.S. West's notice of any evidence of sexual harassment by Coleman that is similar in nature and near in time to his sexual harassment of Doi.[9]

The *Franklin* and *Doi* cases demonstrate that where the harassment is pervasive, courts are more apt to charge the employer with "constructive" knowledge of the presence of harassment in its workplace. The courts assume management must have been aware of pervasive harassing behavior, whether or not the victim of the harassment reported it to management.

In another case, a plaintiff submitted evidence that other female employees had been sexually harassed, but she failed to show that any of those women were harassed by the same individual who harassed her. Moreover, many of the incidents involving the other women occurred well before the acts of harassment she experienced. Under these circumstances, the harassing acts of the other women could not serve as constructive notice that she herself was harassed.[10]

On occasion, as Yvette Hawkins sadly learned, even reported acts of harassment may be inadequate for the purpose of providing notice to the employer of the presence of harassing behavior in its workplace. The Maximus Company hired Hawkins to replace Timothy Bannister as its systems manager. Bannister returned to the company on a temporary consulting basis to train Hawkins and provide Maximus with other technical assistance. Since Bannister was working another job, Hawkins's training sessions were conducted at the end of the regular work day, and on occasion these sessions extended into the late evening hours. While training Hawkins, Bannister continuously complimented her, told her he wanted to take her out, that she "owed" him for the job, that he was sexually frustrated and had sexual needs, and that everyone at Maximus was sleeping with everyone else. Hawkins suspected that Bannister was following her home after evening training sessions. One month later, Hawkins charged Bannister with having raped her.

Maximus could be held liable for Bannister's conduct if it was negligent in having failed to discover and prevent his harassment of Hawkins. The issue presented to the court was whether Hawkins had given

Maximus sufficient information to place it on notice that she was being subjected to harassing conduct. Hawkins had told her project manager that Bannister was a pervert, that he was following her home, and that his behavior "spooked" her. The court ruled that although the information given the project manager was sufficient to place Maximus on notice that Bannister was a "boor," it was insufficient to inform Maximus that a "severe alteration of the terms and conditions of Hawkins's employment was imminent":

> I do not mean to suggest that Maximus would be liable only if it knew that the rape was about to happen; it must have been on notice of sexual harassment in general—severe gender-based conduct that subjectively and objectively alters the terms and conditions of employment. Here Maximus knew only that Bannister was making Hawkins work late, and making suggestive comments to her. The knowledge that Bannister seemed to follow Hawkins home is not enough to put his conduct over the line. As far as Maximus knew, Bannister was a creep . . . not a sex-based discriminator.

Because the court believed Maximus did not know or, in the exercise of reasonable care, could not have learned that Hawkins was being sexually harassed, it dismissed her case.[11]

This is a decision with which it is easy to disagree. Maximus had been advised that Bannister had made suggestive comments and may have been following Hawkins home. This information would appear to be sufficient to activate Maximus's duty to examine Bannister's conduct. Was he harassing her or not? The court, on the other hand, believed that more was required before Maximus reached the "should have known" stage.

Harassment by Nonemployees

An employer's duty to provide its employees with a working environment free of sexual harassment may require it to exercise control, not only over its own employees, but over nonemployees as well. This duty is well illustrated in Sandra Rodriguez-Hernandez's sexual harassment case against her employer, Occidental International. Rodriguez was terminated from her position as office manager after she complained that an executive employee of one of Occidental's most important customers had subjected her to acts of sexual harassment.

Occidental sold electric and industrial equipment in Florida and Puerto Rico. Approximately 80 percent of its business in Puerto Rico was with the Puerto Rico Electric Power Authority. Due to the extent of

Occidental's business with the Authority, Occidental's president and sole stockholder, Omar Chavez, made special efforts to assure good relations between his company and its major customer.

In the main, Chavez employed young, attractive women and instructed them to be especially cordial to Authority employees. Good relations with high-ranking Authority executives, such as Edwin Miranda-Valez, were of first importance for Chavez, and he told Rodriguez "she should be nice" to Miranda and "keep him satisfied." Rodriguez was also instructed to visit Miranda on each occasion she was in the Authority's offices. On one of those visits, Miranda made suggestive comments and unwelcome sexual advances. He invited Rodriguez to dinner and asked her to come to his office after hours and on Friday evenings. On her birthday, he anonymously sent her flowers and a sexually explicit card, and some time later asked her to accompany him to a motel. At that point, Rodriguez complained to Chavez of Miranda's behavior, but Chavez defended Miranda and told Rodriguez she should respond to Miranda "as a woman." Rodriguez rejected this advice, and informed Chavez that unless he intervened to force a change in Miranda's behavior, she would take her complaint to the highest level of Authority executive personnel. Chavez immediately fired Rodriguez.

Rodriguez's subsequent sexual harassment claim culminated in a $200,000 jury award in her favor. When an appellate court later reviewed the jury's verdict, it focused on the question of Occidental's liability for Miranda's conduct. The court noted that Chavez conditioned Rodriguez's continued employment on her agreement to accede to Miranda's sexual advances. Because Chavez failed to take any action to curtail Miranda's sexual demands, he in effect made acceptance of those demands a condition of Rodriguez's employment, thus rendering his company liable under Title VII for sexual harassment. In its decision, the court explained:

> This is a case in which Rodriguez's employer not only acquiesced in the customer's demands, but explicitly told her to give in to those demands and satisfy the customer. This conduct is clearly an example of quid pro quo sexual harassment, as Rodriguez's employer conditioned her future with the company on her responding to the unwanted sexual demands of a customer.[12]

Acts of sexual harassment committed by an employer's clients and customers often remain unreported. Some women decide to ignore the harassment lest they be perceived by their employers as incapable of coping with the conditions of their particular jobs. Female sales representatives are particularly vulnerable to acts of sexual harassment as they often are required to conduct business in hotels, restaurants, and on customers' premises. Since many female workers elect to cope with the harassment of an unruly client or customer rather than seek the intercession of her employer, this type of harassment is far more prevalent than the reported cases appear to indicate.[13]

As in the Rodriguez case, even if a woman reports third-party harassment, her employer may be unwilling to deal with the problem if it believes that by doing so it would unduly disturb a valued client or customer or undermine a profitable business relationship. This was precisely Chavez's reaction to Rodriguez's disclosure that Miranda was harassing her. But an employer is required to deal with the problem if it knows—or should know—of its existence, and in such circumstances it is required to protect its employee from further harassment by implementing immediate and appropriate action.[14] What do the courts consider to be immediate and appropriate action? The answer is found in a most unusual case.

Kelbi Folkerson made her living as a mime. She worked for the Circus Casino in Las Vegas and performed in the guise of a life-size children's wind-up toy named "Kelbi the Living Doll." She was so convincing in her portrayal of a mechanical doll that casino patrons often speculated whether she was human or mechanical, and some patrons tried to touch her to determine if she was a real person. When Folkerson expressed concern to her supervisor that the touching could get out of hand, he directed her to call security whenever she experienced any difficulty of that sort, and as a deterrent to customer touching, the casino provided her with a sign to wear on her back, reading, "Stop, Do Not Touch." The casino also furnished Folkerson with a bodyguard of sorts—another performer dressed as a clown—who accompanied her whenever she performed on the floor of the casino. Other employees also were enlisted by Folkerson to call security if they saw she was in trouble.

Despite these precautions, on one occasion a patron approached Folkerson while apprising bystanders, "I will show you how real she really is," and he lunged toward her with open arms as though intending to embrace her. Folkerson floored him with a left to the jaw. The casino fired Folkerson on the ground that the patron had not sufficiently provoked her to warrant her punching him, but Folkerson alleged her termination was ordered only because she had opposed and rejected a patron's attempt to sexually harass her.

When Folkerson sued the casino alleging sexual harassment, the court agreed with her that her employer could be held liable for a harassing act committed by one of its patrons, but only if the casino management had acquiesced in the harassment by not taking immediate corrective action when it learned of the existence of objectionable conduct. But the facts of the case did not support Folkerson's position. The casino did not acquiesce in touching episodes by its patrons. To the contrary, it undertook reasonable steps to prevent patrons from harassing her. It arranged for its security forces to intervene in the event Folkerson confronted an overly aggressive patron; it provided her with a sign designed to deter touching of her body; and it furnished her with bodyguard protection. The court, therefore, dismissed Folkerson's case.[15]

Victims of harassment rely on the negligence doctrine primarily in co-worker harassment cases. All sexual harassment plaintiffs, however, should consider whether this approach is available to them, for if it is, it may provide them with an additional source for the collection of monetary damages. Many business insurance policies do not provide coverage for employee acts of sexual harassment, but do cover company acts of negligence. If a plaintiff prevails in a negligence suit against an employer, the company's insurance coverage may provide an additional source for recovery of damages, a source generally not available in other types of sexual harassment cases.

CHAPTER THIRTEEN

Constructive Discharge

Even if a court holds an employer liable for acts of sexual harassment, whether committed by a supervisor, co-worker, customer, or client, recovery of damages may be limited in those instances where the victim of the harassment decides to resign from her position rather than continue to work in a hostile and offensive environment.

If a worker quits and later charges her employer with sexual harassment, she may not be able to recover all of her damages, unless she demonstrates that her resignation was involuntary. An involuntary resignation is commonly referred to as a "constructive discharge." Absent a court ruling that the worker's resignation amounted to a constructive discharge, her back pay and other damages may be limited to those that accrued prior to her departure from the company, thus precluding the recovery of damages, such as loss of salary, that may have accrued after her resignation. Whether a woman's departure was in fact a constructive discharge is of major importance in many sexual harassment cases.

The significance of the role of constructive discharge claims in sexual harassment cases was revealed in a study—referred to in chapter 2—undertaken by two law professors who examined every federal district and appellate court decision involving workplace sexual harassment between 1986 and 1995. They found in 89 percent of those cases, the plaintiff was no longer working for the employer at the time of the commencement of the harassment lawsuit.[1] Certainly, some of those plaintiffs left their employers for personal reasons, but it appears likely—given the circumstances a harassment victim typically encounters on the job—a large portion of those workers resigned on account of the harassment and thus were in a position to claim they were constructively discharged. In fact, an earlier survey found that 42 percent of sexually harassed plaintiffs resigned their positions because of the harassment. Another 24 percent were fired for having complained of the harassment.[2]

A court will declare a worker's resignation a constructive discharge if the employer required the worker to perform her job functions under conditions so difficult that any reasonable person laboring under similar circumstances would feel compelled to resign. A worker forced to quit because of "intolerable" working conditions is constructively discharged. In a typical sexual harassment case, a supervisor repeatedly subjects a female subordinate to sexually offensive behavior and his conduct continues until his victim can no longer put up with it and resigns. She "has simply had enough; she can't take it anymore."[3] In those circumstances, the court will consider her to have been constructively discharged.

In evaluating a plaintiff's working conditions to determine whether they are intolerable, the court must apply an objective standard rather than rely on the plaintiff's state of mind. A constructive discharge claim must be supported by evidence that a reasonable person in plaintiff's position would feel she had no alternative but to resign. Under this standard, the worker must demonstrate that she labored under unreasonably harsh conditions, much harsher than those confronted by her co-workers.

What a reasonable person may consider as tolerable or intolerable is an issue often before the courts. If a court determines a worker's resignation occurred under circumstances that were less than intolerable, the worker's damages—particularly back pay damages—that accrue after her resignation may be deleted from a damages award, even if the employer is found guilty of sexual harassment. Conversely, if the court determines her working conditions were intolerable and thus she was constructively discharged, the worker is eligible for the entire panoply of damages and other relief available to any worker unlawfully terminated.

Even if a worker establishes that the sexually harassing conduct she experienced rendered her working conditions intolerable, the court will not sustain her constructive discharge claim unless she also proves the harassment was the primary cause of her resignation. She must establish a causal link between the acts of harassment and her decision to resign. At times, the causal link may be established by considering the time interval between the acts of harassment and the resignation; the shorter the passage of time, the more likely a court will conclude the worker resigned because of the harassment and not for some other reason.

The plaintiff must also prove that prior to resigning she afforded her employer adequate notice of the harassment and it had ample time to investigate her charges and implement remedial measures. If she resigns without giving her employer a reasonable opportunity to address the problem, her constructive discharge claim may be denied.

In addition to requiring proof that (1) the claimant worked in a hostile environment, (2) her working conditions were intolerable, thus forcing her to quit her job, (3) the harassing conduct was the cause of her resignation, and (4) she gave her employer sufficient notice to permit it to eliminate the harassing behavior before she quit, some courts also demand proof of a fifth element: that the worker's employer *intentionally* made her working conditions intolerable thus forcing the termination of her employment. With these elements of proof in mind, we now proceed to an examination of sexual harassment cases involving constructive discharge claims.

Wax Works, the owner and operator of a chain of music and video stores, hired Kerry Ogden as a sales manager for its music store in Sioux City, Iowa. Ogden developed into an outstanding manager, routinely receiving bonuses and awards for her work efforts. About seven years into her employment, Robert Hudson, her district manager, sexually harassed her. She described three occasions on which Hudson was guilty of unwelcome physical advances. On the first, as Ogden and Hudson were leaving a restaurant, an intoxicated Hudson grabbed Ogden by the waist and asked her to his motel room. Ogden pushed him away and told him not to touch her again. On the second occasion, while she and Hudson were in a bar with a group of employees, Hudson, again in a state of intoxication, twice put his arms around her. Each time she rejected his advances. A few weeks later, he approached her again and once more Ogden rebuffed him.

Besides the physical advances, Hudson propositioned Ogden incessantly. He continuously asked her out for drinks after work and to "party" with him at his home. While they were attending a convention, he asked her to accompany him to his motel room. He also exhibited an inappropriate interest in Ogden's personal life, once offering to stay at Ogden's home to "protect" her from her estranged husband. He berated her on learning she had taken a canoe trip with a male companion and on another occasion became angry when another male friend visited her.

Hudson made no secret of his predilection for affairs with Wax Works female employees and boasted he had procured promotions and salary increases for the women with whom he had been involved. Ogden made it clear, however, she was uninterested in engaging in a sexual relationship with him. Eventually, Hudson got the message, but then he began to mistreat her at work, criticizing her performance, screaming at her, and conditioning her performance evaluation and salary increase on her willingness to submit to his advances.

The impact of Hudson's behavior on Ogden's physical and mental health was apparent. On several occasions, she left work in tears. Her personality changed from outgoing to withdrawn. She became depressed, lost interest in all activities, was unable to sleep or eat, and lost some forty pounds over an eight-month period. She began drinking and smoking to excess. She repeatedly fell ill and consequently was unable to report to work for long periods of time.

When Hudson persisted in refusing to complete Ogden's performance evaluation, thus denying her a salary increase, she reported his behavior to management. When no action was taken to halt the harassment, Ogden asked her regional manager whether in light of her allegations against Hudson she should continue to work for the company. He responded, "No, you can't." After having endured Hudson's offensive behavior for nearly fifteen months, Ogden resigned.

Ogden was physically and emotionally devastated by Hudson's harassment and the subsequent loss of her position. Her psychotherapist testified she suffered from post-traumatic stress disorder and depression and attributed these conditions to Hudson's abuse. After spending several months at home recuperating, Ogden secured two part-time positions, earning significantly less than she had as an employee of Wax Works.

During Ogden's employment, Wax Works distributed an employee handbook setting forth its sexual harassment policy. Employees were encouraged "to report any alleged violations of this policy immediately. . . . All such complaints . . . will be investigated thoroughly. Appropriate action will be taken." At the trial of Ogden's sexual harassment case, the evidence clearly showed Wax Works had failed to conduct a thorough investigation of her charges, and it had taken no action to stop the harassment. Instead of following the provisions of its own antiharassment policy, the company minimized Ogden's complaints and focused its investigation on her performance rather than on Hudson's conduct. At the conclusion of the investigation, the company declined to discipline Hudson for his behavior.

Following a five-day trial of Ogden's sexual harassment case, the jury awarded its verdict in her favor. When Wax Works appealed the verdict, it argued before the appellate court that the evidence submitted during the course of the trial was insufficient to support Ogden's constructive discharge claim, and thus the jury's damages award should be reduced. If the appeal had been successful, the reduction would have been significant, for if Ogden had not been constructively discharged, the court could have denied her any recovery of back pay for the period of time extending from her resignation until the date of the trial (see chapter 18). Conversely, if the court determined that she had been constructively discharged, Ogden would be entitled to recover back pay for the period of time after she resigned. This recovery would be substantial, as following her resignation, Ogden had been reduced to working part time, earning considerably less than she earned as a store manager for Wax Works.

The appellate court affirmed the jury's determination that Hudson's conduct had been the cause of Ogden's departure from the company:

> The jury reasonably concluded Hudson's harassment rendered Ogden's working conditions objectively intolerable; and given Ogden's testimony that [the regional manager] told her she could no longer remain with the company in the wake of her allegations, [the jury also concluded] that Wax Works either intended to force Ogden to resign or could have reasonably foreseen she would do so. . . . In addition . . . if an employee quits because she reasonably believes there is no chance for fair treatment, there has been a constructive discharge. . . . The jury could have so concluded here, given Wax Works's response to Ogden's complaints.

The appellate court affirmed a damages award of nearly $950,000.[4]

Ogden presented a particularly strong constructive discharge case. Not all plaintiffs are in a position to offer the court as much evidence as Ogden had available to her. Indeed, in the majority of these cases, the issues are less sharply delineated. Plaintiff-victims nevertheless have been successful, even though they have less evidence to offer. But having stated that, it must be noted that a plaintiff endeavoring to prove a constructive discharge must clearly demonstrate a greater degree of severity or pervasiveness of harassing conduct than that required to prove a hostile working environment.[5] As one court expressed it, "Constructive discharge requires considerably more proof than establishing unpleasant working conditions."[6]

Michelle McCrackin, employed by LabOne, alleged her supervisor subjected her to lewd and sexually suggestive leers, unwanted physical touching, and stalking, and he refused to alter his conduct despite her repeated expressions of discomfort and disapproval. Although management was aware of her supervisor's behavior, it took no action to discipline him or control his behavior. After enduring this treatment for six months, McCrackin complained to two company officials, including the vice president of its human resources department. Other than to suggest she change the location of her desk so as to make it easier for her to avoid her supervisor, the company undertook no remedial or preventative measures. Firmly of the belief the company would not act to alleviate her situation, McCrackin resigned. Her fears that the company would do nothing to eliminate the harassment were confirmed when she picked up her final pay check and the human resources vice president commented, "It's not as if you were raped."

McCrackin sued LabOne, alleging she had been forced to work in an offensive and hostile environment, conditions that ultimately culminated in her constructive discharge. Later in the litigation, LabOne asked the court to dismiss McCrackin's constructive discharge claim, but the court ruled that McCrackin had alleged facts sufficient to show that a reasonable person in her circumstances would have felt compelled to resign. In light of McCrackin's allegations that she had been subjected to a pattern of leers, touchings, and unwelcome advances, management should have done more than merely suggest ways McCrackin might succeed in avoiding her supervisor's offensive behavior. It should have taken action to stop the harassment. Rather than continue to work in such an environment, McCrackin could reasonably and justifiably have felt she had no alternative but to resign. Her belief that management would do nothing to improve her working conditions was heightened and reinforced by management's indifference to the hostility and offensiveness of her work environment and was buttressed by the human resources vice president's "it's not as if you were raped" comment. The court denied LabOne's motion to dismiss McCrackin's constructive discharge claim.[7]

If the supervisor's conduct had been the sole element in the *McCrackin* case, the court might very well have arrived at a different conclusion. A six-month lapse between the first acts of his offensive behavior and McCrackin's resignation suggests her working conditions may have been somewhat less than intolerable. But they became intolerable once she learned management had no intention of changing them. Immediately after learning her working conditions would not improve, McCrackin resigned, thus establishing the requisite causal link between the harassment and her resignation.

Sandra Breeding, a customer service representative employed by Arthur J. Gallagher & Company, alleged that her supervisor used offensive language, made sexually inappropriate comments, and fondled his genitals in her presence. When she reported these incidents, another supervisor minimized the gravity of the supervisor's conduct stating, "That is just the way he is," and nothing was done to alter his behavior. A court later ruled that even if the working conditions Breeding confronted were sufficient to establish a basis for a sexual harassment hostile environment claim, they were insufficient to support a constructive discharge claim. Although the court noted that Breeding's working conditions were difficult and unpleasant, in its opinion they were not so intolerable as to compel a reasonable person to resign.

What one court describes as "difficult or unpleasant" another court characterizes as "intolerable." Indeed, one of the appellate judges sitting on the panel that considered the *Breeding* case dissented from the court's ruling. In the dissenter's opinion, when all of the evidence was considered, especially the nature of the grossly offensive conduct attributed to Breeding's supervisor, a jury could rationally have found she had been "subjected to working conditions that no reasonable, self-respecting woman should be expected to tolerate."[8]

Unfortunately, there are no universal rules applicable to these cases. As we have just seen, a determination that a woman's working conditions are or are not intolerable is dependent, in large part, on the perspective of the judge viewing the evidence. Conduct labeled "intolerable" varies from courtroom to courtroom.

As previously noted, in addition to proving intolerable working conditions, a victim of harassment must establish she notified her employer that she had been subjected to harassing behavior. If she had an avenue of redress within the company and failed to use it, she probably cannot prove she was constructively discharged. In one case, copies of the employer's antiharassment policy were posted at each of its work sites, and each copy included a telephone number of a contact person at corporate headquarters that aggrieved workers could call if a harassment complaint was not resolved satisfactorily on the local level. The plaintiff was aware of the policy provisions and in fact had informed her supervisor she would forward her complaint to corporate headquarters if he failed to act on it. Though aware of her rights under the policy, she failed to abide by its provisions by failing to notify corporate headquarters before quitting. The court dismissed her constructive discharge claim because she failed to follow the reporting procedure establish by her employer, thus denying it a reasonable opportunity to resolve the problems she confronted.[9]

Once a harassment victim has utilized the procedures for reporting harassment established by her employer, she must remain on the job until the employer has had sufficient time to address her complaint. Cynthia Swain, a customer service representative for Roadway Express, alleged she was subjected to unwanted and intimidating sexual comments and physical contact by co-workers. After each incident of harassment, Swain reported it to her supervisor, but Roadway Express declined to take any action and the offensive conduct continued. Eventually, Swain resigned and filed suit against Roadway Express. Until this point in the recitation of facts, it appears that Swain had a solid claim for constructive discharge. But this was not the end of the story. Although it was true that Swain's supervisors at first declined to respond to her complaints, just prior to her resignation, Roadway had taken initial steps to eliminate her hostile working conditions. Management interviewed and admonished two of her co-workers and advised Swain that if she experienced any additional offensive incidents, she was to contact management immediately. Rather than waiting to determine whether these actions were sufficient to bring the harassment to a halt, Swain quit. In these circumstances, Swain's constructive discharge claim was subject to dismissal.[10]

Although a worker must afford her employer a sufficient opportunity to eliminate the harassment, she must be careful not to unduly delay her resignation, lest an element of uncertainty be introduced regarding the intolerableness of her working conditions. Delay may also create doubt with regard to the causal linkage between the harassment and her resignation. She must balance these considerations with her responsibility to furnish her employer with ample time to resolve the issue. If she resigns before her employer has had a reasonable opportunity to implement measures to halt the harassment and eliminate a hostile working environment, the court may conclude the employer, given sufficient time, would have resolved those problems. In those circumstances, a court would probably rule that the worker had failed to establish her working conditions were intolerable. Whether to resign and when to resign are decisions requiring the advice of an attorney well versed in this area of the law.

Constructive discharge also plays a significant role in another area of sexual harassment litigation. In chapter 9, we reviewed the Supreme Court ruling in the *Ellerth* case where the court reaffirmed the distinction between a workplace act of sexual harassment that culminates in a tangible employment action and one that does not. The court's ruling affirmed the employer's liability for a supervisor's acts of sexual harassment that result in a tangible employment action. It also ruled an employer may be responsible for a supervisor's conduct even if the harassment does not result in a tangible employment action, but in those circumstances, the employer must be given the opportunity to establish an affirmative defense that, if proven, would relieve it of liability for the behavior of its supervisors. Thus, if the plaintiff is able to establish she suffered a tangible employment action, the employer will be held strictly liable for the harassing conduct of its supervisor. On the other hand, if she is unable to prove she was subjected to a tangible employment action, the employer, if it successfully establishes the affirmative defense, may avoid liability for the harassing conduct of its supervisor.

The question we must now consider is whether a constructive discharge is a tangible employment action. This is a question of paramount importance in cases involving supervisory harassment, for if a constructive discharge is considered a tangible employment action, the employer will be held strictly liable for the supervisor's harassment. In contrast, if a constructive discharge is not considered a tangible employment action, the employer, in its pursuit of avoiding liability, must be afforded the opportunity to establish the affirmative defense.

The Supreme Court defined a tangible employment action as a "significant change in employment status, such as hiring, firing, failing to promote, reassignment with significantly different responsibilities, or a decision causing a significant change in benefits."[11] Does a constructive discharge fall within that definition? Did the Supreme Court's failure to specifically include a constructive discharge in its list necessarily mean it did not intend to consider it as a tangible employment action? The courts are split on the issue.

Those courts that have ruled a constructive discharge is a tangible employment action often point to the *Ellerth* definition. Since a "firing" is a tangible employment action, a constructive discharge must also fall into that category, as in either case the employee is forced out of her job. Courts that have ruled a constructive discharge is not a tangible employment action point out that a constructive discharge does not occur as the result of a decision made by a supervisory or management employee, and thus it cannot fall within the definition set out in the *Ellerth* ruling.

In its *Ellerth* ruling, the Supreme Court explained that a victim of sexual harassment suffers a tangible employment action when a person acting with the authority of the company inflicts injury upon the worker. As the court noted, although a co-worker may physically injure another worker as readily as a supervisor, and anyone having regular contact with an employee is in a position to inflict psychological injury by his offensive conduct, a co-worker cannot dock another worker's pay or order any other employment action adversely affecting his co-workers.[12] One court specifically relied on this language as a basis for determining that a constructive discharge is not a tangible employment action, reasoning that a tangible employment action occurs only in those instances where the employer is implicated in the harm visited on the victim. But, co-worker harassment may underlie the victim's constructive discharge, and in those instances, the employer is not implicated. Moreover, unlike an ordinary discharge, a constructive discharge is neither ratified nor approved by the employer. For these reasons, the court ruled, a constructive discharge is not a tangible employment action.[13]

Courts have also relied on other aspects of the *Ellerth* ruling to reject the concept that a constructive discharge may be considered a tangible employment action. They note the Supreme Court expressed the view that a tangible employment action is the means by which a supervisor uses the official power of the company to bear on subordinates. Thus, a tangible employment action requires a company act, which in most cases is documented and made subject to review by higher-level supervisors. "The supervisor must obtain the imprimatur of the enterprise and use its internal processes."[14] In cases of constructive discharge, however, no official corporate action takes place. "There is no official act, no documentation, no review, and no use of internal procedure."[15] Instead, a constructive discharge involves an unofficial act of a supervisor that leads a worker to resign in order to avoid intolerable conditions, but this unofficial act does not carry the "imprimatur" of the corporation.

The battle is not yet over, but a trend among the courts appears to favor the proposition that a constructive discharge is not a tangible employment action. Plaintiffs, therefore, must be prepared to deal with the *Ellerth* affirmative defense that employers will continue to assert in constructive discharge cases.

CHAPTER FOURTEEN

Retaliation against Workers Who Charge Their Employers with Sexual Harassment

The reactions of many employers to charges of any sort of employment discrimination—whether it be race, sex, sexual harassment, national origin, religion, age, or disability—does not differ greatly from their responses to whistle-blower charges of fraud, embezzlement, or other criminal activity. Employers are all too prone to strike back at any worker who even so much as utters the words "sexual harassment." Once a supervisor is accused of committing acts of sexual harassment, he is likely to make life extremely difficult for his accuser. The victim of harassment then becomes a victim of retaliation.

The law provides workers with protection from acts of employer retaliation whenever they are engaged in exercising rights provided by Title VII. When Congress enacted Title VII, it decreed it unlawful for an employer to retaliate against a worker who charges it with a discriminatory policy or practice or who participates in a legal or administrative proceeding relating to the company's employment policies or practices. Once a worker has engaged in a protected activity, defined as

- an action opposing an act of discrimination, such as the filing of a charge of discrimination, or
- testifying on behalf of a fellow worker who has asserted a claim of discrimination, or
- participating in an investigation of alleged discriminatory conduct,

an employer is barred from retaliating against that worker on account of her participation in that protected activity. More specifically, Title VII provides that

> It shall be an unlawful employment practice for an employer to discriminate against any of his employees or applicants for employment . . . because [she] has opposed . . . an unlawful practice . . . or because [she] has made a charge, testified, assisted, or participated in any manner in an investigation, proceeding, or hearing under this subchapter.[1]

An employer who ignores its legal duty to refrain from retaliatory acts subjects itself to liability for damages suffered by the worker as a consequence of the retaliation. Charges, alleging retaliation in violation of Title VII precepts, filed annually with the Equal Employment Opportunity Commission, nearly doubled in the ten-year period between 1992 and 2001. In 2001, over 25 percent of all Title VII complaints filed with the EEOC charged employers with acts of retaliation.[2] This steep rise in the filings of retaliation charges reflects an increased tendency on the part of employers to react negatively and irresponsibly to charges of discriminatory conduct, as well as an increased willingness on the part of workers to call their employers to task for acts of retaliatory conduct.

A retaliation claim consists of three components, each of which must be established by the claimant:

1. she participated in a protected activity,
2. she was then subjected to an adverse employment action, and
3. a causal connection exists between her participation in the protected activity and the adverse employment action.

Some plaintiffs find it relatively easy to establish these elements of proof, whereas others fail. The cases that follow consider issues that typically arise in retaliation cases.

After working several years as a loan processor for the Green Tree Credit Corporation, Stephanie Quinn complained to management that two of her supervisors were sexually harassing her, thus forcing her to work in a hostile work environment. Following an investigation of her charges, Green Tree's director of human resources informed Quinn that no evidence had been uncovered substantiating her allegations of sexual harassment. Refusing to accept this finding, Quinn then filed a formal charge of sexual harassment with the New York State Division of Human Rights, the state agency charged with the investigation of worker claims of employment discrimination. Ten days later, Green Tree fired Quinn. She promptly lodged a retaliation charge with the New York State agency, and later filed suit against Green Tree, alleging sexual harassment as well as retaliation. A court later dismissed her sexual harassment claim on the ground the conduct she described as sexual harassing was insufficiently severe or pervasive to support her claim, but it took another tack with regard to her retaliation claim.

Quinn had no difficulty in establishing the second and third elements of proof of retaliation. Her termination obviously was an adverse employment action, thus satisfying the second element. She established the third element by showing the short time interval between her participation in the protected activity and the adverse employment action. The causal connection between a worker's participation in a protected activity and an adverse employment action may in some instances, as in this case, be shown by demonstrating to the court that a relatively short period of time elapsed between the protected activity and the adverse employment action. The closeness in time of the two events raises the inference that there must have been a connection between them. In this case, an elapse of a mere ten days between Quinn's filing of her harassment charge with the State Division of Human Rights and the date of her firing satisfied the third element of proof.

But, it was with the first element of proof that the court had the most difficulty. By definition, an employer is guilty of retaliation if it acts adversely to the interests of a worker who has charged it with a *discriminatory* policy or practice such as sexual harassment. To level such a charge against one's employer is to engage in a protected activity. But in this case the court determined that Green Tree's supervisors had not sexually harassed her, and thus it had not been guilty of a discriminatory policy or practice. In these circumstances, how could it be said that Quinn had participated in a protected activity?

The evidence in the case disclosed that before Quinn formally charged the company with sexual harassment, she consulted with a representative of the State Division of Human Rights concerning the law as it pertained to sexual harassment. It was only after conferring with that representative that Quinn notified the company she intended to file a harassment charge. Although the acts of sexual harassment alleged in her charge were later held by the court to be of insufficient severity or pervasiveness to legally support her charge, they were not totally without substance. Quinn alleged that one of her supervisors had mentioned to her she had been voted the "sleekest ass" in the office and on another occasion he had deliberately touched her breasts with some papers he was holding in his hand. Both supervisors made offensive remarks, referring to their own sexual prowess, to Quinn's body, and to her and her husband's sexual orientation. In addition they pantomimed sexual acts and displayed pornographic materials. Although this evidence may have been insufficient to establish a sexual harassment claim, the court nevertheless believed it may have been adequate to persuade Quinn at the time she was being subjected to acts of a harassing nature.

In order for Quinn to prove the filing of her charge with the New York State agency was a protected activity, she was not required to establish she actually had suffered conduct amounting to a violation of the law. Rather, the court stated, she need only demonstrate she had a "good faith, reasonable belief the underlying challenged actions of the employer violated the law."

> Thus, it is possible for an employee to reasonably believe that specified conduct amounts to harassment, even when that conduct would not actually qualify as harassment under the law. . . . Though we [hold] that Quinn has failed to adduce facts sufficient to establish Green Tree's liability for sexual harassment, we are satisfied that her complaints of sexual harassment . . . included evidence sufficient to sustain a good faith, reasonable belief that Green Tree stood in violation of the law.

Although Quinn's sexual harassment claim ultimately was dismissed, her filing of a discrimination charge with the New York State Division Of Human Rights was a protected activity. Her consultation with a representative of the state agency—an agency charged with administering state laws barring sexual harassment—could have led her to a good faith, reasonable belief that the conduct she experienced was an act of sexual harassment, even though her claim was insufficient to support a legal violation. Green Tree was not guilty of sexual harassment, but it nevertheless had to answer for its conduct in discharging Quinn after she engaged in a protected activity.[3]

Suppose a female employee tells her harasser his conduct is unwelcome and offensive. Has she engaged in a protected activity? Does a woman engage in a protected activity merely by opposing harassing conduct? That was the issue the court confronted in Denise Wildman's harassment suit against Burke Marketing Corporation. Soon after Wildman was hired as a marketing manager, Burke executives instructed her to attend a products exposition in Las Vegas. Prior to leaving for Las Vegas, a female co-worker warned Wildman that Burke's male employees had a history of harassing female workers.

At the conclusion of the first day of the exposition, Wildman and three male Burke regional sales managers were driven back to their hotel. During the course of the ride, two of the sales managers told sexually explicit jokes about President Clinton and commented on the breasts of young girls passing by, while another made a series of offensive remarks displaying his animosity toward homosexuals. Wildman told them she did not want to listen to that type of commentary.

When they arrived at the hotel, Wildman was invited to attend dinner with several Burke employees and customers. During the dinner, one of the regional sales managers suggested that after the dinner Wildman accompany them to a topless show then being presented at the hotel. When Wildman declined to attend, the regional sales manager was visibly angered. On the following day, Wildman's supervisor berated her for objecting to the topless show. He refused to acknowledge the validity of her objections to being present at a show having sexually explicit content.

On the following day, when Wildman was riding back to the hotel with a group of regional sales managers, they again persisted in telling jokes and making sex-related remarks. Wildman ordered the driver to stop the car and she got out. Throughout the remainder of the exposition, Wildman was subjected to repeated incidents of a sexual nature, all of which she found offensive.

On her return from Las Vegas, Wildman asked to speak to her supervisor concerning the behavior she experienced at the exposition, but before she could discuss the matter with him, he fired her, purportedly because she neither "fit in" nor had the right "chemistry" to remain with the company.

When Wildman later sued Burke for sexual harassment and retaliation, the company's lawyers argued that since Wildman had not complained to her supervisor about the conduct of the regional sales managers until after she was fired, she could not prove she had participated in a protected activity, and thus the court should dismiss her retaliation claim. Wildman, on the other hand, contended she had engaged in a protected activity when she declined to attend the topless performance and also when she abstained from participation in the sex-related conduct of the regional sales managers. Wildman, however, did more than merely abstain from this conduct; she resisted it. Despite pressure exerted by a regional sales manager, she refused to view the topless show. She gave up her ride rather than listen to dirty jokes and other sexual commentary. In categorizing her as one who did not "fit in" at Burke Marketing, her supervisor conceded that her responses to the Las Vegas happenings demonstrated her opposition to the behavior of the Burke regional managers.

Although the court was not prepared to hold that Wildman's abstention from the offensive conduct was sufficient in and of itself to establish her participation in a protected activity, it did rule that her active resistance to that conduct was enough.[4] The court established the rule that a woman expressing opposition to sexually offensive conduct engages in a protected activity, and thus satisfies the first element of proof of retaliation.

The second element of proof requires the plaintiff to demonstrate that after participating in a protected activity she suffered an adverse employment action. Retaliatory adverse employment actions come in varied forms: termination; refusal to promote; demotion; disadvantageous transfer; refusal to grant a merited or scheduled pay increase; or issuance of an unwarranted, adverse performance evaluation. Most federal courts have ruled that any materially adverse change in a worker's terms and conditions of employment may provide the basis for a retaliation charge. For example, even if a transfer is not accompanied by a direct economic loss, it still may be considered an adverse employment action if the new position is less prestigious or provides fewer opportunities for advancement. Of course, any material reduction in compensation or benefits also will qualify. Termination, however, appears to be the employers' retaliatory act of choice.

In most instances, plaintiffs have experienced little difficulty in proving the occurrence of an adverse employment action, since the undermining of the victim's employment status is generally apparent. Deanna Haynes's retaliation case against Reebaire Aircraft, however, proved to be the exception.

After two years of employment with Reebaire, Haynes informed the company's human resources director that a co-worker had made sex-related comments in her presence and had engaged in other inappropriate behavior. When confronted with Haynes's allegations, the co-worker admitted certain of his conduct had been improper. The company issued him verbal and written warnings and advised him the occurrence of any future conduct of a similar nature would result in his termination.

About a week later, Haynes met with the human resources director and her supervisor to discuss the co-worker's behavior following the warnings. Haynes complained he was too obvious about avoiding contact with her, for whenever she walked past him he made a scene by jumping out of her way in an exaggerated manner. It was decided the co-worker's antics did not warrant his termination, but he was directed to cease acting in that fashion. A few days later, Haynes's supervisor asked her if she was "still feeling uncomfortable" and offered her two alternative positions within the company. She declined the offer. Subsequently, Reebaire moved Haynes's desk to a location in the office she deemed undesirable and thereafter assigned her tasks she described as menial. Three months later, Reebaire terminated her, purportedly for excessive absenteeism, tardiness, and mismanagement of the company's petty cash fund.

The court had to determine whether Haynes had been subjected to an adverse employment action in retaliation for reporting the co-worker's harassing behavior. It first concluded that a three-month lapse between the protected activity—Haynes's report to the human resources director of the occurrence of the co-worker harassment—and the alleged act of retaliation—her termination—was too great to establish a causal connection. Since the desk move and assignment of menial tasks occurred closer in time to the protected activity, the court turned to those modifications in her employment status to determine whether they amounted to adverse employment actions.

Reebaire ordered changes in Haynes's job functions only after it had filled two vacant office positions. At that time, her duties reverted to those previously assigned to her, but her salary, work hours, and fringe benefits remained the same. The court ruled that these changes in Haynes's employment status were insignificant and insufficient to establish an adverse employment action. Her retaliation claim was dismissed.[5]

Some courts set a fairly high standard of proof for a plaintiff to meet in order to successfully establish her claim that she suffered an adverse employment action. Jeannette Flannery worked as reservation sales agent for Trans World Airlines. After she complained that a supervisor had committed acts of verbal harassment, TWA managers made several decisions Flannery contended were retaliatory. Management changed her work hours, reprimanded her for a dress code violation, moved her parking space further from her work station, unfairly admonished her for an alleged lapse in performance, assigned her to another work station, and removed approximately three hundred complimentary letters and commendations from her personnel file. The court rejected her retaliation claim on the ground these actions merely constituted changes in working conditions and failed to result in any materially significant disadvantage for Flannery.[6]

Each of these actions, if regarded individually, may not have been materially disadvantageous, but in combination—especially the unfair admonishment for a lapse in performance and the removal of the complimentary letters and commendations from her personnel file—appear to have created a barrier to future advancement. Perceived in this light, it appears the court was wrong, that Flannery was indeed subjected to an adverse employment action.

Cynthia Swain sued her employer, Roadway Express, for sexual harassment (see chapter 13), also claiming the company retaliated against her after she reported the harassing conduct of three of her co-workers. According to Swain, after the co-workers learned of her complaints of harassment, they retaliated against her by driving their cars very close to her as if they were attempting to run her over. Other co-workers ostracized her and one actually assaulted her. She failed to allege, however, that any of Roadway's management employees took any direct retaliatory action against her, offering no evidence management instigated, much less knew about, the co-worker antics. The court dismissed her case.[7]

In some retaliation cases the adverse employment action may consist in the continuation and intensification of the acts of harassment. Judy Morris, an employee of the Oldham County Road Department in Kentucky, accused her supervisor, Brent Likins, of engaging in sexually harassing conduct. After Morris complained of Likins's behavior, the Road Department transferred him, directing him not to communicate with Morris unless a third party was present. Despite this directive, Likins repeatedly telephoned Morris and, as she alleged, made these calls solely for the purpose of harassing her. Morris also claimed that Likins drove to her work site on several occasions and sat in his car parked outside her building while staring at Morris's window and making faces at her. On one occasion, he allegedly followed Morris home from work, pulled alongside her mailbox and "gave her the finger." Morris also claimed Likens destroyed the television set in her office and on several occasions threw roofing nails on her driveway. The court concluded the continuing harassing conduct engaged in by Likins clearly constituted an adverse employment action and thus was retaliatory conduct.[8]

The third element of proof requires a complainant to show a causal connection between the protected activity and the adverse employment action. That connection was made in rather unusual circumstances in a retaliation claim asserted by Elizabeth Martini against her employer, the Federal National Mortgage Association ("Fannie Mae"). Martini, director of debt sales in Fannie Mae's treasurer's office, alleged her supervisor, Forrest Kobayashi, repeatedly harassed her, thus creating hostile working conditions.

Martini also claimed Linda Knight, a senior vice president in the treasurer's office and Kobayashi's direct supervisor, ignored her complaints regarding Kobayashi's behavior. Although Fannie Mae's policies required Knight to report Martini's harassment complaints to its office of diversity, Knight failed to abide by that policy. Without informing anyone in a higher position about the harassment complaints, Knight recommended Kobayashi for promotion to vice president. At that point Martini made an informal complaint to personnel working in the office of diversity.

At the time, Knight and Kobayashi were engaged in planning a reorganization of the treasurer's office. After the plan had been formulated but before it was implemented, Martini went one step further, this time formally notifying the office of diversity that Kobayashi was harassing her. When Martini later learned her position was the only one eliminated in the reorganization designed by Knight and Kobayashi, she commenced legal action against Fannie Mae, charging it with sexual harassment and retaliation.

The jury that considered her case perceived the reorganization as a sham, designed to get rid of Martini, and it awarded Martini a huge damages award. The court noted it could readily understand why the jury concluded Martini's job was eliminated as an act of retaliation and punishment for raising the issue of Kobayashi's harassment, especially when one considers that the very person against whom Martini complained, together with that person's supervisor who declined to take any action to address that complaint, designed the reorganization that eliminated her position. But, Fannie Mae argued that Martini's retaliation charge failed because she could not establish a causal link between her harassment complaint and the elimination of her job. It contended that since Martini did not formally complain to the office of diversity until *after* the decision to reorganize had been made, no nexus existed between her formal harassment complaint and the elimination of her position.

If Martini's only protected activity had been the filing of her formal complaint, Fannie Mae's argument would have had merit. However, Martini's informal complaint to the office of diversity also was a protected activity, and that complaint was made *before* Knight and

Kobayashi planned the reorganization. Thus, a nexus between that protected activity and the adverse employment action was established, and the court upheld the jury's verdict.[9]

As the court held in the *Quinn v. Green Tree Credit Corp.* case, the causal connection may be established by relying on the passage of time between plaintiff's participation in a protected activity and her employer's retaliatory action. When that time interval is short, courts are inclined to rule that a plaintiff demonstrates a nexus between the protected activity and the act of retaliation. That, however, is not always the case, as Angela Trezza sadly learned.

Trezza worked as a secretary for The Dilenschneider Group, a public relations firm. Immediately after the firm hired her, she became the target of acts of sexual harassment committed by three men—a co-worker, one of her supervisors, and a company executive. After Trezza complained to one of her female supervisors about the co-worker's conduct, steps were taken to prevent its repetition, and Trezza was instructed to immediately report any reoccurrence. Some time later, Trezza reported incidences of harassing conduct committed by the supervisor and the executive, but on those occasions the firm took no action. After nearly a year elapsed, Trezza requested a meeting with her supervisor to discuss what she claimed to be the occurrence of continuing acts of harassment. Five days later, Trezza was fired.

Trezza maintained that the firm retaliated against her for requesting the meeting to discuss the harassing conduct of the supervisor and the executive. The court rejected her position, noting that if Dilenschneider was motivated to terminate her for requesting a meeting for the purpose of discussing allegations of sexual harassment, it would have fired her when she first reported the co-worker's harassment. Instead of terminating her at that point, the company took appropriate action to eliminate the harassment. Therefore, Trezza could not demonstrate a connection between her request for the later meeting and her firing.[10] The court simply rejected any connection between the request for a meeting and the firing. Although only five days elapsed between Trezza's request for the meeting and her firing, the short time interval was irrelevant to her retaliation claim.

If the court had viewed the facts of this case from another perspective, it may very well have concluded differently. The company promptly took action when Trezza reported the co-worker's harassment, but not when Trezza called attention to the offensive nature of the conduct of her supervisor and the company executive. No steps were undertaken to stop their conduct. When Trezza requested the meeting, company management was aware that, instead of dealing with the harassing conduct of a low-level co-worker, it would be required to confront allegations of sexual misconduct on the part of a supervisor and a member of its executive staff. This time, the firm reacted negatively to Trezza's request for a meeting. They fired her rather than deal with the problem. Examined from this point of view, the causal connection is apparent. It appears as if the court may have committed error in this case.

The courts are split on whether the timing of the retaliatory act, in and of itself, supports a finding of causation, with some courts demanding additional evidence to support a causal connection. Causality may be demonstrated through reliance on other forms of indirect evidence, such as a sudden change in an employer's positive attitude toward a worker to one that is negative. The connection may also be established by showing an employer gave inconsistent reasons for acting adversely to a worker's interests. Then again, a pattern of employer conduct, such as continuous harassment of the worker, may prove adequate for this purpose. Paula Klimiuk's retaliation charge against ESI Lederle is a case in point.

After she was fired, Klimiuk sued Lederle for retaliation. The company asked the court to dismiss her case inasmuch as a year and a half had elapsed between her initial participation in a protected activity—a complaint filed with the company's human resources department—and her termination. Klimiuk argued, however, that the absence of temporal proximity between her participation in a protected activity and the adverse employment action taken against her was not necessarily determinative. She alleged that after she complained to Lederle's human resources department her supervisors had forced her to work in a hostile environment in that they continuously harassed her. Prior to her complaint, her performance was highly rated and she was continuously promoted. After her complaint, her supervisors ridiculed her at project meetings, rated her performance as unsatisfactory, denied her any further promotions, and eventually terminated her. The court ruled that the evidence of continuous acts of adverse treatment over an eighteen-month period was sufficient to raise a genuine issue of fact as to whether a causal connection existed between her complaint to the human resources department and her termination, and thus her case was not subject to dismissal. In the absence of evidence of temporal proximity, a court may search the intervening period for the presence of retaliatory animus as evidence of the requisite nexus. In this case, the court found it.[11]

One final point: In order to establish a retaliation case, a plaintiff must show that her employer actually knew she had engaged in a protected activity. In one case, the employer proved that at the time its supervisor ordered the termination of the plaintiff, he did not know she had previously complained that she had been sexually harassed. Causation could not be established in those circumstances. The court dismissed the retaliation claim.[12]

CHAPTER FIFTEEN

Sexual Harassment of Men by Women

At one time, men were reluctant to assert workplace sexual harassment claims, fearing to be thought of as lacking in manliness or suffering sexual impotence. They no longer appear to be as reluctant. According to an Equal Employment Opportunity Commission statistical compilation, the number of sexual harassment claims filed by men more than doubled between 1992 and 2001.[1] While a portion of those male claims were alleged against other men (see chapter 16), it has been estimated that at least 55 percent of male harassment claims are asserted against women.[2] Although sexual harassment claims filed by women against men are far more often the subject of legal action, lawsuits filed by men, alleging female harassment, will more than likely continue to increase.

The legal principles reviewed in previous chapters—each analyzed in the context of a sexual harassment claim asserted by a woman against one or more men—are equally applicable to male claims of harassment allegedly committed by females. Title VII does not distinguish between the genders of either the harasser or the victim. In the application of Title VII's provisions, however, some courts have favored distinctions based on gender. For example, a court may require a male claimant to demonstrate a greater degree of severity or pervasiveness of harassing conduct than it requires of a woman alleging harassment against a man. The courts also offer widely divergent views regarding the types of female conduct considered to be sufficiently severe or pervasive to support a male sexual harassment claim.

The context in which male claims of female harassment arise differs from that of female claims of male harassment. Women engaged in acts of sexual harassment generally act with greater subtlety than men. Outrageous acts of physical touching are far less likely to be committed by women, while indirect invitations to a sexual liaison are far more common with female workers. The cases that follow illustrate these differences as well as the divergent judicial approaches to male claims of female harassment.

Kenneth Hull worked for APCOA Standard Parking, an operator of a number of parking garages in Chicago. Clarissa Collins, a manager of one of Standard's facilities, and Hull first met when they were co-workers at one of those garages. After Collins was promoted to the position of manager and assigned to another garage, she asked Hull to transfer to her garage to work under her supervision as a shift manager. She repeatedly called him at home and praised his abilities, stating that she needed him as a replacement for one of her shift managers with whose performance she was dissatisfied. Ultimately, her pleas were successful, as Hull agreed to the transfer.

Hull claimed that as soon as he began working in his new position under Collins's management, she expressed an interest in a sexual relationship with him. On the first three days after the transfer, Collins gave him rides home in her car. On the first day, when they reached the building where Hull's apartment was located, Collins, as Hull later described it, "looked him up and down as if he was some type of beef that she was about to purchase." She questioned him about the floor location of his apartment, and as she turned to look up at the apartment, she pressed up against his chest with her upper body. On the second day when they arrived at Hull's apartment building and had to double-park, Collins remarked that they should find a parking space. Hull interpreted this comment to mean that Collins wanted to accompany him to his apartment. Hull, however, thanked her for the ride and got out of the car. On the third day, as they parted in front of his apartment building, Hull said, "See you tomorrow," and Collins replied, "Okay" and drove off. Hull believed that Collins's behavior on that occasion reflected her disappointment in his lack of interest in her as well as an effort to save face. Subsequently, Hull did not accept her offers of a ride home.

According to Collins, it was not unusual for her to offer garage employees rides home after work. She frequently made such offers when an employee was without a car or had been required to work overtime. She accommodated Hull only because at the time he did not own a car and she lived close by.

Hull claimed that Collins changed her work schedule to coincide with his. On a number of occasions, she asked him out on a date, and on one occasion commented, "I need a good man." On her birthday, she reiterated the remark that she needed a man, and added that she wanted to get married. Hull rejected each of her suggestions and invitations, and informed her he was happy with his personal life. Hull also alleged that Collins continuously and unnecessarily touched him, finding excuses to come into physical contact with him whenever they were in close quarters in the garage premises.

Collins continued to suggest that they associate socially, and Hull continued to reject her overtures. Finally, Collins said to him, "Okay, Ken, if you and I can't go out together, . . . will you at least consider escorting me?" Hull's response again was negative. That was the last occasion Collins directly asked Hull to date her, but she continued to make references to her social activities, intimating that he was welcome to join her.

Over time, Collins began to question Hull's performance as a shift manager. Before his transfer to Collins's garage, Hull's performance evaluation was highly rated, a "4" out of a possible "5". Collins, however, found fault with the manner in which he performed his job functions, and when these faults persisted, Collins fired him. Hull then filed suit against the garage company for quid pro quo sexual harassment, alleging that Collins had made submission to her sexual demands a condition of his employment.

The court set out the standard it would use in determining the adequacy of Hull's allegations. To establish the basic elements of a quid pro quo sexual harassment claim, Hull had to show that (1) he was a member of a protected class, (2) Collins's sexual advances were unwelcome, (3) the harassment was sexually motivated, and (4) after he rejected her advances, he suffered an adverse employment action.

No dispute existed with regard to the first, second, and fourth factors: Hull, as a male, was a member of a protected class; Collins's advances clearly were unwelcome; and Hull's termination, obviously, was an adverse employment action. Standard Parking argued, however, that Hull could not satisfy the third factor because no aspect of Collins's conduct was sexually harassing. Although the court agreed that some components of her behavior fell outside the category of sexual harassment, it pointed to several aspects of her conduct that clearly were sexually harassing:

- Collins told Hull she needed a man and they should go out together.
- She repeatedly asked Hull to date her.

- Collins asked Hull to be her escort.
- She repeatedly asked him to socialize with her.
- She touched him unnecessarily.
- Collins's view of Hull's job performance changed after he rejected her invitations.

The court concluded that Collins's alleged conduct was sexually motivated, that Collins was interested in a sexual relationship with Hull, and that she conditioned his continued employment on his acceding to her sexual demands.[3]

In another case, a claim against a female supervisor was upheld although the male plaintiff offered little evidence of severe or pervasive conduct. In his sexual harassment case against Omega Optical Company, Thomas Dornfeld claimed he was terminated after he failed to respond to the sexual advances of his female supervisor. He alleged that one evening when he and the supervisor were entertaining clients in a local night club, she, without his consent, sat on his lap and rubbed the inside of his thigh for several minutes. He did not respond to her advances. One week later, Dornfeld was fired. At the trial of his harassment case, the supervisor denied she had harassed Dornfeld, but admitted she had sat on his knee on the evening in question. Nothing else happened, she testified. The jury accepted Dornfeld's version of the evening's events and returned a verdict in his favor.[4]

The *Hull* and *Dornfeld* cases were decided in favor of the male plaintiffs, even though the severity and pervasiveness of the alleged female harassing conduct was, at best, questionable. These decisions are typical of a line of cases that does not require evidence of seriously offensive female misconduct to support a verdict for a male plaintiff. The two cases that follow, however, are typical of another line of cases that requires male plaintiffs to submit substantial evidence of materially offensive female conduct before a verdict is rendered in favor of a male plaintiff.

Thomas Bowman, formerly a star college football player, was hired by Shawnee State University to fill the position designated as Coordinator of Sports Studies, a position that fell within the jurisdiction of Dr. Jessica Jahnke, the university's Dean of Education. Bowman claimed that over a period of four years, Jahnke committed numerous acts of sexual harassment, including the following:

- On one occasion, while Jahnke was in Bowman's office, she rubbed his shoulder.

- At a Christmas party Jahnke held in her house, she grabbed Bowman's buttocks. Bowman commented that if someone were to do that to her, she would fire him. Jahnke replied that "she controlled [Bowman's] ass and she would do whatever she wanted with it."
- While Bowman was at Jahnke's house repairing her deck, Jahnke urged him to complete the job quickly so that the two of them could use her whirlpool.
- Jahnke, after inviting Bowman and his girlfriend to swim in her pool, suggested to him that the next time he ought to come unaccompanied and enjoy himself.
- Jahnke called Bowman at his home on various occasions, and although he claimed the calls to be harassing, Jahnke's conversation was neither abusive nor sexual in nature.
- Jahnke wrote a memo chastising Bowman for missing classes he was scheduled to teach even though he had not missed any.
- After emphasizing the importance of teaching every class, Jahnke reprimanded Bowman for not attending a scheduled meeting, although in order for him to have attended the meeting he would have had to miss a class.
- At a meeting in her office, Jahnke, irate because Bowman had lied to her about a class he was teaching at another university, pushed him out of her office.
- A number of other incidents of a nonsexual nature also occurred that Bowman characterized as abusive and harassing.

Matters came to a head when Jahnke informed Bowman that because he had lied to her about teaching a course at another university, she was stripping him of his responsibilities as Coordinator of Sports Studies. The university later rescinded that order, and although Bowman did not suffer any loss of compensation, he sued the university, claiming Jahnke had sexually harassed him.

Was Jahnke's conduct sufficiently severe or pervasive to create a hostile working environment for Bowman? Although Bowman recited a litany of perceived slights and abuses that fell into the category of gender harassment, the court rejected these because Bowman was unable to prove they were based on his status as a male. Thus, all charges of a nonsexual nature, including claims Jahnke chastised Bowman for missing classes and that she reprimanded him for failing to attend a scheduled meeting, were rejected by the court as acts of harassment:

> Bowman has not alleged that Jahnke made a single comment evincing an anti-male bias. . . . Bowman has not shown that the non-sexual conduct he

complains of had anything to do with his gender. While he may have been subject to intimidation, ridicule, and mistreatment, he has not shown that he was treated in a discriminatory manner because of his gender.

The only incidents that the court considered as "arguably" hostile were the incidents involving the shoulder rubbing, the Christmas party, the whirlpool, the swimming pool, and the meeting in Jahnke's office. Although these incidents were serious, in the court's view they were neither severe nor pervasive. Since Bowman's work environment was not hostile, the court rejected his claim.

Did the court correctly decide this issue? For guidance, we return to the sexual harassment suit alleged by Lynn Fall against the South Bend branch of the University of Indiana and its chancellor (see chapter 2). On one occasion, the chancellor put his arms around Fall, kissed her, and forced his hands down her blouse and groped her breasts. Although Fall alleged only this single act of sexual harassment, the court ruled that an incident involving physical assault, such as that experienced by Fall, may sufficiently alter the conditions of the victim's employment and thus create a hostile work environment.[5] Was Jahnke's buttocks-grabbing incident at her Christmas party sufficient to alter the conditions of Bowman's employment? Apparently, the court felt that it was not, since it failed even to refer to the issue in its decision. Thus, in this court's view, a single act of sexual harassment, involving the physical touching of a male by a female, is not sufficiently severe to alter the terms of the male's employment.[6]

Question: Would the court have arrived at the same decision if the gender roles were reversed and a male supervisor had grabbed the buttocks of a female subordinate and told her "he controlled her ass and would do whatever he pleased with it?"

If a male worker is unsuccessful in pleading a sexual harassment claim that involves an incident of intimate physical contact, what hope does he have if he alleges only verbal acts of harassment? Not much, as John Wolf discovered when he sued the Northwest Indiana Symphony Society, alleging that its president and CEO, Cheryl Cox, sexually harassed him. He alleged that immediately after the symphony hired him as its operations manager, Cox began to sexually harass him. Cox made comments such as, "Girls, we have to watch ourselves. We have a man in the office," and that she liked having "muscle in the office." According to Wolf, Cox generally denigrated men and held them to be untrustworthy. She repeatedly assigned him menial tasks such as carrying boxes and assembling office furniture.

Wolf believed that Cox desired to initiate a sexual relationship with him. She informed him she "hadn't been with a man in over six years." She gave him her house keys because, as she put it, he would "never know when [he] might need them." Wolf alleged that on one occasion Cox phoned him at home late at night and told him she was sitting in the dark in her nightgown, in her king-sized bed, and she was alone and afraid. She frequently held his arm when he walked with her to her car at the end of the day. She once reserved a hotel room for him and took a shower in the room before a concert. Wolf interpreted these incidents as invitations to have sex with her, although he admitted that Cox never explicitly requested him to enter into a sexual relationship with him.

Were these acts sufficiently severe or pervasive that a reasonable person would find them hostile or abusive? No, said the court:

> Cox never did make any explicit comment to Wolf inviting him to have a sexual relationship with her. Perhaps Cox crassly let Wolf know that she was lonely, but only someone mysteriously aloof from American popular culture in all its sex-saturated vulgarity would find Cox's sexual overtures, if they even can be identified as such, substantially distressing.

The court then dismissed Wolf's case.[7]

The *Bowman* and *Wolf* cases were decided in favor of the alleged female harassers, even though the severity and pervasiveness of their harassing conduct appear to be beyond question. The courts that decided these cases are representative of those requiring overwhelming evidence of seriously offensive female misconduct. Unlike the courts that decided the *Hull* and *Dornfeld* cases, they represent the other extreme.

One court employed another approach in assessing the severity and pervasiveness of the harassing conduct of a female worker. AT&T temporarily assigned James Casiano, one of its customer representatives, to a trainee position in its education department. Casiano claimed that while he was assigned to the trainee position, Susie Valenzuela, a course administrator in the education department, demeaned him by continuously asking him to bring her food, beverages, and personal items. She also referred to him in the presence of others as "honey" or "James, my honey," and on at least fifteen occasions during a four-month period, initiated sexual conversations, including requests that he engage in sex with her. Valenzuela denied each of Casiano's allegations.

The court had to determine whether Valenzuela's alleged behavior—if it were established—was severe or pervasive. Supposing, the court suggested, the roles of the two antagonists in the case were reversed.

Suppose the trainee was female and the course administrator was male. Then assume the male course administrator calls the female trainee "honey" in the presence of other workers, repeatedly demands that she bring him coffee, cold drinks, snacks, and personal items, frequently initiates discussions of sex-related matters, and propositions her to engage in extramarital sex. In these circumstances, the court asked, could anyone possibly conclude that such behavior would not constitute severe or pervasive sexual harassment? The court answered the question merely by asking it.[8]

If the courts in the *Hull, Dornfeld, Bowman,* and *Wolf* cases had approached the severity and pervasiveness issues in this manner, might not those courts have arrived at more equitable conclusions? Their approaches to the severity and pervasiveness issues would have been more balanced and in line with harassment cases reviewed earlier in the book. Even though the particulars of the harassing conduct of a female worker may differ somewhat from that of a male worker, the criteria used by the courts to assess the severity and pervasiveness must remain the same, regardless of the gender of the harasser or of the victim of the harassment.

If such an approach had been used in Brandon Hosey's sexual harassment case against McDonald's, his claim probably would have been upheld rather than dismissed. Hosey, eighteen years old when he started working at McDonald's as a "crew person," alleged that one of the restaurant's female supervisors made unwanted sexual advances. The female supervisor, also eighteen, on numerous occasions asked him out on dates and made offensive comments, such as "she would like to know what it felt like to have [him] inside her." In addition, there were several incidents of offensive touching, such as buttocks-grabbing.

The court determined that the argument advanced in support of Hosey's claim that the supervisor's offensive conduct was severe as well as pervasive was unpersuasive. It noted it is common for teenagers to ask each other for dates and they often use "unprofessional" language. Moreover, the offensive touching incidents did not occur often enough to be considered severe or pervasive. Hosey's work environment, therefore, was not hostile.[9]

Suppose Hosey was a woman and the supervisor a man. It is doubtful that this court—any court, for that matter—would find evidence of a male supervisor's persistent, unwelcome requests for dates, offensive sexual remarks, and instances of touching, including touching of the female worker's buttocks, anything but severe and pervasive.

Lest the reader conclude that I have been overly critical of the courts that have considered these types of harassment cases, other courts—in addition to the one that decided the *Casiano* case—have demonstrated a sensible approach to the severity and pervasiveness issues. David Papa's harassment case against Domino's Pizza is a case in point. Papa, a store manager, worked under the supervision of Beth Carrier, a Domino corporate area supervisor. While under Carrier's jurisdiction, Papa was promoted twice and nominated "Manager of the Year." During that time, Carrier subjected Papa to numerous sexual advances.

- When Carrier was present in Papa's store, she was accustomed to rubbing his neck and back, and while standing beside him to place her arm around his waist.
- On two occasions, she told him he had a nice ass, that he turned her on, and on another occasion she squeezed his buttocks.
- Carrier knew Papa was experiencing marital difficulties and that he and his wife were separated. She asked him if he was interested in entering into a sexual relationship with her.
- She told him she loved him and cared about him.
- Carrier told Papa she would never treat him like his estranged wife did. "Just think," she said, "you could become a supervisor, and I could stay home and take care of [your son]."
- On one occasion, when Carrier was present in the store, she told him her bra had slipped off and she wanted to know if that turned him on.
- She made it clear he was more than welcome to come live with her.

After Carrier had made one too many advances, Papa ordered her out of his office and threatened to report her conduct to her supervisor. On leaving the store, Carrier told Papa she would "get him." Six days later, Papa was fired, purportedly for violating company policies, but management was unable to substantiate any of the charges levied against him.

The court began its analysis of the case with the general principle that a claimant must show a change in the conditions of his or her employment. Certainly, Carrier's harassment was sufficiently severe to create a hostile and abusive work environment which affected a "term, condition or privilege" of Papa's employment:

> As the Supreme Court explained . . . there is no precise test for determining whether conduct created a hostile and abusive atmosphere. [We have previously provided] guidance however, by stating that "Whether an environment is 'hostile' or 'abusive,' can be determined only by looking at all the circumstances. These may include the frequency of the discriminatory conduct; its severity; whether it is physically threatening or humiliating or

a mere offensive utterance; and whether it unreasonably interferes with an employee's work performance."

Unquestionably, Carrier's conduct was unwelcome to Papa. In fact, he specifically informed her that she was not to touch him. Her behavior embarrassed him and made him feel uncomfortable. His discomfort was so acute that he instructed other employees to remain in his presence whenever Carrier visited the store. The terms and conditions of Papa's employment clearly were altered when it became impossible for him to confer with his supervisor in a normal fashion, but instead had to resort to requiring the presence of other employees so as to prevent her from engaging in physical contact with him. Carrier's conduct was the cause of an adverse change in the terms of Papa's employment. The court ruled that Carrier sexually harassed Papa, and it awarded him damages of nearly $240,000.[10]

In cases of sexual harassment of men by women, the courts need to acquire a more balanced approach. A male victim should not be required to prove conduct that is more severe or pervasive than that underlying female sexual harassment claims. Conversely, a female defendant has every right to expect a court to judge her conduct without reference to her gender. The laws were written to apply equally to male and female claimants and to male and female victims of harassment. Conduct considered severe and pervasive in cases of male harassment of women should also be similarly considered when the gender roles are reversed. On the other hand, a court should not make it a requirement of male plaintiffs to provide evidence of a greater degree of hostile conduct than that required of female plaintiffs.

CHAPTER SIXTEEN

Same-Sex Sexual Harassment

In 1981, Donald Wright, an employee of Methodist Youth Services, a not-for-profit corporation providing social services to minors residing in Illinois, alleged that during the course of his employment his male supervisor made overt homosexual advances toward him, and as a result of his resistance to those advances, he was terminated. Prior to the *Wright* case, no litigant had proposed the notion that same-sex sexual harassment violated Title VII precepts. Without any direct precedent to rely on, the court that considered the *Wright* case turned for guidance to female sexual harassment claims alleging the occurrence of adverse employment actions following the rejection of sexual advances of a male supervisor. Resolution of those cases, as earlier chapters of this book attest, has been predicated on the premise that a male supervisor's sexual demands on a female employee are demands that would not be made of a male employee, and thus are sex discriminatory and actionable under Title VII. The court reasoned in the *Wright* case that since the homosexual supervisor's sexual demands on Wright would not have been made on a female worker, Wright's claim also was based on discrimination on account of sex and thus actionable under Title VII.[1]

Following the *Wright* case, federal district and appellate courts seized on wildly divergent positions regarding the viability of same-sex harassment claims. Some courts rejected the rationale of the *Wright* ruling, holding that same-sex sexual harassment claims are never cognizable under Title VII, while other courts held that those claims are actionable only if the harasser is homosexual. Some courts required the plaintiff to prove that the harassment was motivated by sexual desire, and still others expressed the opinion that workplace sexual harassment is always actionable, regardless of the harasser's sex, sexual orientation, or motivation. It remained for the Supreme Court to sort this out, and an opportunity to do so arose in a case involving same-sex harassment claims asserted by Joseph Oncale against his employer, Sundowner Offshore Services.

Oncale worked as a member of an eight-man crew on an oil platform in the Gulf of Mexico. He alleged that on several occasions, in the presence of the rest of the crew, he was forcibly subjected to sex-related, humiliating actions by a co-worker and two supervisors, and that they sexually assaulted him and threatened him with rape. When Oncale's complaints to supervisory personnel failed to produce remedial action, he resigned. When later asked the reasons for his resignation, Oncale responded, "I felt that if I didn't leave my job, that I would be raped or forced to have sex."

The "bewildering variety of stances" adopted by district and appellate courts prior to the *Oncale* case offered little assistance to the Supreme Court in determining whether workplace sexual harassment violated Title VII in those situations where the harasser and the harassed employee are of the same sex. The court began its analysis with the wording of the statute itself, that it "shall be an unlawful employment practice for an employer . . . to discriminate against any individual . . . because of such individual's . . . sex."[2] This language, the court previously had held, demonstrated a congressional intent to strike at the entire spectrum of discriminatory acts against men and women in employment.[3] Consequently, the courts may not exclude from Title VII coverage *any* workplace conduct based on sex. Since same-sex harassment claims may be based on sex, Congress must have intended Title VII to encompass those claims.

But, Title VII comes into play only in instances of discriminatory conduct. Can it be said that Title VII even recognizes the possibility that a man may discriminate against another man, or that a woman may discriminate against another woman? In responding to this query, the court noted that just as one may not presume an employer will not discriminate against members of his or her own race, one may not presume men will refrain from discriminating against other men, or women against other women.

The court concluded that there was no justification in the statutory language to categorically exclude same-sex harassment claims from the coverage of Title VII. The court emphasized, however, that the plaintiff who asserts a same-sex sexual harassment claim must always prove the harassment occurred because of his or her sex.

Courts and juries have found the inference of discrimination easy to draw in most male-female sexual harassment situations, largely because the challenged conduct involves explicit or implicit proposals of sexual activity, thus making it reasonable to assume those proposals would not have been made to someone of the same sex. But, as we have seen, harassing conduct need not be motivated by sexual desire to support an inference of discrimination on the basis of sex. For example, if a female victim is harassed in such sex-specific and derogatory terms by another woman as to make clear that the harasser is motivated by general hostility to the presence of women in the workplace, then the harasser's action may be discriminatory. Since a female harasser in such instance is not motivated by hostility to the presence of men in the workplace, the female plaintiff may establish that the basis for the harassing conduct is her sex.

The same-sex sexual harassment plaintiff must always prove that the conduct at issue was not merely tinged with offensive sexual connotations, but actually constituted discrimination because of sex. The court emphasized this point, and it cannot be overly underscored here, as the issue arises time and again in same-sex harassment cases.

In its *Oncale* decision, the Supreme Court issued a caveat. Its recognition of liability for same-sex sexual harassment was not intended to transform Title VII into a "general civility code for the American workplace." Title VII does not address genuine but innocent differences in the ways men and women routinely interact with members of the same and of the opposite sex:

> The prohibition of harassment on the basis of sex requires neither asexuality nor androgyny in the workplace; it forbids only behavior so objectively offensive as to alter the "conditions" of the victim's employment. "Conduct that is not severe or pervasive enough to create an objectively hostile or abusive work environment . . . is beyond Title VII's purview. . . ." We have always regarded that requirement as crucial, and as sufficient to ensure that courts and juries do not mistake ordinary socializing in the work-

place—such as male-on-male horseplay or intersexual flirtation—for discriminatory "conditions of employment."

The court further noted that common sense and an appropriate sensitivity to social context will enable courts and juries to distinguish between simple teasing or roughhousing among members of the same sex, and conduct which a reasonable person would find severely hostile or abusive.[4]

Thus, in summary, the court, while leaving the door open to same-sex harassment claims, ruled that this type of claim always requires the plaintiff to show he or she was treated differently because of gender, and it emphasized that ordinary workplace socializing must not be mistaken for conduct that is truly sexually harassing. We now proceed to an examination of issues that have arisen in same-sex sexual harassment cases after the Supreme Court rendered its *Oncale* decision.

Under What Circumstances May Sexual Commentary Provide a Basis for a Same-Sex Sexual Harassment Claim?

While serving as a supervisor for Coastal International Security, Wallace Davis disciplined two subordinate Coastal employees for various on-the-job infractions. Believing they had been unfairly punished, the two workers launched a retaliatory campaign against Davis, which they began by repeatedly slashing his tires. Some time later, one of the workers approached Davis, made a kissing gesture while holding his crotch, and used a phrase describing oral sex. This type of episode was twice repeated, and both workers continued to direct lewd remarks and comments at Davis. More than three years after these events began, Davis filed suit alleging that the behavior of the two workers constituted sexual harassment in violation of Title VII.

The court dismissed Davis's claim, observing that although Davis and the two workers "were fighting like scorpions in a bottle," the behavior of the two workers had nothing to do with sexual harassment. The fact that anatomical references were part of the harassment did not make it sexual harassment. The two workers were motivated by a grudge, not sexual attraction. Obscene expressions uttered by men while conversing with one another often are unrelated to sexual acts to which they make reference. In such circumstances, the plaintiff in a same-sex sexual harassment case must clearly establish that the harassment occurred only because he is a man, that is, because of sex. Davis failed to prove this.[5]

May Sexual Stereotypes Provide the Basis for a Same-Sex Harassment Claim?

Antonio Sanchez worked for Azteca Restaurant Enterprises, an operator of a chain of restaurants in Washington and Oregon. Throughout his tenure at Azteca, Sanchez was subjected to a relentless campaign of insults, name-calling, and vulgarities. Male co-workers and a male supervisor referred to Sanchez as "she" and "her," called him a "faggot" and a "female whore," mocked him for walking "like a woman" and derided him for not having sexual intercourse with a waitress he had befriended. In Sanchez's harassment case alleged against Azteca, the court was confronted with the issue of causation. Was Sanchez harassed because of sex?

Sanchez maintained that the verbal abuse he suffered was based on the perception that he was effeminate and failed to conform to male stereotypes. Thus, he argued, the source of the harassing conduct of his male co-workers and supervisors was his gender. In support of his position, he directed the court's attention to a previous Supreme Court case involving, not a man, but a woman. In that case, the Price Waterhouse accounting firm denied Ann Hopkins a partnership position because a number of male partners perceived her as too aggressive, as "macho," as in need of a "course in charm school," as a "lady using foul language," and as a "tough-talking somewhat masculine hard-nosed manager." After her rejection for partnership, Hopkins's supervisor advised her that she could improve her chances for partnership in the future if she were to "walk more femininely, talk more femininely, dress more femininely, wear makeup, have her hair styled, and wear jewelry." The Supreme Court ruled that an employer who acts on the basis of belief that a woman is overtly masculine, or its evaluation of her otherwise reflects negative stereotypes of female workers in general, acts on the basis of sex.[6]

Sanchez contended that the ruling in the *Hopkins* case applied with equal force to a man harassed for appearing too feminine. The court agreed. The vulgar name-calling was cast in female terms, and the systematic abuse directed at Sanchez reflected co-worker belief that he failed to act as a man should act. The court concluded that this verbal abuse was closely linked to gender, and thus the harassing conduct occurred because of sex.[7]

What Is the Distinction between Same-Sex Sexual Harassment and Horseplay, Simple Teasing, and Roughhousing?

Charles English, a new car sales consultant for a Lexus new and used car dealership, alleged that he was harassed by Joseph Dutchburn, employed by the dealership as a used-car consultant. Dutchburn was well known among his co-workers for lewd comments and annoying conduct, but his colleagues generally tolerated his behavior. When one of them complained to him that his conduct was especially annoying, Dutchburn generally would desist from further behavior of that sort.

At first, English thought Dutchburn's conduct was amusing, but then Dutchburn commenced a daily campaign of lewd behavior directed solely at English. On one occasion, Dutchburn walked up behind English, wrapped his arms around him, and said, "I am going [to lunch] with you." He questioned English about his home life and intimate sexual relations with his wife. After telling English "they needed to bond," Dutchburn approached English, while seated at his desk, and pressed his genitals against English's shoulder. The following day, Dutchburn again asked English if he wanted to bond with him. When English called him a "wacko," Dutchburn retorted, "I love you," winked, and then added, "like a step-son." Dutchburn made other comments of similar ilk, all occurring over a three-day period.

When English filed a same-sex sexual harassment claim against the car dealership, the court regarded the context in which Dutchburn acted as significant as what he said, noting that in the *Oncale* case the Supreme Court had emphasized that in same-sex harassment cases the court must carefully consider the social context in which particular behavior occurs. The Supreme Court had used this example:

A professional football player's working environment is not severely or pervasively abusive . . . if the coach smacks him on the buttocks as he heads onto the field—even if the same behavior would reasonably be experienced as abusive by the coach's secretary (male or female) back at the office.[8]

The circumstances in which Dutchburn cavorted was more of the nature of a men's locker room than a business environment. His antics transpired in the car dealership's showroom, populated mostly by men, and his behavior was known to all those working at the car dealership. He occasionally enlisted other workers to carry out obnoxious pranks, and some co-workers encouraged Dutchburn's behavior toward English. Under these circumstances, the court concluded that English could not prove that his tormentor acted because of sex:

> Reviewing the "constellation of surrounding circumstances," and applying basic "common sense," [citing the *Oncale* opinion] the record reveals that Dutchburn's conduct directed toward English and other co-workers, amounted to expressions of juvenile provocation and offensive behavior driven by Dutchburn's desire to tease or humiliate English and others. But English does not provide sufficient evidence for a reasonable jury to infer that such conduct was driven by an unlawful design such as gender discrimination.[9]

It is not unusual for a court to take into account the circumstances in which sexually harassing conduct surfaces. In chapter 2, we reviewed Lynn Fall's sexual harassment case involving allegations of harassment committed by the chancellor of the South Bend branch of Indiana University. In that case, the court observed that the social context in which the chancellor's offensive acts were committed was a significant factor that should be considered. The chancellor did not approach Fall in a social setting or out in public where she could have more readily deterred or escaped his physical advances. Instead, his attack occurred behind closed doors within the confines of his office, and thus concealed from public view.[10] If Dutchburn's conduct had taken place in a much less public setting, the court might very well have concluded that he acted because of sex. But, due to the public arena atmosphere in which it took place, the court characterized his behavior as "horseplay."

Does the Harassment of a Worker on Account of His or Her Sexual Orientation Violate Title VII?

In its *Oncale* decision, the Supreme Court did not suggest that male harassment of other males or female harassment of other females *always* violates Title VII. Rather, as has been stressed here, the court insisted that every victim of same-sex harassment must demonstrate he or she was harassed because of his or her sex. The critical issue "is whether members of one sex are exposed to disadvantageous terms or conditions of employment to which members of the other sex are not exposed." Thus, when postal worker Dwayne Simonton, a homosexual, sued the Postal Service for sexual harassment, alleging that his co-workers harassed him, not because he was a man but because of his sexual orientation, the court dismissed his claims.

Simonton tried to resurrect his case with the argument that the abuse he suffered was akin to discrimination based on sexual stereotypes, which under the *Price Waterhouse v. Hopkins* rationale may rise to the level of discrimination based on sex. He maintained that the *Hopkins* theory of sexual stereotyping should apply to his case, since he was targeted for harassing conduct on account of his failure to conform to gender norms. But no evidence in the court record indicated that Simonton had behaved in a stereotypical feminine manner or that the harassment he endured was based on anything other than his sexual orientation. If Simonton had available to him evidence of sexual stereotyping, he might have emerged victorious.[11]

Although in some cases a homosexual plaintiff may successfully establish the source of his harassment as his failure to conform to gender norms, in other cases the nature of the harassment will identify the source as his sexual orientation. As an example, such statements as "everyone knows you're a faggot," or "you are as queer as a three dollar bill" clearly target the plaintiff's sexual orientation rather than his sex.[12]

In another case, workers maligned a colleague because they perceived him to be a homosexual and suspected that he desired some sort of physical intimacy with them. Their stereotypical comments expressed their hostility to his homosexuality: they did not indicate an intent to harass him because of his gender. Again, in these circumstances, sexual orientation was the source of the harassment, and thus the workers' harassing conduct was not actionable under Title VII.[13]

Until September 2002, courts barred claimants alleging harassment on account of sexual orientation from validly asserting a same-sex sexual harassment claim under Title VII. At that time, however, the U.S. Court of Appeals for the Ninth Circuit—the federal appellate court having jurisdiction over appeals from federal district courts sitting in nine western states—held that an employee's sexual orientation is irrelevant for purposes of Title VII. The issue arose in litigation involving Medina Rene and his employer, the MGM Grand Hotel, located in Las Vegas.

Rene, an openly gay man, worked for the hotel as a butler on its twenty-ninth floor, where he served wealthy, high-profile, and famous guests for whom the twenty-ninth floor was reserved. All the other butlers on the floor, as well as their supervisor, were men. Rene provided evidence that his supervisor and several of his fellow butlers harassed him by whistling and blowing kisses at him, calling him "sweetheart," telling him crude jokes, and forcing him to look at pictures of naked men having sex. They also caressed and hugged him, grabbed his crotch and poked their fingers through his clothing into his anus. When Rene was asked what he believed motivated this harassing behavior, he responded that he was harassed because he was gay.

The lower court rejected Rene's case, relying on the law as it then stood. "Title VII's prohibition of sex discrimination applies only [to] discrimination on the basis of gender and is not extended to include discrimination based on sexual preference." Rene appealed to the Ninth Circuit Court of Appeals.

The Ninth Circuit court ruled that the conduct Rene suffered was so severe and pervasive as to constitute an abusive working environment. The conduct of his co-workers and supervisor was clearly of a sexual nature. "Rene's tormentors did not grab his elbow or poke their fingers in his eye. They grabbed his crotch and poked their fingers in his anus." In such circumstances, the sexual orientation of the victim of the harassing behavior is irrelevant:

> The premise of a sexual touching hostile work environment claim is that the conditions of the work environment have been made hostile "because of . . . sex." . . . The physical attacks to which Rene was subjected, which targeted body parts clearly linked to his sexuality, were "because of . . . sex." Whatever else those attacks may, or may not, have been "because of" has no legal consequence. . . . Why the harassment was perpetrated . . . is beside the point.

The offensive conduct was sexual and it was discriminatory. Since this is precisely what Title VII forbids, Rene's sexual orientation was not a relevant factor for the court to consider.[14]

Since September 2002, claims asserted by gays or lesbians that they have been sexually harassed because of their sexual orientation may be cognizable under Title VII precepts provided they are able to establish that they were subjected to offensive same-sex physical conduct of a sexual nature, that is, offensive conduct that is clearly discriminatory and forbidden by Title VII. In othe circumstances, such claims will be denied. Ultimately, the Supreme Court will be required to resolve the issue whether sexual orientation, in and of itself, is a valid basis for a Title VII sexual harassment claim.

Does the Conduct of a Worker Who Harasses Both Men and Women Violate Title VII Principles?

Steven and Karen Holman, husband and wife, worked in the maintenance department of the Indiana Department of Transportation under the supervision of Gale Uhrich. Each claimed that Uhrich sexually harassed them. Karen Holman alleged that Uhrich touched her body, was accustomed to standing too close to her, asked her to go to bed with him, and made sexist remarks in her presence. Steven Holman alleged that Uhrich asked him to engage in sexual conduct with him.

Since Title VII was enacted to eliminate workplace discrimination, inappropriate conduct inflicted on both sexes, or inflicted regardless of sex, is not conduct that discriminates on the basis of sex, and thus does not fall within the ambit of the statute. The bisexual or "equal opportunity" harasser does not treat one sex better or worse than the other, but treats them similarly. Bisexual behavior, such as Uhrich's, does not discriminate on the basis of sex. As a result, the unfortunate objects of such harassment, such as the Holmans, are without a Title VII remedy.[15]

A gay male worker and a lesbian female worker, both working under the same supervisor, charged him with sexually harassing them both. They attempted to avoid the bisexual harasser dilemma by alleging that the supervisor couched his harassment in terms of their homosexuality, arguing that since he treated employees that he thought were homosexual differently than he treated employees he thought were heterosexual, that his conduct was based on sex. But in pleading their case in this fashion, they ran afoul of the rule of law that harassment on the basis of sexual orientation is not harassment on account of gender. The court dismissed their claims.[16]

Can a Plaintiff Establish a Sexual Harassment Claim If the Conduct Complained of Is Equally Offensive to Both Sexes?

In a case decided before *Oncale* (but the outcome of which would not have changed had it been decided after that decision was rendered),

Kimberley Fair, associate director of administration for the nonprofit Guiding Eyes for the Blind, charged the corporation's executive director, Martin Yablonski, with sexual harassment. Fair contended that Yablonski continuously engaged in conversations about his homosexuality and other topics pertaining to sexual preference.

- Yablonski referred to a male acquaintance as a "bitch" and complained that he had the gall to have sexual relations with a woman.
- He challenged Fair's support for the pope because of his views on homosexuality.
- He advised Fair not to drink a particular brand of orange juice on account of the antihomosexuality remarks made by a spokesperson for that product.
- He mentioned attending an event with Fred, his lover.

Fair's reluctance to converse with Yablonski on sexual matters such as these led to a deterioration in their working relationship, eventually culminating in her termination. Yablonski replaced her with a man. Fair claimed she was unfairly discharged because of her refusal to discuss sexual matters with her superior.

Fair presented a weak case, as the severity of Yablonski's conduct was questionable. But she faced an even more serious problem. At the foundation of a sexual harassment case is the claim that a worker, because of his or her sex, was singled out for adverse treatment. If the conduct of the harasser is equally offensive to both sexes, then the worker is unable to claim to have been singled out because of sex. Fair presented no evidence suggesting that Yablonski's comments were any more offensive to a heterosexual woman than to a heterosexual man, and thus she was unable to show she was treated differently on account of her sex. The court dismissed her case.[17]

In another case, after a school principal sent letters, containing offensive sexual content, to female and male school personnel, two female teachers sued the school district for sexual harassment. The court later ruled that since the principal sent offensive materials to both men and women, the workplace, while offensive, was not any more offensive or hostile to women than to men. Inasmuch as the female plaintiffs were exposed to terms and conditions of employment that were not any more disadvantageous than those extended to the male recipients of the letters, they were not entitled to relief under title VII.[18]

What Type of Evidence Is Probative in Demonstrating That Sex Was the Basis for Acts of Same-Sex Harassment?

Scott Preston worked for the City of Danville in Kentucky. Over a period of several years, Preston's supervisor, Ralph Greer, gave him gifts, loaned him money, purchased him groceries, bought him meals, and made his car payments. Preston's co-workers teased and taunted him, asserting that Greer was baiting him and treating him favorably only because he wanted to have sex with him. Ultimately, Greer sexually assaulted Preston, but when he reported the incident to another supervisor, Greer denied the attack, and the city undertook no action. Co-workers continued to taunt Preston and accused him of being Greer's lover.

When Preston later sued for same-sex sexual harassment, the city asked the court to dismiss his lawsuit on the ground that the co-worker harassment had not been occasioned by Preston's gender, but rather on account of personality conflicts as well as miscellaneous work issues. But the court rejected the city's position. Inasmuch as the co-worker taunts had centered on assertions of homosexual activity and allegations that Preston had engaged in sexual acts with Greer, the court ruled that Preston had offered sufficient evidence to show the source of the harassment was his sex.

But another issue remained—did Preston establish that he was forced to work in a hostile environment? The evidence of teasing and taunting alone was insufficiently severe to establish a hostile work environment, but, when combined with evidence of Greer's sexual assault and the subsequent taunts of a sexual nature, there appeared to be little question that Preston had offered sufficient proof of hostility to defeat the city's motion to dismiss his case.[19]

While Preston had more than sufficient evidence to convince the court that his harassment occurred because of sex, Estelle West had little or no probative evidence to offer the court to support her same-sex harassment claim. West, employed as a secretary for Dr. Joyce Shriver at Mt. Sinai Medical Center in New York City, alleged that Dr. Shriver repeatedly victimized her with sexual advances. Although Shriver never directly propositioned her, West claimed she often did nice things for her, such as buy her yogurt, offered to take her to the theater, brought her food, and contrary to hospital regulations, allowed her to eat at her desk. West also alleged that Shriver occasionally inquired about her weekend plans and sat close to her when others were not present. West interpreted these gestures as sexual advances.

The court observed that West's complaints were totally devoid of even a hint of sexual innuendo:

> Even if there were evidence suggesting that Dr. Shriver is homosexual [which there was not] it is hard to see how a [jury] could conclude that Dr. Shriver's alleged actions were anything other than simple friendly gestures, not veiled sexual advances. . . . The complete lack of sexual innuendo in Dr. Shriver's alleged conduct, coupled with the lack of evidence that she is homosexual, leaves no basis whatsoever . . . to conclude that Dr. Shriver's actions were motivated by [West's] sex.

The court then dismissed West's complaint.[20]

The cases reviewed here disclose that same-sex harassment claims are most likely to succeed in two sets of circumstances. First, where the evidence points to a harasser who sexually desires the victim, such as when a gay or lesbian supervisor treats a same-sex subordinate in a sexually charged manner, it is reasonable to infer that the harasser acts in that fashion because of the victim's sex. Second, when it is established that the harassment was motivated by a belief that the victim did not conform to gender stereotypes, the courts are likely to attribute the victim's sex as the basis for the harasser's conduct. The advancement of other types of same-sex claims are less likely to succeed.

Same-sex sexual harassment cases appear with increasing frequency.[21] But, as we have seen, current court limitations regarding the scope of Title VII have severely restricted the applications of its protections to workers subjected to conduct not clearly directed against one gender rather than the other. Workers finding themselves in those circumstances must await less restrictive interpretations of the statute, or legislative amendments expanding Title VII to include that type of harassment claim.

CHAPTER SEVENTEEN

The Role of Arbitration in Sexual Harassment Cases

Certain procedural matters need to be reviewed before we consider the role arbitration plays in sexual harassment cases. The litigation of a Title VII sexual harassment case begins with the filing of a discrimination charge with the Equal Employment Opportunity Commission (EEOC). After Congress adopted the Civil Rights Act of 1964, barring discrimination in employment by reason of race, color, sex, national origin, and religion, it assigned primary enforcement of the statute to the newly created EEOC. At the time, Congress anticipated that nearly all Title VII discrimination charges would be resolved administratively in EEOC proceedings, but that has not proved to be the case. Workers file thousands of Title VII employment discrimination cases each year in federal and state courts across the country. Each of these cases, however, begins with a charge filed with the EEOC.

An EEOC investigation of a discrimination charge generally culminates in one of two findings: (1) a determination that reason exists to believe that the worker has been subjected to discriminatory conduct (a "for cause" finding), or (2) a determination that no reason exists to believe the employer has engaged in such conduct (a "no cause" finding). A finding of "no cause" effectively terminates the EEOC's involvement in the worker's charge. Conversely, a finding of "for cause" leads to further EEOC action, such as conciliation and settlement.

The EEOC reported it "resolved" 15,792 sexual harassment charges in 2002. It disposed of 47 percent of those charges with a "no cause" finding and dismissed another 33 percent for various other reasons. Thus, 80 percent of the harassment charges resolved that year were dismissed at an early stage of the EEOC's administrative process. Of the remaining 20 percent, approximately 11 percent were settled with employers before the EEOC made a "for cause" or a "no cause" determination, and the remaining 9 percent (1,463 of 15,792) were granted a "for cause" determination. Only 455 of these charges were successfully conciliated.[1] These statistics reflect the shortcomings of the EEOC process. Since very few workers achieve success at the administrative level, those who wish to proceed further with their claims must turn to the courts.

Although Congress intended for the major portion of Title VII employment discrimination claims to be resolved administratively, it nevertheless granted the EEOC the authority to initiate judicial proceedings on behalf of discrimination claimants. Even though the EEOC has the option of filing suit on behalf of a claimant, it rarely does, generally leaving it to the claimant to proceed in the courts. Six months after a charge is filed with the EEOC, a worker may demand a right-to-sue notice, and the EEOC must comply and issue the notice, even if it has not completed its investigation or even if it has concluded its investigation with a "no cause" determination. The issuance of the right-to-sue notice divests the EEOC of jurisdiction over the charge and provides the worker with entry to the judicial system.

As a practical matter, workers who believe they have been victimized by discriminatory employment conduct must pursue their claims in the courts, with little or no direct assistance from the EEOC. Consequently, more than 95 percent of the employment discrimination cases adjudicated in the federal courts are shepherded through the court system by attorneys retained by workers.[2] For the sexually harassed worker, litigation is often the best if not the only route to pursue to attain the recovery of damages for the suffering endured at the hands of a harasser.

The basic elements of proof in litigated sexual harassment cases have been set forth in previous chapters. The plaintiff must prove she was the subject of unwelcome harassing acts, such as sexual advances, requests for sexual favors, or other conduct of a sexual nature (see chapter 3) or conduct exhibiting a bias against women (see chapter 7); that these acts were sufficiently severe or pervasive to alter the terms and conditions of her employment, thus creating a discriminatorily hostile or abusive working environment (see chapter 4); and that a legal basis exists for holding her employer liable for the harassment (see chapters 9, 10, 11, and 12).

As the cases in the next chapter demonstrate, plaintiffs who successfully litigate their cases in the courts can reasonably expect to attain a
significant measure of relief. Jurors sitting in employment discrimination
cases appear most concerned with the element of fairness and thus identify with the unfairly treated worker. In harassment cases, jurors tend to
view acts of sexual harassment from the perspective of the victim rather
than from that of the harasser. As a consequence, claimants are at times
made the recipients of huge damage awards. Thus it is not surprising that
employers abhor jury trials and will do almost anything to avoid them.
On the other hand, attorneys representing harassment claimants, recog-
nizing the advantages to be attained, nearly always insist on jury trials
for their clients. Unfortunately for harassed workers, employers have
available to them the means of excluding juries from ruling on worker
claims. In effect, employers possess the power to diminish, if not extin-
guish, the role of the judicial system in the resolution of employment discrimination claims.

An employer may avoid a jury determination of its employment disputes by requiring its employees, at the time of their hiring, to sign
agreements containing language such as, "I agree to arbitrate any dispute, claim, or controversy that may arise between me and the company
during the course of my employment." This type of agreement, commonly referred to as a "compulsory" or "predispute" arbitration agreement, bars an employee from litigating employment disputes, including
sexual harassment claims, in the courts. With this type of agreement in
hand, an employer may compel a worker to process her harassment
claim in an arbitral rather than a judicial forum, and if a worker initiates litigation in the courts in violation of that agreement, the employer
may obtain a court order compelling the worker to submit her claim to
arbitration, thus assuring the company that no jury will ever hear the
worker's case.

Workers have argued that compulsory or predispute agreements to arbitrate employment discrimination claims are inconsistent with the statutory scheme contemplated by Congress in enacting Title VII. Prior to
1991, the courts generally agreed, ruling that a worker could not waive
his or her rights to litigate civil rights claims. But in that year the
Supreme Court changed course, ruling that no inconsistency existed between predispute agreements to arbitrate employment discrimination
claims and the legal and social issues fostered by the federal employment
discrimination laws.[3]

Once given Supreme Court approval, predispute arbitration agreements quickly became the employers' most favored method of resolving employment disputes. One plaintiff's lawyer labeled this unfolding change as "one of the most pernicious developments in employment law today,"[4] and most workers' counsel agree. For those sexually harassed, arbitration is not a viable alternative to judicial resolution of their complaints.

For a number of reasons, compulsory, predispute arbitration is an unacceptable method for resolving discrimination complaints. A predispute arbitration agreement is basically nonnegotiable. The worker is required, as a condition of employment, or as a condition to remaining employed, to consent to the arbitration of all disputes occurring during the course of the employment relationship. Provisions for arbitration appear (or sometimes are buried) in employment agreements, employment application forms, and employee handbooks. In all events, the worker is presented with a take-it-or-leave-it situation: "Agree to arbitration, or you don't get the job." Negotiation of these terms is not allowed; the worker must accept them, or be denied employment.

By agreeing to the arbitration of employment disputes in return for a job, a worker waives her statutory right to a judicial determination of any Title VII discrimination claim she may later assert. But the law clearly provides that a waiver of a statutory right is valid only if it is made *knowingly* and *voluntarily*. When the choice is between the acceptance of arbitration as a method of resolving future disputes and the relinquishment of a job offer, the worker's agreement to arbitrate should never be considered voluntary. It defies common sense to argue otherwise. In agreeing to arbitrate employment disputes, the worker consents to the resolution of disputes that have not yet occurred and the nature and identity of which are purely conjectural. Such an agreement cannot be considered as having been made knowingly. Yet worker agreements to arbitrate future disputes are routinely enforced by the courts.

An unemployed job applicant cannot afford to be overly concerned about problems that may never occur during the employment relationship. First and foremost, the worker needs a job. Thus, in the hiring process, the possibility of future employment disputes is not a relevant factor for most workers. Freedom of contract in those circumstances is a fiction. The enforcement of an agreement to arbitrate—an agreement imposed on a worker as a condition of employment—cannot be justified merely by arguing that the worker must have acted voluntarily and knowingly, else she would not have agreed to arbitrate. Nonetheless, employers, aided by the Supreme Court, have found a near fail-proof method of avoiding jury trials of cases involving workers' allegations of employment discrimination, including allegations of sexual harassment.

The arbitral forum lacks the protections of the judicial forum. In her or his lifetime, a worker more likely than not will be involved only once in an employment dispute requiring resolution by a third party, such as an arbitrator. Employers, however, who require their workers to submit disputes to arbitration, appear before the same arbitrators time and again. Because an arbitrator is paid for his services, he wants to be selected for future arbitrations, and an employer is far more likely to nominate an arbitrator who has previously decided in its favor. Inasmuch as it is unlikely that the worker will appear more than once in an arbitrated dispute, an arbitrator has no reason to be troubled about the possibility that the worker may fail to nominate him in the future. In these circumstances, the worker is justifiably concerned that an arbitrator may be biased in favor of the employer. At the very least, an appearance of a conflict of interest exists in these circumstances.

Some years ago, when arbitration was first offered as an alternative to the judicial resolution of disputes, it gained favor with the business community, primarily because it was commonly believed that business disputes could be more readily resolved by arbitrators familiar with the particulars of the industry in which disputes arose. The knowledge and experience of the arbitrators were driving forces behind the arbitral concept. But arbitrators are totally inexperienced in the nuances of the laws barring employment discrimination, and they are especially unprepared to render judgment in matters involving claims of sexual harassment. The basic, underlying reason and motivation for the arbitration of these disputes, therefore, is absent.

The arbitral forum lacks another basic protection offered by the judicial forum. When an arbitrator makes a mistake, the error probably will remain uncorrected, as the judicial review of arbitration decisions is severely limited by law. A case in point involved Rosalind Smith's sexual harassment claims against her employer, PSI Services. Smith claimed she was subjected to the sexually harassing acts of a co-worker and later discharged in retaliation for complaining about them to her supervisors. Her harassment claim was subject to a provision in her employment contract providing for the arbitration of all employment disputes arising between Smith and the company. The arbitrator designated to rule on Smith's claim found several instances of inappropriate behavior on the part of the co-worker, including:

- asking Smith for a "one night stand,"
- making vulgar and sexually suggestive comments about her body,
- asking her whether her fiancé sexually satisfied her,
- peering down her blouse, and
- writing her a menacing note.

The arbitrator rejected Smith's harassment claim on the ground that since she offered no evidence demonstrating she had been subjected to harassing acts on a daily basis, the co-worker's harassing behavior could not be considered as either severe or pervasive. When Smith appealed the arbitrator's decision, a federal court judge agreed with her that the arbitrator had erred, that sexual harassment need not occur on a daily basis to be considered severe or pervasive. In fact, as we have seen, a single act of harassing conduct may, in some circumstances, be considered severe and pervasive. The highly offensive behavior attributed to the co-worker was clearly sufficient to satisfy the tests of severity and pervasiveness.

The arbitrator clearly misapplied the law, and her error, if she had been a judge sitting in a judicial forum, was the type an appellate court would have been compelled to correct. But the arbitrator's error was insufficient to require a reversal of her decision rejecting Smith's claim. As the court noted, a judicial reversal of an arbitrator's decision is justified under the law only if the decision is rendered "in manifest disregard of the law."

"Manifest disregard of the law" is the judicially created ground for vacating arbitration awards. It contemplates more than the commission of an error of fact or of law. Its application is reserved for situations where an arbitrator recognizes a clearly governing legal principle and then proceeds to ignore it or pay it little attention. Misapplication of the law to the facts, in and of itself, does not constitute a manifest disregard of the law. In the *Smith* case, the court ruled that the arbitrator, although she wrongly applied the tests for severity and pervasiveness, had not acted in manifest disregard of the law. Although she applied the test wrongly, she did not disregard it. The court upheld the arbitrator's decision rejecting Smith's harassment claim.[5]

Even though the arbitrator was clearly wrong, the court was barred under the "manifest disregard of the law" concept from correcting the mistake. If Smith had been able to litigate her claim in the courts, she would have achieved a different result. This provides Smith with little solace; her arbitration claim was rejected and she had no further recourse.

Arbitration favors the employer in another respect. Prehearing discovery in arbitral proceedings is considerably more limited than the pretrial discovery available in court cases. Arbitral procedures generally allow only minimal discovery, while the Federal Rules of Civil Procedure provide for very broad discovery. To the extent that the worker's discovery is limited, the probability of success is reduced. Denying a worker access to an employer's investigative reports and its other documents and records may materially undermine the development of her case. Under these circumstances, the employer will be free to use its own documents for its own advantage, while preventing the worker from obtaining documents that may support her position. As an example, the personnel records of other female employees, sexually abused by the same supervisor that harassed the plaintiff, could significantly strengthen a harassment claim, especially in those instances where the harasser denies that he committed acts of harassment against the plaintiff. In a judicial proceeding, the court would more than likely order these records made available to the worker. In an arbitral proceeding, their availability to the worker is far less likely.

In the federal court system, the appointment of a magistrate judge to oversee pretrial discovery gives both the worker and the employer a measure of assurance that discovery will be conducted fairly, while affording both parties discovery broad enough in scope to allow them to properly develop their cases. Nothing of a similar nature exists in the arbitral system. Arbitrators, wholly inexperienced in the area of employment discrimination, not having the slightest inkling of the importance of discovery in the preparation of a sexual harassment case, are particularly ill-suited to determine the appropriate scope of discovery in the pre-arbitration hearing process. The inability of an arbitrator to serve a meaningful role in this process redounds to the benefit of the employer, while materially undermining the worker's ability to present a viable case.

The arbitral process, as it now exists, is governed by few rules and standards. Rules and standards serve the purpose of guaranteeing fairness to both sides to a dispute. Without meaningful rules of procedure, the potential for abuse by the stronger party is considerable. The arbitral process cannot substitute for the judicial process in guaranteeing fair procedures.

In 1997, the EEOC announced it was firmly opposed to the enforcement of arbitration agreements imposed on workers as a condition of employment. It felt compelled to announce this policy, publicly and formally, since it noted an increasing number of employers were requiring workers, as a condition of gaining employment, to give up their rights to pursue employment discrimination claims in court, and to agree instead to the resolution of these disputes through arbitration.

The EEOC prefaced its policy statement by reminding the public that federal civil rights laws, including the laws prohibiting discrimination in employment, have played a unique role in American jurisprudence: "They flow directly from core Constitutional principles, and this nation's history testifies to their necessity and profound importance." The EEOC then stated that an analysis of the mandatory arbitration of rights, guaranteed by these laws, must "be squarely based in an understanding of the history and purpose of these laws."

While the EEOC is the primary federal agency responsible for enforcing the employment discrimination laws, it recognizes that the courts have been vested with the final responsibility for statutory enforcement, through the interpretation of the statutes while adjudicating claims. In its policy statement, the EEOC enumerated the reasons why that responsibility must remain with the courts:

- Many of the principles governing the application of these laws have been developed through judicial interpretations and case precedents. Without the courts, doctrines essential to free the workplace of unlawful discrimination will not continue to develop.
- The courts are public bodies; the exercise of judicial authority is subject to public scrutiny. When courts fail to apply these laws in accordance with public values, they are subject to correction by higher courts and by Congress.
- The courts also play a critical role in preventing violations of the law. Court decisions give guidance to those covered by the laws, thus enhancing voluntary compliance with them. By issuing orders and decisions, later made known to the public, the courts identify violators of the law and their conduct. "As has been illustrated time and again, the risks of negative publicity and blemished business reputation can be powerful influences on behavior."
- The courts cannot fulfill their enforcement responsibilities if workers do not have access to the courts. Individual workers act as "private attorneys general" in bringing claims to the courts, serving not only in their own private interest, but also serving as instruments of deterrence of would-be violators of the statutes.

The EEOC expressed its concern that predispute arbitration "privatizes" the enforcement of the employment discrimination laws. The nature of the arbitral process allows for minimal public accountability of arbitrators, since they answer to the private parties to the dispute, but not to the public. The arbitrator is part of a system of self-government, created by and for private parties. Because the decisions of arbitrators are private, employers are not held publicly accountable for their violations of the law, and this lack of public disclosure weakens deterrence of further violations. The EEOC also observed that the arbitral process does not allow for the development of the law. Arbitration decisions are usually not written and in any event are not made public. As a result, there is virtually no opportunity for the courts to correct errors of statutory interpretation.

The EEOC confirmed long-held concerns of employment lawyers. Arbitrators are often biased in favor of the employer, discovery is unduly limited, and arbitration is imposed on workers simply because employers stand a greater chance of success in arbitration than in a court before a jury.

The EEOC concluded that further use of arbitration agreements as a condition of employment should be barred, because it harms both the civil rights of the claimant and the public interest in eradicating discrimination:

> Those whom the law seeks to regulate should not be permitted to exempt themselves from federal enforcement of civil rights laws. No one should be permitted to deprive civil rights claimants of the choice to vindicate their statutory rights in the courts—an avenue of redress determined by Congress to be essential to enforcement.[6]

Although workers have forcefully argued that compulsory arbitration denies them their civil rights under Title VII and the other antidiscrimination statutes, and the EEOC has announced its opposition to the use of arbitration to resolve employment discrimination disputes, the Supreme Court nevertheless recently reaffirmed its decision upholding the validity of predispute arbitration agreements.[7] Unless Congress takes action to amend Title VII to bar employers from requiring workers to submit employment discrimination disputes to arbitration, employers will undoubtedly continue to require mandatory arbitration as a condition of employment. However, all hope has not faded. In certain circumstances a worker may still be able to have her claim processed in the courts. We turn now to cases where plaintiffs have successfully avoided arbitration.

In its 1991 decision empowering employers to require arbitration of employment disputes, the Supreme Court noted that a worker who submits her claims to arbitration does not relinquish her rights provided her by the civil rights statutes, and so long as it is possible for the worker to achieve vindication in the arbitral forum, the goals of those statutes are not frustrated. Plaintiffs have relied on this language to support the argument that an arbitration agreement that fails to provide access to the rights and remedies of Title VII is not enforceable. Those were the circumstances in the gender and sexual harassment case filed by Susan Rosenberg against Merrill Lynch.

Rosenberg, at the time she entered Merrill Lynch's training program for financial consultants, was required to complete and sign a standardized registration form generally required of employees in the securities industry. That form included a commitment "to arbitrate any dispute, or claim or controversy that may arise between me and my firm . . . that is required to be arbitrated under the rules, constitutions, or by-laws of the organizations [listed below]." Among the organizations listed was the New York Stock Exchange.

Later in her employment, Rosenberg charged her supervisor with having sexually harassed her, and she also accused Merrill Lynch of having committed other sex discriminatory acts. When she filed suit against the firm, Merrill Lynch asked the court to compel Rosenberg to submit her claims to arbitration, arguing that the rules of the New York Stock Exchange required her claims to be resolved in arbitration rather than in the courts. Indeed, at the time, the New York Stock Exchange rules stated that *all* employment disputes were to be arbitrated. But no one had explained to Rosenberg that the standardized registration form, signed at the time of her hiring, encompassed disputes relating to her employment with the firm. The words "employment disputes" did not appear in the registration form. It merely referred to "any dispute, claim or controversy." Although the Stock Exchange rules specifically referred to "employment disputes," Merrill Lynch had failed to provide Rosenberg with a copy of those rules before she was required to sign the standard registration form through which she agreed to arbitration. Furthermore, Merrill Lynch did not advise Rosenberg that management interpreted the registration form's requirement to arbitrate "disputes, claims and controversies" to also include employment discrimination claims. Management had been totally silent in that regard.

The court ruled that since the registration form failed to define the range of claims subject to arbitration, except in that it referred to the rules of the New York Stock Exchange, a copy of those rules should have been furnished Rosenberg before she was required to sign the form. In fact, the form explicitly contemplated that Merrill Lynch would provide

Rosenberg with knowledge of the Stock Exchange rules. The court, therefore, denied Merrill Lynch's motion to compel Rosenberg to arbitrate her charges against the firm and her case then proceeded to be litigated in the courts.[8]

As noted, by consenting to the arbitration of a statutory claim, such as a claim asserted under Title VII, a claimant does not thereby waive her substantive rights afforded by the statute; she only agrees to submit her claims for resolution in an arbitral rather than in a judicial forum. Accordingly, prior to requiring an employment discrimination claimant to proceed in the arbitral forum, a court will closely examine both the wording of a predispute arbitration agreement and the means of its implementation. If any evidence exists indicating that the claimant will be denied access to the rights and remedies provided by Title VII, the court, rather than compelling the arbitration of those claims, will order them to proceed in the judicial forum. As an example, one court ruled that if a claimant were to be held responsible for the payment of substantial arbitrator fees or other costs, ordinarily not incurred in a judicial forum, arbitration would not be compelled, since in those circumstances arbitration does not provide the claimant with an effective mechanism for the vindication of her Title VII rights.[9]

In one case, at the time of her hiring, a worker was required to sign an agreement that read:

> I agree to the grievance and arbitration provisions set forth in the [employee manual]. I understand that I am waiving my right to a trial, including a jury trial, in state or federal court of the class of disputes specifically set forth in the grievance and arbitration provisions [of the employee manual].

The employee manual specifically included Title VII disputes. When the worker charged the company with sex discrimination, the court refused to require her to arbitrate her claim. Why? Because the agreement to arbitrate was worded solely in terms of the worker's obligations: "I agree," "I understand," and "I am waiving." Although the worker was obligated under the agreement to proceed only in arbitration, the employer was not. The agreement contained no commitment of the employer to be bound by arbitration. A one-sided agreement to arbitrate is not enforceable.[10]

Another worker agreed to arbitrate employment disputes, but in order to invoke the arbitration procedures mandated by the employer, he had to pay one-half of the arbitrator's fee. The worker was financially incapable of paying his portion of the fee. When the employer asked the court to order the worker to submit his discrimination claim to arbitration, the court refused, noting that the agreement to arbitrate placed the plaintiff "between the proverbial rock and a hard place." On the one hand, the agreement prohibited use of the judicial forum, where the plaintiff would not be required to pay for a judge's services, and on the other hand it forced him to incur prohibitive costs for use of the arbitral forum. In effect, the agreement to arbitrate failed to provide the worker an accessible forum in which to resolve his statutory rights, thus undermining the remedial functions of the federal antidiscrimination laws.[11]

In some instances, courts have refused to compel arbitration because the employer drafted unfair arbitration rules and procedures,[12] and in others instances because the arbitral procedures failed to provide the full complement of relief granted by Title VII.[13] Unless the arbitration procedures are fair and neutral and the range of relief provided by those procedures is equal to that available through litigation, the agreement to arbitrate will not be enforced.

Several lessons may be drawn from our review of the roles the EEOC administrative process, litigation, and arbitration play in sexual harassment cases. First, a claimant should not rely solely on the EEOC. Adequate relief is far more likely to be gained in litigation than in administrative proceedings conducted by the EEOC. A claimant may proceed to litigation by demanding a right-to-sue letter from the EEOC, and such a demand may be made six months after she files her charge. Any claimant intent on recovering damages for the ills suffered at the hands of those who engage in sexual harassment, should avail herself of the opportunity to proceed to litigate her case in the courts at the earliest possible point in time.

Second, if the opportunity is presented, a claimant should always choose litigation over arbitration. In addition to the procedural disadvantages common to the arbitral process, a jury is far more likely than an arbitrator or a panel of arbitrators to award a claimant substantial damages. Claimants should be guided by the knowledge that employers greatly favor arbitration, because historically they have fared better in that forum than in the courts, while workers have experienced the opposite.

Third, if the employer claims that a worker is bound by the terms of a predispute or compulsory agreement to arbitrate, the worker should always examine the terms and provisions of that agreement as well as the arbitration procedures established by the employer. A path to the courts may still exist. Generally, an agreement to arbitrate will not be enforced unless the employer can prove the following:

- The claimant was not subjected to fraud or duress when she signed an arbitration agreement; that she knowingly and voluntarily agreed to arbitrate employment disputes.
- The claimant and the employer are equally bound by the terms of the arbitration agreement.
- The arbitrator is obligated to apply Title VII, both as to the substance of the claim and its remedy.
- The claimant is not inhibited from proceeding in arbitration by reason of the costs involved.
- The arbitration rules of procedure are fair and even-handed, thus ensuring the neutrality of the proceedings.
- The claimant is provided with a fair and simple method to secure information necessary to the presentation of her claim.

The claimant and her attorney, however, should not limit their examination and review to these specific areas. Evidence of any unfairness at any point in the arbitral process may prove sufficient to persuade a court to deny an employer's motion to compel arbitration.

CHAPTER EIGHTEEN

Compensatory and Punitive Damages and Other Remedies

The cases reviewed in the preceding chapters establish beyond doubt that women are often subjected to severe and pervasive acts of harassment, acts that corrupt their workplaces and create extremely hostile working conditions. Although most women survive corrupt and hostile working environments without experiencing severe psychological damage, others suffer long-lasting, acute pain and mental suffering.

In chapter 2 we reviewed the case of Cynthia Stoll, a young, single mother who worked at the Sacramento post office for six years before fleeing her workplace to escape multiple acts of sexual harassment committed by an entire network of male workers. Male co-workers and supervisors asked her to perform oral sex, followed her into the women's bathroom, asked her to go on vacation with them, fondled her body and rubbed up against her, and generally stalked her throughout the post office facility, and ultimately one of her supervisors raped her. As a consequence, Stoll suffered severe depression and later made four attempts to end her life. At the trial of her sexual harassment case, a psychiatrist testified that Stoll was scarred for life, would never again be able to work, and probably would continue to try to commit suicide.[1] How is it possible for a court or jury to determine the proper measure of damages to be awarded a woman experiencing suffering of this magnitude?

In computing the damages recoverable by a victim of sexual harassment, the courts apply a fundamental legal principle common to all employment discrimination cases: the worker who successfully establishes she had been made the object of discriminatory conduct is entitled to be made "whole." She is entitled to be placed in those circumstances she would have been in if she had not been discriminated against, and thus the remedy ordered by the court should remove from her work life all adverse effects of the discriminatory conduct.

Despite the near universal acceptance of the "make whole" standard of relief, the remedies available to a sexually harassed female worker are materially deficient in two respects in certain circumstances: a woman may be denied full recovery of the punitive and compensatory damages awarded by a jury and, on occasion, she may even be denied recovery of all damages.

Until 1991, Title VII did not specifically authorize a court to grant recovery of monetary damages to recompense a victim of harassment for her pain and suffering—commonly referred to as "compensatory damages." Moreover, the statute failed to provide for the recovery of punitive damages. Although Congress had broadly defined the remedies available under Title VII, it failed specifically to designate compensatory and punitive damages as appropriate forms of relief for victims of discriminatory acts. As a consequence, nearly all federal courts denied litigants the right to recover these damages. In sexual harassment cases, where the primary damages suffered by victims of harassment are nearly always of a compensatory and punitive nature, claimants were effectively deprived of any remedy under Title VII. The plight of the pre-1991 sexually harassed victim is well illustrated by the circumstances Lisa Maturo encountered in her sexual harassment lawsuit alleged against her employer, National Graphics.

Maturo and her co-worker Harold Peters, hired by National Graphics at approximately the same time in 1984, occupied adjacent work areas. Soon after they began working for the company, Peters made sexually explicit remarks in Maturo's presence, inquired about her sex life, and repeatedly expressed an interest in having sex with her. Maturo demanded that he desist from engaging in this type of conversation, but Peters persisted, and throughout the remaining months of 1984, his remarks became increasingly more vulgar and sexually aggressive.

The following year, Peters continued to subject Maturo to a steady stream of comments, expressed in starkly graphic language, relating to his desire to have oral sex with her and to the various sexual positions he planned to use when they had intercourse. The remarks intensified throughout the year to the point where they became a daily occurrence. To make matters worse for Maturo, Peters was promoted to be her supervisor, and he thereafter repeatedly informed her that if she pleased him sexually he could obtain for her pay raises and additional vacation time. On one occasion, he invited her to go on a "love weekend," and promised her that in return for having sex with him he would secure additional job benefits for her.

Peters's continuing harassing behavior brought Maturo embarrassment and humiliation. On many occasions, she had to vacate her work area to avoid Peters's abusive behavior. In addition, she grew frightened of him because of the increasingly aggressive nature of his comments, as well as the threat he posed to her continued employment.

Maturo did not remain silent in the face of Peters's verbal onslaught. Throughout 1985, she complained to National Graphics' plant manager and also to the president and CEO of the company, but they did nothing to restrain Peters. Apparently interpreting the inaction of management as permission to elevate the offensiveness of his conduct, Peters on two occasions physically assaulted Maturo. Maturo filed a criminal complaint against him, and although Peters was later arrested and charged with sexual assault, National Graphics continued to employ him. Even while the criminal charges were pending against him, Peters continued to harass Maturo, and ultimately she fled the work site in panic and never returned. She later wrote to the president of the company advising him that due to management's continued refusal to provide her with a harassment-free working environment, it was no longer possible for her to continue her employment with the company.

Subsequently, Maturo suffered serious emotional problems, a condition still existent three years later when her sexual harassment suit against National Graphics reached trial. During that three-year period, she grew depressed, had difficulty sleeping and eating, and withdrew from family and friends. She suffered from nightmares, experienced a high level of anxiety and stress as well as a general feeling of unease. She was unable to engage in ordinary daily activities, could not work because of her inability to cope with normal job stresses, and was forced to seek psychological counseling.

Although it was evident Maturo had suffered greatly, the court, by reason of the status of the law as it then existed, was limited in the damages it was authorized to grant her. In 1989, at the time of the trial of her sexual harassment charges against National Graphics, Title VII did not permit an assessment of damages against an employer to compensate a victim of sexual harassment for her mental suffering, nor did it allow a court to award her punitive damages. Although the circumstances of the

Maturo case demonstrated that compensatory and punitive damages were clearly warranted, the only item of damage the court was authorized to grant (other than recovery of her legal expenses incurred during the course of the litigation) was back pay. The court awarded Maturo twenty-three thousand dollars to compensate her for the loss of salary suffered during the time she was unable to work after leaving National Graphics. The court was barred from compensating her for her anxiety, depression, eating and sleeping disorders, and her inability to perform normal daily activities. Although acute and long-lasting, her suffering did not provide a legal basis for the recovery of damages, and thus National Graphics escaped liability for a major portion of the damages Maturo suffered as a consequence of Peters's harassment.[2]

The absence in the statute of any provision granting a remedy for the type of mental suffering experienced by Maturo and other women subjected to sexually harassing conduct disclosed a major deficiency in Title VII. The statute had to be amended. In 1991, Congress, admitting its error in failing to provide for compensatory and punitive damages when it enacted Title VII in 1964, amended the statute to provide specifically for the recovery of these damages. The amendment, however, failed to completely resolve the issue. As a concession to the American business community, Congress included in the amending legislation an adjustable scale of upper limits on the combined amounts of compensatory and punitive damages recoverable by a successful litigant. The upper limit, or cap, ranges from $50,000 for small employers, having between 15 and 100 employees, to $300,000 for employers with more than 500 employees.[3] This limitation on awards of compensatory and punitive damages denies adequate relief to harassment victims, particularly those subjected to egregious acts of harassing conduct. Cynthia's Stoll's case against the post office is a case in point. A $300,000 recovery—the maximum Stoll could have recovered under federal law—would be wholly inadequate to compensate that poor woman in light of the injury done to her.

In some circumstances, a successful litigant may avoid the limitations of Title VII's damages cap. If the circumstances of her case permit, a plaintiff may plead violation of a state civil rights statute in addition to a violation of Title VII. If the standard of liability under the state statute is similar to that under Title VII, the court may allocate to the state statute that portion of the damages that exceeds the Title VII cap.[4] Thus, in those states that do not limit the recovery of damages, or limit damages less restrictively than the caps established by the amendments to Title VII, a large jury award may be preserved in whole or part.

The statutory limitation on the recovery of compensatory and punitive damage awards is not the only obstruction litigants confront in their endeavors to attain adequate recoveries of damages, as the courts have created barriers of their own. A judge is not required to accept a jury's determination regarding the measure of damages it deems appropriate. Rather, a judge is required to ascertain whether the trial evidence supports the jury's award, and if it does not, he may either reduce the award to that he considers supportable by the evidence or, alternatively, order a new trial on the issue of damages.

The criteria governing a trial judge's evaluation of the appropriateness of the amount of a jury award have been articulated from a number of perspectives. A jury award should stand without change unless *grossly excessive*, bearing no rational relationship to the evidence. A judge should not interfere with a jury award unless a *miscarriage of justice* would result if he were not to intercede. A jury award should not be overturned unless the amount of the award *shocks one's conscience* and cries out to be voided. It should stand unless it appears to be so excessive as to suggest that the jury was *motivated by passion or prejudice* rather than by a reasoned assessment of the evidence presented at the trial.

Thus, a judge should refrain from wholly usurping the jury's function in assessing damages and, provided a reasonable basis exists to support the award, he should uphold that award. Moreover, a judge should not overturn an award merely because he would have granted a lesser amount if he had been conducting the trial without a jury, since a judge's belief or opinion that the jury was unduly generous affords an insufficient basis to warrant the court's intercession.

On balance, the application of these standards has more often worked in favor of employers and contrary to the interests of worker claimants. Too often, a court's position on damages appears more closely allied with that espoused by the business community. In some instances, judges have exhibited a total inability to relate to workplace problems commonly experienced by workers, and thus court decisions appear at times to be totally divorced from workplace reality. Consequently, large jury awards in favor of sexual harassment claimants are frequently reduced if not overturned. In some instances, these awards must be reduced in accordance with the limitations established by Congress, but other times they have been reduced on the ground that they were so excessive as to suggest that the juries were motivated by passion or prejudice rather than by a reasoned assessment of the trial evidence.

State court jury awards often meet the same fate. Damage awards, based on violations of state antidiscrimination laws lacking a provision limiting damages, are ruthlessly slashed by short-sighted judges to a fraction of the amount determined appropriate by a jury. Thus, when a jury grants a substantial award of compensatory or punitive damages, the claimant should anticipate that the award will be closely scrutinized by the trial and appellate courts and that one or both of those courts may intervene to her detriment.

A *National Law Journal* study revealed that during a two-year period approximately 80 percent of employment case jury verdicts of $1 million and more (verdicts that were not subject to statutory caps) were either reduced by the trial court or reversed by an appellate court. The study also found that the greater the award, the more vulnerable it was to reduction by a court. During those two years (1996–1997), juries awarded sixteen verdicts of more than $6 million to plaintiffs alleging discrimination, harassment, wrongful termination, or retaliation. Nine of the sixteen awards were later reduced, two others were reversed, and in two cases, a reduction of the jury's award was under consideration. Only three of the awards survived the trial court intact: but, two of those were on appeal, and the other had been settled.[5] What is the explanation for this dismal record? How can it be justified?

Plaintiffs' lawyers believe that jurors are more apt than judges to understand and relate to the workplace problems experienced by workers. Jurors themselves may have confronted discrimination in the workplace and are thus sympathetic to the plight of those who suffer the consequences of biased employer practices and conduct. Some judges, on the other hand, appear incapable of relating to worker concerns and seem more disposed to identify with employers.

Even with statutory and judicial limitations, the recovery of punitive damages may significantly increase the total damages a successful sexual harassment litigant may recover. The standard a court must apply in deciding whether punitive damages may be awarded under Title VII was established by Congress in its 1991 amendments to the statute. Punitive damages may be awarded to a worker when the evidence discloses that a defendant employer acted "with malice or with reckless indifference to the federally protected rights" of its workers.[6] Stated more simply, an employer may be held accountable to its workers for punitive damages if it acted maliciously in response to reports of sexually harassing conduct or without any concern for the antidiscrimination protections afforded employees by Title VII.

Proving employer malice or reckless indifference presents a significant evidentiary hurdle for claimants. The Supreme Court, moreover, raised the evidentiary bar even higher when in a 1999 decision it created an affirmative defense an employer may assert to defeat a punitive damages claim. On that occasion, the court ruled that when an employer is able to establish that it made "good faith efforts to comply with Title VII," it may not be held liable for punitive awards assessed in connection with the discriminatory conduct of its managerial employees. If the conduct of a management employee is contrary to his employer's good-faith efforts to comply with Title VII, the employer may not be held liable for punitive damages.[7] Thus, even though a woman may have been cruelly harassed, she may be denied recovery of punitive damages if the defendant employer successfully establishes this affirmative defense.

What are "good faith efforts?" The Supreme Court, consciously or unconsciously, failed to formulate a definitive standard to identify employer measures that qualify as acts of good-faith compliance with Title VII, thus leaving it to the lower federal courts to ponder the issue. One of the first cases in which the issue arose involved Lynn Cadena's sexual harassment claim against the Pacesetter Corporation.

Soon after Pacesetter, a home improvement company, hired Cadena as a telemarketer in its Lenexa, Kansas, office, Charles Bauersfeld, a telemarketing manager and Cadena's supervisor, subjected her to a barrage of verbal and physical acts of harassment. When Cadena complained to another manager about Bauersfeld's conduct, he responded "Lynn, that's the way he is. . . . There's nothing nobody can do about it. That's Charlie for you. What can I say?" He also intimated that company officials at corporate headquarters were aware of Bauersfeld's conduct but declined to confront him because he made a good deal of money for the company. He suggested that if Cadena was unhappy with her lot, she should seek other employment.

Cadena then reported Bauersfeld's harassment to the general manager of the Lenexa office, but he advised her that she should view Bauersfeld's conduct as a compliment to her physical attractiveness, and he offered her an increase in salary if she would agree not to persist in asserting a harassment claim against the company. Cadena rejected the offer, resigned, and sued the company for sexual harassment.

After a three-day trial, a jury awarded Cadena $50,000 in compensatory damages for her emotional distress and $700,000 in punitive damages. The court then reduced the total award to $300,000 in accordance with the statutory cap. Pacesetter appealed, arguing that the trial court should have entered judgment in its favor on the issue of punitive damages since the evidence demonstrated that Bauersfeld's harassing conduct was contrary to Pacesetter's good faith efforts to comply with Title VII and to its efforts to prevent sexual harassment from occurring in its workplace.

Arguing in support of its position, Pacesetter asserted that it had initiated and had consistently maintained a strong policy against sexual harassment and that it had adequately trained its employees in the implementation and enforcement of that policy. But the evidence was to the contrary. For example, the Lenexa office manager responsible for sexual harassment training testified that she conducted monthly meetings among employees to discuss harassment issues. Other employees, however, testified that no such meetings had ever occurred. More significantly, the office manager also testified that it was her opinion that a male supervisor who exposed his genitalia to a female subordinate or grabbed her breasts would not be guilty of sexual harassment so long as he apologized to her after such an incident. Based on such admitted ignorance concerning basic sexual harassment concepts, the appellate court ruled that Pacesetter had failed to make a good faith effort to adequately educate its employees about its sexual harassment policy.

Even with an adequate antiharassment policy, Pacesetter still was required to establish that it enforced its provisions by addressing alleged Title VII violations as soon as management learned of them. But Cadena presented substantial evidence that Pacesetter knew about Bauersfeld's sexually harassing actions but failed to undertake any action to stop them. Thus Pacesetter failed to prove that it made a good faith effort to comply with the statutory demands, and the appellate court upheld the punitive damages award.[8]

The mere existence of a sexual harassment policy is not enough to establish an employer's good faith attempt to comply with Title VII. The employer will be unable to establish that it exerted a good faith effort to comply with the demands of the statute if the evidence discloses that managerial employees:

- disregarded the company's sexual harassment policy in making employment decisions,
- minimized the significance of harassment complaints by performing cursory investigations of the harassment charges asserted by female employees,
- focused their investigation on the victim's performance or conduct rather than on the harasser's conduct, or
- disregarded reported acts of harassment.[9]

To prove that it made a good faith effort to comply with the statute, an employer must demonstrate that after adopting a sexual harassment policy, it fully implemented and enforced all its provisions. Employers who have failed to exercise a good faith effort have suffered the consequences. The Baker & McKenzie law firm, in an earlier case, can attest to that.

Martin Greenstein, a Baker & McKenzie partner, worked in its Chicago office for many years. In 1987, a secretary employed in that office complained to the firm's director of administration that Greenstein had sexually harassed her, and she threatened legal action against the firm. After the chairman of the firm's Chicago office reviewed her allegations, he prepared a memorandum listing the accusations made against Greenstein but, inexplicably, failed to arrange for a copy of the memorandum to be placed in Greenstein's personnel file.

The following year, one of the firm's young female attorneys reported several incidents of sexual harassment committed by Greenstein. At the time, no investigation was undertaken, but a memorandum outlining the accusations against Greenstein was prepared, and although a copy was placed in the file of the complaining female attorney, again, none was placed in Greenstein's file. Subsequently, Greenstein transferred to the firm's office in Palo Alto, California. On five separate occasions during the ensuing three years, female staff members complained that Greenstein had subjected them to various acts of sexual harassment. Although on each occasion the accusations of harassment were reported to Greenstein's superiors, they abstained from ordering any disciplinary action with regard to any of the charges leveled against Greenstein by these women.

In the summer of 1991, the firm hired Rena Weeks to work as Greenstein's secretary. Three weeks after she was hired, Weeks had lunch with several employees, as well as Greenstein, at a local restaurant. As they left the restaurant, Greenstein gave Weeks some M&M candies, which she placed in her blouse pocket. As they walked to their car, Greenstein put his arm over Weeks's shoulder, put his hand in her blouse pocket, and dropped more candies into the pocket. He then placed his knee in her lower back, pulled her shoulders back, and said, "Let's see which breast is bigger." On another occasion, Weeks unintentionally ran into Greenstein as he was carrying a box through the office. After putting the box down, Greenstein lunged toward Weeks with his hands cupped. When she moved back, crossing her hands over her chest, he asked her if she was afraid that he was about to grab her. On another occasion he did grab her—but this time it was her buttocks, not her breasts. At that point, Weeks reported Greenstein's conduct to the manager of the Palo Alto office. A copy of the office manager's notes of her conversation with Weeks was placed in Weeks's personnel file but not in Greenstein's. The firm then assigned Weeks to work for another attorney, but a few weeks later she resigned from the firm.

When Weeks filed a sexual harassment suit against both Greenstein and Baker & McKenzie, the jury had little difficulty in concluding that Greenstein had been guilty of sexually harassing conduct. With evidence that Baker & McKenzie had continued to employ Greenstein even though it had been repeatedly apprised of his egregious acts of harassing conduct, the jury determined that the firm had intentionally disregarded the continuing threat of sexual abuse to its female employees. Accordingly, the jury awarded punitive damage awards of $225,000 against Greenstein and $6.9 million against Baker & McKenzie. The court later reduced the punitive damage award against the firm to $3.5 million, but Weeks was able to recover this entire sum as she and her attorneys had based her lawsuit on violations of California's antidiscrimination law which, unlike Title VII, did not limit the punitive damage award granted in her favor.[10]

On the basis of the evidence demonstrating that Baker & McKenzie's management knew that Greenstein posed a danger to female employees, the jury was persuaded to grant a huge punitive damages award against the firm. Greenstein held a position of power in the firm, while the victims of his harassment were clerical staff or junior attorneys. Evidence of the firm's failure to take any action to curtail Greenstein's harassing behavior or to discipline him illustrated the firm's indifference to the plight of its female employees. The inaction of the firm's managing partners was attributable to their desire to protect one of their own. The firm's managers were well aware of Greenstein's continuous harassment of young female workers long before Weeks was hired, but they still proceeded to assign Weeks to work for him. Without any forewarning, Weeks was assigned to the lion's den.

If the *Weeks* case had been litigated in a federal court pursuant to the provisions of Title VII, the jury could very well have found that Baker & McKenzie had not exerted a good faith effort to comply with Title VII and that it had had acted "with malice or with reckless indifference to the federally protected rights" of its workers. Prior knowledge of a supervisor's predilection for sexually harassing behavior is likely to culminate in a punitive damage award. Indeed, in a case decided before the Supreme Court's "good faith" ruling, a court ruled an employer's unresponsiveness to reported complaints that one of its supervisor's conduct was rife with foul language, sexual innuendo, and sexual advances readily led to an inference that it had acted recklessly and without regard to the rights of its female workers, thus rendering it liable for punitive damages.[11]

Sexual harassment cases are sometimes settled for enormous sums. A family-owned importing firm in New Rochelle, New York, agreed to pay $2.6 million to 104 of its female workers who were sexually harassed by the seventy-nine-year-old owner and president of the company.[12] The EEOC reached a major settlement with the Ford Motor Company, providing nearly $8 million in payments to female workers who were sexually and racially harassed.[13] After the Mitsubishi Company was accused of ignoring—and even encouraging—acts of sexual harassment committed against female employees working in its automobile assembly plant, it agreed to pay $34 million to the harassed women.[14]

In addition to compensatory and punitive damages, the successful sexual harassment litigant may be entitled to recover other forms of damages. In a case where a worker is forced to resign her position in order to escape acts of harassment—in other words, in a case of a constructive discharge—the plaintiff may be entitled to recover back pay and, under certain circumstances, front pay as well.

Back pay is the monetary loss sustained by a worker subsequent to the termination of her employment and during the period extending to the trial of her sexual harassment suit against her employer. The award is computed by first calculating the salary and other employee benefits she would have been paid had she not been terminated or otherwise forced from her position and then by reducing that amount by the compensation she actually received in other employment.

An award of back pay should reflect increases in salary the worker would have received if her employment had not been terminated. In that regard, the court may assume a worker's salary would have continued to increase at the same rate it had increased in the past. If her salary history discloses annual increases averaging 5 percent a year, that average may be used in the back pay award computation.

Other financial benefits that would have accrued to the worker had she not been terminated also should be included in the back pay award. As an example, courts customarily increase a damage award to compensate the worker for reduced pension benefits and increased costs of health and medical benefits and life insurance premiums.

The "make whole" doctrine requires the court to examine all other circumstances that follow on an unlawful act of discrimination. For example, the court may order an employer to reinstate a constructively discharged worker. In many instances, however, reinstatement to the worker's former position is not feasible, either because of the possibility of renewed acts of harassment or on account of the hostility that often develops between worker and employer in the course of the litigation of a sexual harassment case. If the court determines that reinstatement is not an appropriate remedy, the successful claimant may then apply for a front pay award.

A claim for front pay seeks the recovery of the loss of salary and benefits the worker contends she will sustain subsequent to the trial. While an award of back pay is based on what already has occurred, an award of front pay is based on what *may* happen in the future, and thus an element of uncertainty is innate to a claim of this nature. In computing a front pay award for a plaintiff who remains unemployed at the time of the trial, the court must determine when it is likely she will again become gainfully employed and at what salary. Based on its conclusions to these inquiries, the court will then compute the award. If the worker, on the other hand, has obtained new employment but at a lower salary than that paid to her while employed by the defendant, the court must determine at what point it is likely she will again be compensated on a scale comparable to that she was paid by the defendant employer. In either event, the court is dealing with uncertainties. Because the computation of a front pay award involves factors that may or may not occur, the court may be asked to make assumptions it is reluctant to make. Thus, to the extent a worker is able to furnish the court with facts that tend to reduce the degree of uncertainty, the more likely the court will be agreeable to an award of front pay.

The primary goal of nearly all sexual harassment claimants is the recovery of monetary damages in compensation for the emotional pain and economic losses suffered as a consequence of the harassment. Injunctive relief, designed to prevent future acts of harassment, is less apt to be sought in a suit brought by an individual complainant. It is far more likely to be the subject of broad-based class actions and EEOC-initiated cases, especially in cases where the employer is alleged to continue to engage in unlawful employment practices. But, in those cases where the sexually harassed claimant remains in the employ of the defendant, the court may grant some form of injunctive relief so as to assure the claimant that she may continue to work for the defendant without threat of further harassment.

In one case, a labor union local was ordered "to adopt, implement, and enforce a policy and procedure for the prevention and control of sexual harassment." The court further ordered the union local (1) to set forth in its antiharassment policy that acts of sexual harassment violate Title VII and EEOC regulations and that it was unlawful to retaliate against any worker who complained about acts of harassment, (2) to develop appropriate sanctions or disciplinary measures for union members found to have engaged in sexually harassing conduct, and (3) to formulate appropriate means of educating its officers and members about the particulars of its sexual harassment policy. The court-ordered injunctive relief was expressed in specific terms because the court believed that if it were simply to enjoin the union from creating a hostile work environment, its order would prove to be insufficient if not fruitless.[15]

Finally, the successful litigant, pursuant to statute,[16] is entitled to recover her reasonable attorney's fees. The fee-recovery statute assures a complainant her damage award will not be diminished by reason of the expenses incurred in the litigation. Absent such a statutory provision, many sexual harassment claims would not be pursued, since a large number of those claims are asserted after the claimant is constructively discharged, is out of work, and thus lacks the financial means to support a lawsuit. Lawyers often agree to some form of contingency fee arrangement with workers finding themselves in such circumstances. But, in instances where a large damage award is improbable, and hence a contingency fee arrangement is less meaningful, the statutory fee award may provide the only means for a lawyer to obtain adequate payment for his services.

Sexual harassment litigation is complex—in the factual issues underlying each case as well as in the variety of legal issues frequently arising in these cases. Moreover, employers vigorously defend themselves against sexual harassment charges, and while the worker more often than not retains a sole practitioner or a small law firm, employers nearly always rely on a goliath law firm, with hundreds of lawyers and multitudinous support staff. In such circumstances, the worker and her counsel need all the assistance they can obtain. The fee award statute is Congress's recognition that the worker and her attorney must be granted that assistance if Title VII is to be adequately enforced.

Conclusion

The sexually harassed woman, because her workplace role is reduced to that of an object of male sexual desire or is undermined by anti-female bias, suffers a diminishment in her status as a worker. She also suffers diminishment as a person. "Sexual harassment limits women in a way men are not limited. It deprives them of opportunities that are available to male employees without sexual conditions."[1] Sexually harassing behavior also tends to confirm and intensify male control of the workplace, and thus "replicates and perpetuates a sexual hierarchy in which men possess and maintain their power by virtue of their ability to define women in terms of their sexuality."[2]

As we have seen in the cases reviewed in previous chapters, the question of what constitutes sexual harassment presents complex issues of fact and law. Since Americans have not developed a uniform attitude toward the role of sex in the workplace, whether particular workplace behavior crosses the line separating licit from illicit conduct is the subject of continuing disagreement.

The right to be free from unwanted sexual attention is of fundamental importance to workers, female and male alike. "Nothing is more destructive of human dignity than being forced to perform sexual acts against one's will."[3] At the same time, unfounded charges of sexual harassment, or charges based on misconceptions, can readily destroy the career of one accused.

Since men and women working side by side often find that sexual attraction ensues, workplace romantic relationships are common, giving birth to many marriages. But in these circumstances, the opportunity to take unfair advantage of a subordinate also occurs. Because of economic reasons, most harassed workers cannot simply abandon their employment. Since they cannot just quit and turn to other employment, their primary defense to unlawful sexual conduct lies in the law. Title VII and the various state antiharassment statutes stand as the workers' primary—and often, the only—protection from sexual intimidation and repression.

Although litigation may not be the ideal way to cope with a hostile and offensive work environment, it is the best means currently available. Litigation enlightens: it provides men with a broader awareness of the types of conduct women find offensive. Moreover, the fear of public disclosure in a legal forum undoubtedly deters men from engaging in harassing conduct and encourages employers to adopt preventive measures and place greater emphasis on dealing with sexual harassment sooner rather than later. The more common the occurrence of sexual harassment lawsuits, the less hesitant women are to report harassing behavior. More litigation today may diminish its need tomorrow.

As this book reaches its conclusion, the Michigan Court of Appeals has affirmed a $21 million jury award granted to a female worker subjected to crushing sexual abuse over a period of years.[4] Media sources have reported this award as the largest recovery of damages by an individual sexual harassment plaintiff in United States history.[5] Awards of this size can only motivate employers to clean up their workplaces. When the cost of defending against sexual harassment cases exceeds the cost of implementing effective antiharassment procedures, the American workplace will be well on its way to becoming harassment free.

The efforts exerted by women to exclude sexual harassment from the workplace have redefined the relationship between working men and women. That relationship differs vastly from that which existed before the advent of the concept that unwelcome sex has no rightful place at the work site. In many respects, the workplace has been revolutionized. Women who have pursued sexual harassment claims pursuant to Title VII have succeeded in changing previously held perceptions of acceptable workplace conduct.

It cannot be stated with certainty, of course, that litigation ultimately will eradicate sexual harassment from the workplace. But, without the threat of legal sanctions against employers, sexually harassing conduct will continue to corrupt the workplace. Currently, the threat of litigation provides the only realistic incentive for employers to act to prevent and remove harassing behavior from their workplaces. Women must continue to avail themselves of the opportunity for redress provided by our legal system. The power of the law resides in women who rely on and use it to its fullest extent.

Notes

Introduction

1. Catharine A. MacKinnon, *Sexual Harassment of Working Women* (New Haven: Yale University Press, 1979), 1.
2. Ibid., 25.
3. Deborah L. Rhode, *Speaking of Sex: The Denial of Gender Inequality* (Cambridge: Harvard University Press, 1997), 96.
4. Kathryn Abrams, "The New Jurisprudence of Sexual Harassment," *Cornell Law Review* 83 (1998): 1169, 1205.
5. Ann Juliano and Stewart J. Schwab, "The Sweep of Sexual Harassment Cases," *Cornell Law Review* 86 (2001): 548, 578–580, referring to the works of Anita Bernstein, Katherine Franke, Kathryn Abrams, and Vicki Schultz.
6. Law review articles discussing the "power, not sex" concept are legion. Far fewer are those that discuss the erotic component of sexual harassment. One of the latter was written by Mark McLaughlin Hager, "Harassment as a Tort: Why Title VII Hostile Environment Liability Should Be Curtailed," *Connecticut Law Review* 30 (1998): 375, 379–380.
7. Katherine M. Franke, "What's Wrong with Sexual Harassment?" *Stanford Law Review* 49 (1997): 691, 728.
8. *Campbell v. Board of Regents*, 770 F. Supp. 1479 (D. Kan. 1991).
9. *Rabidue v. Osceola Refining Co.*, 805 F.2d 611 (6th Cir. 1986).
10. *Oncale v. Sundowner Offshore Services, Inc.*, 523 U.S. 75 (1998).
11. This view, that of an attorney who represents employers, is quoted by Kathleen Neville, *Internal Affairs* (New York: McGraw-Hill, 2000), 19–20.
12. Barbara A. Gutek, *Sex and the Workplace* (San Francisco: Jossey-Bass, 1985), 96.

1. Sexual Harassment in the Workplace

1. Barbara A. Gutek, *Sex and the Workplace* (San Francisco: Jossey-Bass, 1985), 44.
2. William Petrocelli and Barbara Kate Repa, *Sexual Harassment on the Job* (Berkeley, Calif.: Nolo Press, 1999), 1–10, citing the *National Law Journal*, 12/20/93.

3. Susan Estrich, "Sex at Work," *Stanford Law Review* 43 (1991): 813, 821, citing United States Merit Systems Protection Board, "Sexual Harassment in the Federal Workplace: Is It a Problem?" (1981), 2–3.

4. Catharine A. MacKinnon, *Sexual Harassment of Working Women* (New Haven: Yale University Press, 1979) 26, citing a survey conducted by *Redbook* magazine.

5. Deborah S. Brenneman, "From a Woman's Point of View: The Use of the Reasonable Woman Standard in Sexual Harassment Cases," *Cincinnati Law Review* 60 (1992): 1281, 1297, quoting Chairman James Hanley, Hearings Before the Subcommittee on Investigations of the Committee on Post Office and Civil Service, 96th Congress, 1st Session 3 (1979).

6. MacKinnon, *Sexual Harassment of Working Women*, 28. MacKinnon's work has been described as "one of the most influential law books of the late twentieth century." Jeffrey Toobin, "The Trouble with Sex," *New Yorker*, February 9, 1998, 48, 50.

7. Equal Employment Opportunity Commission Sexual Harassment Charges: EEOC and FEPAs Combined: FY 1992–FY 2001, available at http://www.eeoc.gov/stats/harass.html.

8. Nijole V. Benokraitis and Joe R. Feagin, *Modern Sexism: Blatant, Subtle, and Covert Discrimination, 2d ed.* (Englewood Cliffs, N.J.: Prentice Hall, 1995), 31, citing Chris Swingle, "Sexism Still an Obstacle," *USA Today*, June 30, 1993.

9. Marion Crain, "Women, Labor Unions, and Hostile Work Environment Sexual Harassment: The Untold Story," *Texas Journal of Women and Law* 4 (1995) 9, 28–29.

10. Ibid., 28.

11. MacKinnon, *Sexual Harassment of Working Women*, 47.

12. Rosa Ehrenreich, "Dignity and Discrimination: Toward a Pluralistic Understanding of Workplace Harassment," *Georgetown Law Journal* 88, no. 1 (1999): 1, 16.

13. *Robinson v. Jacksonville Shipyards, Inc.*, 760 F. Supp. 1486 (M.D. Fla. 1991).

14. Mona Harrington, *Women Lawyers: Rewriting the Rules* (New York: Plume, 1995), 105, 115.

15. Gutek, *Sex and the Workplace*, 8–9.

16. I owe this terminology to Crain, "Women, Labor Unions, and Hostile Work Environment Sexual Harassment," 22–23.

17. MacKinnon, *Sexual Harassment of Working Women*, 48.

18. Crain, "Women, Labor Unions, and Hostile Work Environment Sexual Harassment," 21–25.

19. Barbara A. Gutek, *Sex and the Workplace*, 96–97.

20. Congressman's Smith's attempt to defeat enactment of Title VII has been widely reported, including David L. Rose, "Twenty-Five Years Later: Where Do We Stand on Equal Employment Opportunity Law Enforcement," *Vanderbilt Law Review* 42 (1989) 1121, 1131.

21. Alfred W. Blumrosen, *Modern Law: The Law Transmission System and Equal Employment Opportunity* (Madison: University of Wisconsin Press, 1993) 45.

22. Title VII, Civil Rights Act of 1964, 42 U.S.C. Sections 2000e et seq.

23. MacKinnon, *Sexual Harassment of Working Women*, 4.

24. Ibid., 193.

25. Ibid., 4.

26. *Tomkins v. Public Service Electric & Gas Company*, 422 F. Supp. 553 (D. N.J. 1976); reversed 568 F.2d 1044 (3rd Cir. 1977).

27. *Barnes v. Train*, 13 FEP Cases 123 (D. D.C. 1974), reversed 561 F.2d 983 (D.C. Cir. 1977).

28. *Corne v. Bausch and Lomb, Inc.*, 390 F. Supp. 161 (D.C. Ariz. 1975), reversed on other grounds 562 F.2d 55 (9th Cir. 1977).

29. *Tomkins v. Public Service Electric & Gas Company*, supra.

30. *Barnes v. Costle*, 561 F.2d 983 (D.C. Cir. 1977).

31. Court of Appeals opinion, reversing the lower court in *Tomkins v. Public Service Electric & Gas Company*, supra.

32. *Henson v. City of Dundee*, 682 F.2d 897 (11th Cir. 1982).

33. *Meritor Savings Bank v. Vinson*, 477 U.S. 57 (1986).

34. 29 C.F.R. Section 1604.11 (a) (1) and (2).

35. Ann Juliano and Stewart J. Schwab, "The Sweep of Sexual Harassment Cases," *Cornell Law Review* 86 (2001): 548, 565.

36. EEOC Policy Guidelines on Current Issues of Sexual Harassment, No. N-915–050 (3/19/90) Available at http://www.eeoc.gov/doc). See also *Lancaster v. Sheffler Enterprises*, 19 F. Supp.2d 1000 (W.D. Mo. 1998).

2. Various Forms of Sexual Harassment

1. *Barnes v. Costle*, 561 F.2d 983 (D.C. Cir. 1977).

2. This case was reported under the name *Johnson v. Indopco, Inc.*, 846 F. Supp 670 (N.D. Ill. 1994).

3. See, for example, *Glickstein v. Neshaminy School District*, 80 F.E.P. Cases 67 (E.D. Penn. 1999).

4. *Stoll v. Runyon*, 165 F.3d 1238 (9th Cir. 1999).

5. *Jenson v. Eveleth Taconite Co.*, 130 F.3d 1287 (8th Cir. 1997).

6. *Meritor Savings Bank v. Vinson*, 477 U.S. 57 (1986).

7. *Nichols v. Frank*, 42 F.3d 503 (9th Cir. 1994). The court ruled, however, that the Postal Authority could not be held liable for hostile environment harassment because it was unaware that Francisco was harassing Nichols. In light of latter developments in the law with regard to employer liability (see chapter 9), this ruling is questionable.

8. *Fall v. Indiana University Board of Trustees*, 12 F. Supp.2d 870 (N.D. Ind. 1998); new trial granted on other grounds, 33 F. Supp.2d 729.

9. EEOC Policy Guidance on Sexual Harassment, EEOC Policy Guidance Manual.

10. *Blackmon v. Pinkerton Security & Investigative Services*, 182 F.3d 629 (8th Cir. 1999).

11. *Baskerville v. Culligan International Co.*, 50 F.3d 428 (7th Cir. 1995).

12. Ann Juliano and Stewart J. Schwab, "The Sweep of Sexual Harassment Cases," *Cornell Law Review* 86 (2001): 548, 566. The authors of this article examined every federal district and appellate court decision between 1986 and 1995 involving sexual harassment in the workplace—nearly 650 cases in all.

13. *Robinson v Jacksonville Shipyards, Inc.*, 760 F. Supp.1486 (M.D. Fla. 1991).

14. *O'Rourke v. City of Providence*, 235 F.3d 713 (1st Cir. 2001).

15. *Broderick v. Ruder*, 685 F. Supp.1269 (D.C. D.C. 1988).

16. *Mallinson-Montague v. Pocrnick*, 224 F.3d 1224 (10th Cir. 2000).

17. Barbara A. Gutek, *Sex and the Workplace* (San Francisco: Jossey-Bass, 1985), 56.

18. *Bryson v. Chicago State University*, 96 F.3d 912 (7th Cir. 1996).

19. *Jew v. University of Iowa*, 749 F. Supp. 946 (S.D. Iowa 1990).

3. The Welcomeness Issue

1. *Meritor Savings Bank v. Vinson*, 477 U.S. 57 (1986).

2. *Kotcher v. Rosa & Sullivan Appliance Center, Inc.*, 957 F.2d 59 (2d Cir. 1992).

3. Senate Judiciary Committee Confirmation Hearing, as quoted in Anne C. Levy and Michele A. Paludi, *Workplace Sexual Harassment* (Upper Saddle River, N.J.: Prentice Hall, 1997), 45.

4. *Kouri v. Liberian Services, Inc.*, 55 FEP Cases 124 (E.D. Va. 1991), affirmed 960 F.2d 146 (4th Cir. 1992).

5. *Chamberlin v. 101 Realty, Inc.*, 915 F.2d 777 (1st Cir. 1990).

6. *Morton v. Steven Ford-Mercury of Augusta, Inc.*, 162 F. Supp. 2d 1228 (D. Kan. 2001).

7. *Gan v. Kepro Circuit Systems*, 28 FEP Cases 639 (E.D. Mo. 1982).

8. *Weinsheimer v. Rockwell International Corp.*, 754 F. Supp 1559 (MD. Fla. 1990), affirmed 949 F.2d 1162 (11th Cir. 1991). See fn. 12 of the lower court decision.

9. *Loftin-Boggs v. City of Meridian*, 633 F. Supp. 1323 (S.D. Miss. 1986), affirmed 824 F.2d 971 (5th Cir. 1987).

10. *Nuri v. PRC, Inc.*, 13 F. Supp. 2d 1296 (M.D. Ala. 1998).

11. *Swentek v US Air, Inc.*, 830 F.2d 552 (4th Cir. 1987).

12. *Carr v. Allison Gas Turbine Division*, 32 F.3d 1007 (7th Cir. 1994).

13. *Burns v. McGregor Electronic Industries, Inc.*, 989 F.2d 959 (8th Cir. 1993).

14. Kathleen Neville, *Internal Affairs* (New York: McGraw-Hill, 2000), 21.

15. *Sarro v. City of Sacramento*, 78 F. Supp. 2d 1057 (E.D. Cal.1999).

16. *Wolak v. Spucci*, 217 F.3d 157 (2d Cir. 2000).

17. *Rodriguez-Hernandez v. Miranda-Valez*, 132 F.3d 848 (1st Cir. 1998).

18. *Federal Rules of Evidence*, 412.

19. *Meritor Savings Bank v. Vinson*, supra.

20. *Federal Rules of Evidence*, 412 (a) (2).

21. William Petrocelli and Barbara Kate Repa, *Sexual Harassment on the Job,* 4th ed., (Berkeley, Calif.: Nolo Press, 1999), 2/23.

22. Susan Estrich, "Sex at Work," *Stanford Law Review* 43 (April 1991): 813, 828.

23. *Kahn v. Objective Solutions International*, 86 F. Supp.2d 377 (S.D. N.Y. 2000).

24. James J. McDonald Jr. and Daniel S. Fellner, "A Plaintiff's Obligation to 'Avoid Harm Otherwise': New Life for the Welcomeness Defense," *Employee Relations Law Journal* 25, no. 2, (1999): 17, 26.

4. Severe or Pervasive Conduct

1. *Meritor Savings Bank v. Vinson*, 477 U.S. 57 (1986).

2. *Harris v. Forklift Systems, Inc.*, 510 U.S. 17 (1993).

3. Ibid.

4. *Fall v. Indiana University Board of Trustees*, 12 F. Supp. 2d 870 (N.D. Ind. 1998); new trial granted on other grounds, 33 F. Supp.2d 729.

5. *Worth v. Tyer*, 276 F.3d 249 (7th Cir. 2001).

6. EEOC Policy Guidance on Current Issues of Sexual Harassment, No. 915–050 (3/19/90), available at http://www.eeoc.gov/doc.

7. *Roberts v. University of Pennsylvania*, 87 FEP Cases 837 (E.D. Pa. 2001).

8. *McKenzie v. Illinois Department of Transportation*, 92 F.3d 473 (7th Cir. 1996).

9. *Baskerville v. Culligan International Co.*, 50 F.3d 428 (7th Cir. 1995).

10. *Bishop v. Interim Industrial Services*, 77 FEP Cases 1598 (N.D. Tex. 1998).

11. *EEOC v. A. Sam & Sons Produce Co., Inc.*, 872 F. Supp. 29 (W.D.N.Y. 1994).

12. *Smith v. Norwest Financial Acceptance, Inc.*, 129 F.3d 1408 (10th Cir, 1997).

13. *EEOC v. R&R Ventures*, 244 F.3d 334 (4th Cir. 2001).

14. *Butler v. Ysleta Independent School District*, 161 F.3d 263 (5th Cir. 1998).

15. *Hurley v. Atlantic City Police Department*, 174 F.3d 95 (3d Cir. 1999).

16. *Bonora v. UGI Utilities, Inc.*, 85 FEP Cases 853 (E.D. Penn. 2000).

17. *Danna v. New York Telephone Co.*, 752 F. Supp. 594 (S.D.N.Y. 1990).

18. *Harris v. Forklift Systems, Inc.*, supra.

19. *Clark County School District v. Breeden*, 532 U.S. 268 (2001).

20. *Taylor v. Regeneration Technologies, Inc.*, 86 FEP Cases 112 (N.D. Fla. 2001).

21. *Mendoza v. Borden, Inc.*, 195 F.3d 1238 (11th Cir. 1999).

22. *Oncale v. Sundowner Offshore Services, Inc.*, 523 U.S. 75 (1998).

23. *Scott v. Sears, Roebuck & Co.*, 798 F.2d 210 (7th Cir. 1986).

24. *Lindblom v. Challenger Day Programs, Ltd.*, 37 F. Supp. 2d 1109 (N.D. Ill. 1999).

25. *Adusumilli v. City of Chicago*, 164 F.3d 353 (7th Cir. 1998).
26. *Prigmore v. Houston Pizza Ventures, Inc.*, 189 F. Supp. 2d 635 (S.D. Tex. 2002).
27. *Steiner v. Showboat Operating Co.*, 25 F.3d 1459 (9th Cir. 1994).

5. A Woman's Rights When Other Women Are Harassed

1. *Priest v. Rotary*, 634 F. Supp. 571 (N.D. Cal.1986).
2. *Toscano v. Nimmo*, 570 F. Supp. 1197 (D. Del. 1983).
3. EEOC "Policy Guidance on Employer Liability under Title VII for Sexual Favoritism," N-915.048 (1/12/90).
4. *Broderick v. Ruder*, 685 F. Supp. 1269 (D. D.C. 1988).
5. *Hirase-Doi v. U.S. West Communications, Inc.*, 61 F.3d 777 (10th Cir. 1995).
6. *Leibovitz v. New York City Transit Authority*, 4 F. Supp. 2d 1444 (E.D.N.Y. 1998), reversed (see note 7).
7. *Leibovitz v. New York City Transit Authority*, 252 F.3d 179 (2d Cir. 2001).
8. *Garvey v. Dickinson College*, 64 FEP Cases 156 (M.D. Penn. 1991).
9. *Cruz v. Coach Stores, Inc.*, 202 F.3d 560 (2d Cir. 2000).
10. Lisa A. Fried, "Hostile-Environment Case is Praised, Criticized," *National Law Journal* (5/15/2000): B-4.
11. *Andrews v. City of Philadelphia*, 895 F.2d 1469 (3d Cir. 1990).

6. Sexual Harassment in Other Settings

1. 29 C.F.R. Section 1604.11(a).
2. *Rabidue v. Osceola Refining Co.*, 584 F. Supp. 419 (E.D. Mich 1984), affirmed 805 F.2d 611 (6th Cir. 1986).
3. *Gross v. Burggraf Construction Co.*, 53 F.3d 1531 (10th Cir. 1995).
4. Amie L. Vanover, "Williams v. General Motors Corporation: Giving Sexual Harassment Plaintiffs a Chance," *Ohio State Law Journal* 61 (2000): 1559, 1576–1577.
5. *Williams v. General Motors Corp.*, 187 F.3d 553 (6th Cir. 1999).
6. *Oncale v. Sundowner Offshore Services, Inc.*, 523 U. S. 75 (1998).
7. Christine A. Amalfe and Kerrie R. Heslin, "Courts Start to Rule on Online Harassment," *National Law Journal* (1/24/2000): C-3.
8. *Coniglio v. City of Berwyn*, 2000 WL 967989 (N.D. Ill. 2000).
9. Anheuser-Busch, Inc. is one such company. *Schwenn v. Anheuser-Busch, Inc.*, 1998 WL 166845 (N.D. N.Y. 1998).
10. Ann Juliano and Stewart J. Schwab, "The Sweep of Sexual Harassment Cases," *Cornell Law Review* 86 (2001): 548, 563.
11. *Tomka v. Seiler Corp.*, 66 F.3d 1295 (2d Cir. 1995).
12. *Enders v. Associated Co., Inc.*, 1995 WL 580052 (D. Kan. 1995).
13. *P.F. v. Delta Air Lines, Inc.*, 83 FEP Cases 442 (E.D.N.Y. 2000), reversed (see note 14).
14. *Ferris v. Delta Air Lines, Inc.*, 277 F.3d 128 (2d Cir. 2001).
15. *Huitt v. Market Street Hotel Corp.*, 62 FEP Cases 538 (D. Kan. 1993).
16. *McGuinn-Rowe v. Foster's Daily Democrat*, 74 FEP Cases 1566 (D. N.H. 1997).

7. Gender Harassment

1. 29 C.F.R. Section 1604.11(a).
2. *Hall v. Gus Construction Co.*, 842 F.2d 1010 (8th Cir. 1988).
3. *Durham Life Insurance Co. v. Evans*, 78 FEP Cases 1426 (E.D. Pa. 1997), affirmed 166 F.3d 139 (3d Cir. 1999).

4. EEOC Policy Guidance on Current Issues of Sexual Harassment, No. N-915–050 (3/19/90), Section C (4).

5. Amie L. Vanover, "Williams v. General Motors Corporation: Giving Sexual Harassment Plaintiffs a Chance," *Ohio State Law Journal* 61 (2000): 1559.

6. The term *gender harassment* was first used in *Cline v. General Electric Capital Auto Lease, Inc.*, 748 F. Supp. 650 and 757 F. Supp. 923 (N.D. Ill. 1991).

7. Lex K. Larson, 3 *Employment Discrimination*, 2d ed. (Newark, N.J.: Lexis Nexis, 2002), Section 46.03[4].

8. *Kopp v. Samaritan Health System, Inc.*, 13 F.3d 264 (8th Cir. 1993).

9. *Smith v. First Union National Bank*, 202 F.3d 234 (4th Cir. 2000).

10. *Delgado v. Lehman*, 665 F. Supp. 460 (E.D. Va. 1987).

11. *Galloway v. General Motors Service Parts Operation*, 78 F.3d 1164 (7th Cir. 1996).

12. *Walk v. Rubbermaid, Inc.*, 913 F. Supp. 1023 (N.D. Ohio 1994), affirmed 76 F.3d 380 (6th Cir. 1996).

13. *Cline v. General Electric Capital Auto Lease, Inc.*, supra.

8. The Reasonable Person and Reasonable Woman Standards

1. *Lipsett v. University of Puerto Rico*, 864 F.2d 881 (1st Cir. 1988).

2. Barbara A. Gutek, *Sex and the Workplace* (San Francisco: Jossey-Bass, 1985), 88–92.

3. Rosemary Agonito, *Dirty Little Secrets: Sex in the Workplace* (Syracuse: New Futures, 2000), 159–160.

4. Kathryn Abrams, "Gender Discrimination and the Transformation of Workplace Norms," *Vanderbilt Law Review* 42 (1989): 1183, 1205.

5. Catharine A. MacKinnon, *Sexual Harassment of Working Women* (New Haven: Yale University Press, 1979), 199.

6. *Rabidue v. Osceola Refining Co.*, 805 F.2d 611 (6th Cir. 1986).

7. *Ellison v. Brady*, 924 F.2d 872 (9th Cir. 1991).

8. *Ebert v. Lamar Truck Plaza*, 715 F. Supp. 1496 (D. Colo. 1987), affirmed 878 F.2d 338 (10th Cir. 1989).

9. EEOC Policy Guidelines on Current Issues of Sexual Harassment, No. N-915–050 (3/19/90). Available at http://www.eeoc.gov/doc. *Fall v. Indiana University Board of Trustees*, 12 F. Supp.2d 870 (N.D. Ind. 1998); new trial granted on other grounds 33 F. Supp. 2d 729.

10. *Ebert v. Lamar Truck Plaza*, supra.

11. *Caleshu v. Merrill Lynch, Pierce, Fenner & Smith, Inc.*, 737 F. Supp. 1070 (E. D. Mo.1990), affirmed 985 F.2d 564 (8th Cir. 1991).

12. *Ellison v. Brady*, supra.

13. *Harris v. Forklift Systems, Inc.*, 510 U.S. 17 (1993). The case was remanded to the lower court where the parties to the suit later resolved the remaining issues.

14. EEOC Guidance on Harris v. Forklift, No. N-915–002 (3/8/94) Available at http://www.eeoc.gov/docs.

15. Ibid.

16. *Rabidue v. Osceola Refining Co.*, supra.

17. *Fuller v. City of Oakland*, 47 F.3d 1522 (9th Cir. 1995).

18. Deborah L. Rhode, *Speaking of Sex: The Denial of Gender Inequality* (Cambridge: Harvard University Press, 1997), 106.

19. *Dey v. Colt Construction & Development Company*, 28 F.3d 1446 (7th Cir. 1994).

20. *Martin v. Howard University*, 81 FEP Cases 964 (D. D.C. 1999).

21. Professor Abrams was quoted by Katherine M. Franke, "What's Wrong with Sexual Harassment?" *Stanford Law Review* 49 (1997): 691, 751.

9. Employer Liability for Workplace Sexual Harassment

1. Civil Rights Act of 1964, Title VII, 42 U.S.C. Sections 2000e et seq.
2. *Burlington Industries, Inc. v.. Ellerth*, 524 U.S. 743 (1998). See also *Faragher v. City of Boca Raton*, 524 U.S. 775 (1998).
3. *Burlington Industries, Inc. v. Ellerth*, supra.
4. *Faragher v. City of Boca Raton*, supra.
5. EEOC Enforcement Guidance: Vicarious Employer Liability for Unlawful Harassment by Supervisors, No.915.002 (6/18/99), Section III A.1. Available at http://www.eeoc.gov/docs/harassment.html.
6. EEOC Enforcement Guidance, supra, Section III A.2.
7. *Parkins v. Civil Construction of Illinois*, 163 F.3d 1027 (7th Cir. 1998).
8. *Sowers v. Kemira, Inc.*, 701 F. Supp. 809 (S.D. Ga. 1988).
9. EEOC Enforcement Guidance, supra, Section III B.
10. *Burlington Industries, Inc. v. Ellerth*, supra.
11. EEOC Enforcement Guidance, supra, Section IV B.
12. *Durham Life Insurance Co. v. Evans*, 166 F.3d 139 (3d Cir. 1999).
13. *Molnar v. Booth*, 229 F.3d 593 (7th Cir. 2000).
14. *Bryson v. Chicago State University*, 96 F.3d 912 (7th Cir. 1996).
15. EEOC Enforcement Guidance, supra, Section IV B.
16. *Hasbrouck v. BankAmerica Housing Services, Inc.*, 105 F. Supp. 2d 31 (N.D. N.Y. 2000).
17. *Nichols v. Frank*, 42 F.3d 503 (9th Cir. 1994).
18. EEOC Enforcement Guidance, supra, Section IV B.
19. *Jin v. Metropolitan Life Insurance Co.*, 295 F.3d 335 (2d. Cir 2002).
20. *Reinhold v. Commonwealth of Virginia*, 151 F.3d 172 (4th Cir.1998).
21. EEOC Enforcement Guidance, supra, Section IV B, fn.32.
22. *Glickstein v. Neshaminy School District*, 80 F.E.P. Cases 67 (E.D. Pa. 1999).
23. *Watts v. Kroger Co.*, 170 F.3d 505 (5th Cir. 1999).

10. The Employer's Duty to Prevent and Promptly Correct Acts of Sexual Harassment

1 EEOC Enforcement Guidance: Vicarious Employer Liability for Unlawful Harassment by Supervisors, No.915.002 (6/18/99), Section V.C.-1 Available at http://www.eeoc.gov/docs/harassment. html.
2. *Smith v. First Union National Bank*, 202 F.3d 234 (4th Cir. 2000).
3. *Meritor Savings Bank v. Vinson*, 477 U.S. 57 (1986).
4. *Miller v, Woodharbor Molding & Millworks, Inc.*, 80 F. Supp.2d 1026 (N.D. Iowa 2000).
5. EEOC Enforcement Guidance, supra, Section V. C.-1(c).
6. EEOC Enforcement Guidance, supra, Section V.C.-1(d).
7. The case is pending. Thus the availability of the affirmative defense to the employer has not yet been determined.
8. *Faragher v. City of Boca Raton*, 524 U.S. 775 (1998).
9. *Barrett v. Applied Radiant Energy Corp.*, 240 F.3d 262 (4th Cir. 2001).
10. *Miller v, Woodharbor Molding & Millworks, Inc.*, supra.
11. *Baty v. Willamette Industries, Inc.*, 172 F.3d 1232 (10th Cir. 1999).
12. *Smith v. First Union National Bank*, supra.
13. *Fall v. Indiana University Board of Trustees*, 12 F. Supp. 2d 870 (N.D. Ind. 1998); new trial granted on other grounds, 33 F. Supp. 2d 729 (N.D. Ind.1998).
14. *Sarro v. City of Sacramento*, 78 F. Supp.2d 1057 (E.D. Cal. 1999).
15. *Haynes v. Reebaire Aircraft, Inc.*, 161 F. Supp. 2d 985 (W.D. Ark. 2001).

16. *Carmon v.Lubrizol Corp.*, 17 F.3d 791 (5th Cir. 1994).
17. *Swenson v. Potter*, 271 F.3d 1184 (9th Cir. 2001).
18. *Wal-Mart Stores, Inc. v. Davis*, 78 FEP Cases 278 (Tex. Ct. Appeals 1998).
19. Ibid.
20. *Desmarteau v. City of Wichita*, 64 F. Supp. 2d 1067 (D. Kan. 1999).
21. *Shaw v. AutoZone, Inc.*, 180 F.3d 806 (7th Cir. 1999).

11. An Employee's Duty to Take Advantage of Her Employer's Preventive and Corrective Measures

1. *Faragher v. City of Boca Raton*, 524 U.S. 775 (1998).
2. EEOC Enforcement Guidance: Vicarious Employer Liability for Unlawful Harassment by Supervisors, No.915.002 (6/18/99), Section V, D. Available at http://www.eeoc.gov/docs/harassment.html.
3. Ibid. See also *Burlington Industries, Inc. v. Ellerth*, 524 U.S. 743 (1998).
4. *Scrivner v. Socorro Independent School District*, 169 F.3d 969 (5th Cir. 1999).
5. Barbara A. Gutek, *Sex and the Workplace* (San Francisco: Jossey-Bass, 1985) 71–72.
6. William Petrocelli and Barbara Kate Repa, *Sexual Harassment on the Job* (Berkeley, Calif.: Nolo Press, 1999), 3/3.
7. *Riffle v. The Sports Authority, Inc.*, 80 FEP Cases 897 (D. Mary. 1999), affirmed 210 F.3d 361 (4th Cir. 2000).
8. *Hylton v. Norrell Health Care of New York*, 53 F. Supp.2d 613 (S.D.N.Y. 1999).
9. *Barrett v. Applied Radiant Energy Corp.*, 70 F. Supp. 2d 644 (W.D. Va. 1999), affirmed in relevant part 240 F.3d 262 (4th Cir. 2001).
10. *Shaw v. AutoZone, Inc.*, 180 F.3d 806 (7th Cir. 1999).
11. *Alberter v. McDonald's Corp.*, 70 F. Supp.2d 1138 (D. Nev. 1999).
12. *Matvia v. Bald Head Island Management, Inc.*, 259 F.3d 261 (4th Cir. 2001).
13. *Sims v. Health Midwest Physician Services Corp.*, 196 F.3d 915 (8th Cir. 1999).
14. *Watts v. Kroger Co.*, 170 F.3d 505 (5th Cir. 1999).
15. *Montero v. AGCO Corp.*, 192 F.3d 856 (9th Cir. 1999).
16. *Gawley v. Indiana University*, 276 F.3d 301 (7th Cir. 2001).
17. *Hill v. American General Financial, Inc.*, 218 F.3d 639 (7th Cir. 2000).
18. *Savino v. C.P. Hall Co.*, 199 F.3d 925 (7th Cir. 1999).
19. *Greene v. Dalton*, 164 F.3d 671 (D. D.C. 1999).
20. *Corcoran v. Shoney's Colonial, Inc.*, 24 F. Supp.2d 601 (W.D. Va. 1998).
21. *Mathers v. Sherwin-Williams Co., Inc.*, 82 FEP Cases 755 (E.D. Pa. 2000).
22. *Scrivner v. Socorro Independent School District*, supra.
23. *O'Dell v. Trans World Entertainment Corp.*, 153 F. Supp. 2d 378 (S.D. N.Y. 2001).
24. *Faragher v. City of Boca Raton* and *Burlington Industries, Inc. v. Ellerth*, supra.
25. *Brown v. Perry*, 184 F.3d 388 (4th Cir.1999).
26. Lex K. Larson, 3 *Employment Discrimination* (Newark, LexisNexis, 2002), Section 46.07 [5] [c], n.96.

12. Other Forms of Employer Liability

1. EEOC Enforcement Guidance: Vicarious Employer Liability for Unlawful Harassment by Supervisors, No.915.002 (6/18/99), Section VI, B. Available at http://www.eeoc.gov/docs/harassment. html.
2. *Burns v. McGregor Electronic Industries*, 989 F.2d 959 (8th Cir. 1993).
3. *Harrison v. Eddy Potash, Inc.*, 158 F.3d 1371 (10th Cir. 1998).

4. *Burlington Industries, Inc. v. Ellerth*, 524 U.S. 743 (1998).

5. *Lintz v. American General Finance, Inc.*, 50 F. Supp. 2d 1074 (D.C. Kan. 1999).

6. *Sharp v. City of Houston*, 164 F.3d 923 (5th Cir. 1999).

7. *Burlington Industries, Inc. v Ellerth*, supra.

8. *Franklin v. King Lincoln-Mercury-Suzuki, Inc.*, 51 F. Supp. 2d 661 (D.C. Mary. 1999)

9. *Hirase-Doi v. U.S. West Communications, Inc.*, 61 F.3d 777 (10th Cir. 1995).

10. *Fuller v. Caterpillar, Inc.*, 124 F. Supp. 2d 610 (N.D. Ill. 2000).

11. *Hawkins v. Maximus, Inc.*, 84 FEP Cases 1217 (N.D. Ill. 2000).

12. *Rodriguez-Hernandez v. Miranda-Valez*, 132 F. 3d 848 (1st Cir. 1998).

13. Robert J. Aalberts and Lorne H. Seidman, "Sexual Harassment of Employees by Non-Employees: When Does the Employer Become Liable?" *Pepperdine Law Review* 21 (1994): 447.

14. EEOC Guidelines, 29 C.F.R. Section 1604.11 (e).

15. *Folkerson v. Circus Circus Enterprises, Inc.*, 107 F.3d 754 (9th Cir. 1997).

13. Constructive Discharge

1. Ann Juliano and Stewart J. Schwab, "The Sweep of Sexual Harassment Cases," *Cornell Law Review* 86 (2001): 548, 560.

2. Ibid., citing "The Impact of Sexual Harassment on the Job," a report issued by the Working Women's Institute (1979).

3. *Draper v. Coeur Rochester, Inc.*, 147 F.3d 1104 (9th Cir. 1998).

4. *Ogden v. Wax Works, Inc.*, 214 F.3d 999 (8th Cir. 2000).

5. *Metcalf v. Metropolitan Life, Inc.*, 961 F. Supp. 1536 (D. Utah 1997).

6. *Woodward v. City of Worland*, 977 F.2d 1392 (10th Cir. 1992).

7. *McCrackin v. LabOne, Inc.*, 74 FEP Cases 1018 (D. Kan. 1995). McCrackin's case was later dismissed on other grounds. 903 F. Supp. 1430.

8. *Breeding v. Arthur J. Gallagher & Co.*, 164 F.3d 1151 (8th Cir. 1999).

9. *Howard v. Burns Bros., Inc.*, 149 F.3d 835 (8th Cir. 1998).

10. *Swain v. Roadway Express, Inc.*, 71 FEP Cases 71 (D. Mary. 1996).

11. *Burlington Industries, Inc. v. Ellerth*, 524 U.S. 743 (1998).

12. Ibid.

13. *Caridad v. Metro-North Commuter R.R.*, 191 F.3d 283 (2d Cir. 1999).

14. *Burlington Industries, Inc. v. Ellerth*, supra.

15. *Scott v. Ameritex Yarn*, 72 F. Supp. 2d 587 (D. S.C. 1999).

14. Retaliation against Workers Who Charge Their Employers with Sexual Harassment

1. 42 U.S.C. Section 2000e-3 (a).

2. Equal Employment Opportunity Commission Charge Statistics FY 1992 Through FY 2001. Available at http://www.eeoc.gov/stats/charges/.html.

3. *Quinn v. Green Tree Credit Corp.*, 159 F.3d 759 (2nd Cir. 1998).

4. *Wildman v. Burke Marketing Corp.*, 120 F. Supp. 2d 1182 (S.D. Iowa 2000).

5. *Haynes v. Reebaire Aircraft, Inc.*, 161 F. Supp. 2d 985 (W.D. Ark. 2001).

6. *Flannery v. Trans World Airlines, Inc.*, 160 F.3d 425 (8th Cir. 1998).

7. *Swain v. Roadway Express, Inc.*, 71 FEP Cases 71 (D. Mary. 1996).

8. *Morris v. Oldham County Fiscal Court*, 201 F.3d 784 (6th Cir. 2000).

9. *Martini v. Federal National Mortgage Association*, 977 F. Supp. 464 (D. D.C. 1997); reversed on other grounds, 178 F.3d 1336 (D.C. Cir. 1999).

10. *Trezza v. Dilenschneider Group*, 84 FEP Cases 1345 (S.D.N.Y. 2000).

11. *Klimiuk v. ESI Lederle, Inc.*, 84 FEP Cases 971 (E.D. Penn. 2000).
12. *Taylor v. Regeneration Technologies, Inc.*, 86 FEP Cases 112 (N.D. Fla. 2001).

15. Sexual Harassment of Men by Women

1. Equal Employment Opportunity Commission Sexual Harassment Charges, EEOC and FEPAs Combined: FY 1992 through FY 2001, available at http://www.eeoc.gov/stats/charges/.html.
2. Ernest F. Lidge, III, "The Male Employee Disciplined for Sexual Harassment as Sex Discrimination Plaintiff," *University of Memphis Law Review* 30 (2000): 719, fn.10. Other commentators, however, disagree, arguing that most male sexual harassment cases are filed against other men. See, e.g., Reed Abelson, "Men, Increasingly, Are the Ones Claiming Sex Harassment by Men," *New York Times*, June 10, 2001.
3. *Hull v. APCOA/ Standard Parking Corp.*, 82 FEP Cases 247 (N.D. Ill. 2000).
4. *Dornfeld v. Omega Optical Co.*, 76 FEP Cases 759 (E.D. La. 1998).
5. *Fall v. Indiana University Board of Trustees*, 12 F. Supp.2d 870 (N.D. Ind. 1998); new trial granted on other grounds, 33 F. Supp. 2d 729.
6. *Bowman v. Shawnee State University*, 220 F.3d 456 (6th Cir. 2000).
7. *Wolf v. Northwest Indiana Symphony Society*, 250 F.3d 1136 (7th Cir. 2001).
8. *Casiano v. AT&T Corp.*, 213 F.3d 278 (5th Cir. 2000).
9. *Hosey v. McDonald's Corp.*, 71 FEP Cases 201 (D. Md. 1996); affirmed 113 F.3d 1232 (4th Cir. 1997).
10. *EEOC v. Domino's Pizza, Inc.*, 909 F. Supp.1529 (M.D. Fla. 1995); affirmed 113 F.3d 1249 (11th Cir. 1997).

16. Same-Sex Sexual Harassment

1. *Wright v. Methodist Youth Services, Inc.*, 511 F. Supp. 307 (N.D. Ill. 1981).
2. 42 U.S.C. Section 2000e-2(a)(1).
3. *Meritor Savings Bank v. Vinson*, 477 U.S. 57 (1986).
4. *Oncale v. Sundowner Offshore Services*, 523 U.S. 75 (1998).
5. *Davis v. Coastal International Security, Inc.*, 275 F.3d 1119(D.C. Cir. 2002).
6. *Price Waterhouse v. Hopkins*, 490 U.S. 228 (1989).
7. *Nichols v. Azteca Restaurant Enterprises, Inc.*, 256 F.3d 864 (9th Cir. 2001). Sanchez and two other Azteca employees brought this action. This opinion considered only Sanchez's claim.
8. *Oncale v. Sundowner Offshore Services*, supra.
9. *English v. Pohanka of Chantilly, Inc.*, 190 F. Supp.2d 833 (E.D. Va. 2002).
10. *Fall v. Indiana University Board of Trustees*, 12 F. Supp. 2d 870 (N.D. Ind. 1998); new trial granted on other grounds, 33 F. Supp. 2d 729.
11. *Simonton v. Runyon*, 232 F.3d 33 (2d Cir. 2000).
12. *Bibby v. Philadelphia Coca Cola Bottling Co.*, 260 F.3d 257 (3d Cir. 2001).
13. *Spearman v. Ford Motor Co.*, 231 F.3d 1080 (7th Cir. 2000).
14. *Rene v. MGM Grand Hotel, Inc.*, 305 F.3d 1061 (9th Cir. 2002).
15. *Holman v. State of Indiana*, 211 F.3d 399 (7th Cir. 2000).
16. *Fitzpatrick v. Winn-Dixie Montgomery, Inc.*, 153 F. Supp. 2d 1303 (D. Ala. 2001).
17. *Fair v. Guiding Eyes for the Blind, Inc.*, 742 F. Supp. 151 (S.D. N.Y. 1990).
18. *Butler v. Ysleta Independent School District*, 161 F.3d 263 (5th Cir. 1998).
19. *Preston v. City of Danville*, 84 FEP Cases 1043 (E.D. KY 2000).
20. *West v. Mt. Sinai Medical Center*, 88 FEP Cases 1270 (S.D. N.Y. 2002).

21. Reed Abelson, "Men, Increasingly, Are the Ones Claiming Sex Harassment by Men," *New York Times*, June 10, 2001.

17. The Role of Arbitration in Sexual Harassment Cases

1. EEOC Sexual Harassment Charges: EEOC & FEPAs Combined: FY 1992–FY 2002; available at http://www.eeoc.gov/stats/harass.html.
2. Michael Selmi, "The Value of the EEOC: Reexamining the Agency's Role in Employment Discrimination Law," *Ohio State Law Journal* 57 (1996): 6, n. 17.
3. *Gilmer v. Interstate/Johnson Lane Corp.*, 500 U.S. 20 (1991).
4. Pearl Zuchlewski, 3 *Employee Rights Litigation: Pleading and Practice* (New York: Matthew Bender, 2000), 16–2.
5. *Smith v. PSI Services II, Inc.*, 84 FEP Cases 1409 (E.D. Pa. 2001).
6. "EEOC Policy Statement on Mandatory Arbitration," EEOC Notice No. 915.002 (7/10/97).
7. *Circuit City Stores, Inc. v Adams*, 532 U.S. 105 (2001).
8. *Rosenberg v. Merrill Lynch, Pierce, Fenner & Smith, Inc.*, 170 F.3d 1 (1st Cir. 1999).
9. *Ball v. SFX Broadcasting, Inc.*, 165 F. Supp. 2d 230 (N.D. N.Y. 2001).
10. *Gibson v. Neighborhood Health Clinics, Inc.*, 121 F.3d 1126 (7th Cir. 1997).
11. *Shankle v. B-G Maintenance Management of Colorado, Inc.*, 163 F.3d 1230 (10th Cir. 1999).
12. *Hooters of America, Inc. v. Phillips*, 173 F.3d 933 (4th Cir. 1999).
13. *Paladino v. Avnet Computer Technologies*, 134 F.3d 1054 (11th Cir. 1998).

18. Compensatory and Punitive Damages and Other Remedies

1. *Stoll v. Runyon*, 165 F.3d 1238 (9th Cir. 1999).
2. *Maturo v. National Graphics, Inc.*, 722 F. Supp. 916 (D. Conn. 1989).
3. 42 U.S.C. Section 1981a. The complete limitation is as follows: $50,000 for employers with 15 to 100 employees; $100,000 for employers with 101 to 200 employees; $200,000 for employers with 201 to 500 employees; and $300,000 for employers with more than 500 employees.
4. *Passantino v. Johnson & Johnson Consumer Products, Inc.*, 212 F.3d 493 (9th Cir. 2000).
5. Margaret Cronin Fisk, "Judges Slash Worker Awards," *National Law Journal* (April 20, 1998).
6. 42 U.S.C. Section 1981a.
7. *Kolstad v. American Dental Association*, 527 U.S. 526 (1999).
8. *Cadena v. Pacesetter Corp.*, 224 F.3d 1203 (10th Cir. 2000).
9. *Luu v. Seagate Technology, Inc.*, 86 FEP Cases 595 (D. Minn. 2001).
10. *Weeks v. Baker & McKenzie*, 76 FEP Cases 1219 (Cal. Ct. of Appeals, 1998).
11. *Jonasson v. Lutheran Child & Family Services*, 115 F.3d 436 (7th Cir. 1997).
12. Monte Williams, "$2.6 Million to End Sex Harassment Suit," *New York Times*, June 4, 1999.
13. EEOC Press Release (September 7, 1999). (Available at http://www.eeoc.gov).
14. Reed Abelson, "Can Respect Be Mandated? Maybe Not Here," *New York Times*, September 10, 2000.
15. *Stair v. Lehigh Valley Carpenters Union*, 66 FEP Cases 1473 (E.D. Pa. 1993), amended in part, 855 F. Supp. 90 (1994), affirmed 43 F.3d 1463 (3d Cir. 1994).
16. 42 U.S.C. Section 2000e-5(k).

Conclusion

1. Catharine A. MacKinnon, *Sexual Harassment of Working Women* (New Haven: Yale University Press, 1979), 193.

2. Katherine M. Franke, "What's Wrong with Sexual Harassment?" *Stanford Law Review* 49 (1997): 691, 728.

3. *Nichols v. Frank*, 42 F.3d 503 (9th Cir. 1994).

4. *Gilbert v. DaimlerChrysler Corp.*, 2002 WL 1767672 (Mich. Ct. of Appeals, 2002).

5. Adam Liptak, "Pain-and-Suffering Awards Let Juries Avoid New Limits," *New York Times*, October 28, 2002.

Index